THE UNITY OF PICASSO'S ART

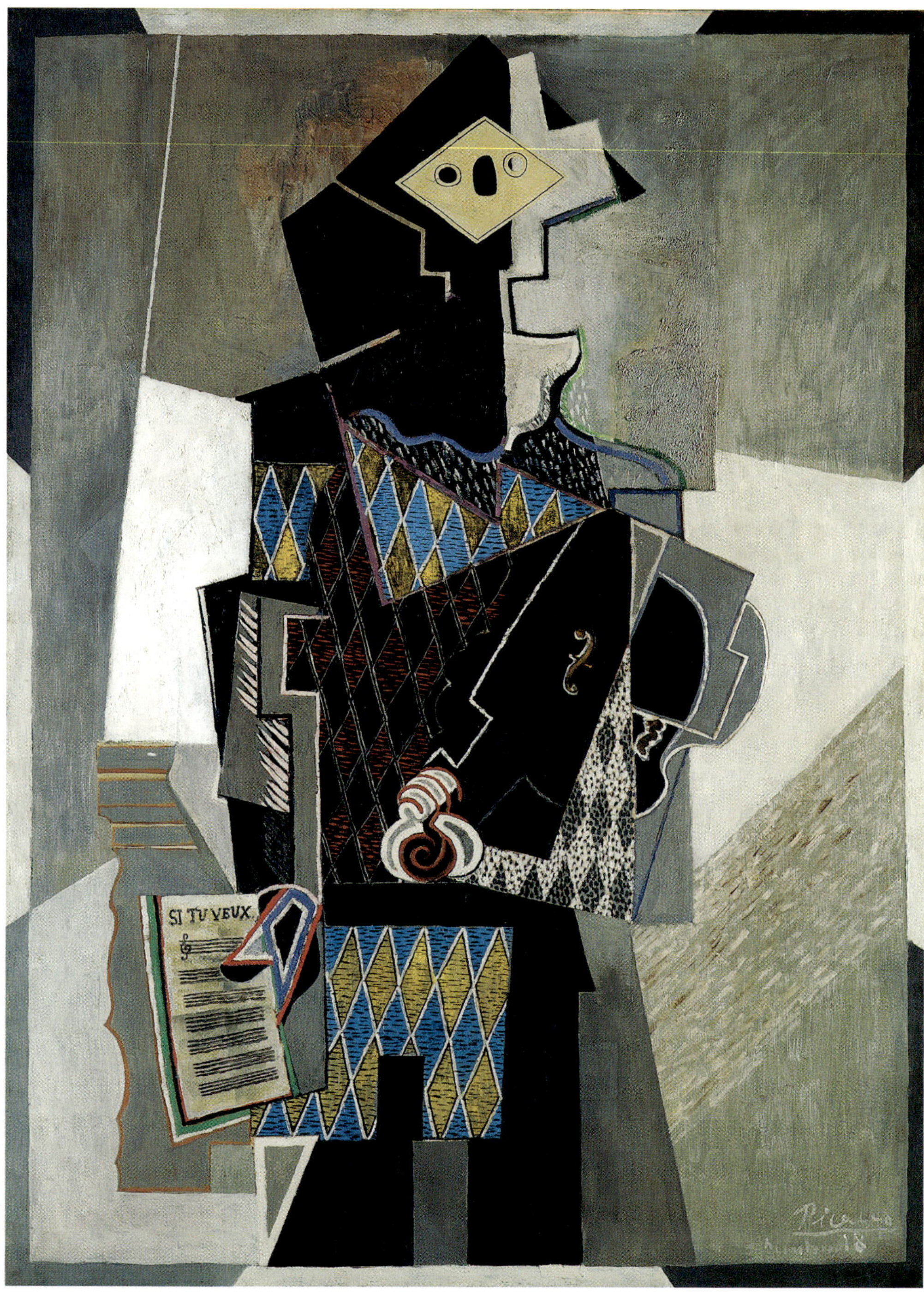
SI TU VEUX
Picasso

THE UNITY OF PICASSO'S ART

Meyer Schapiro

GEORGE BRAZILLER / NEW YORK

All works illustrated in this volume are by Pablo Picasso, unless otherwise noted.

First published in 2000 by George Braziller, Inc.

For information, please write to the publisher:

George Braziller, Inc.
171 Madison Avenue
New York, New York, 10016

Library of Congress Cataloging-in-Publication Data:

Schapiro, Meyer, 1904-96
The unity of Picasso's art / Meyer Schapiro.
p. cm.
Includes index.
ISBN 0-8076-1479-3 (cl)
1. Picasso, Pablo, 1881–1973—Criticism and interpretation. 2. Picasso, Pablo, 1881–1973. Guernica. 3. Cubism. 4. Einstein, Albert, 1879–1955—Aesthetics. I. Title.

N6853.P5 S33 2000
709'—dc21 00-034318

Frontispiece: Pablo Picasso, *Harlequin with Violin ("Si tu veux")*, 1918, oil on canvas, 56 x 39½" (142.2 x 100.3 cm), The Cleveland Museum of Art, Leonard C. Hanna, Jr., 1975.2.

Designed by Rita Lascaro
Printed in Hong Kong

FIRST EDITION

CONTENTS

PREFACE

In 1928 the author of these three essays published an illustrated text on Picasso, Braque, and Cubism in Columbia University's "Introduction to Contemporary Civilization in the West" syllabus. He also lectured on the subject at the Museum of Modern Art in New York in 1934. For this volume I selected three later lectures. There remains unpublished, among other texts, a lengthy one on *Guernica*.

The author lectured on "The Unity of Picasso's Art" at Brandeis University in April, 1969, and at the Albright-Knox Art Gallery in Buffalo in December, 1973. The present text, which consists of sections from the Brandeis and Albright-Knox lectures, was first prepared by the author in 1985 for the Metropolitan Museum of Art's Video Collection.

The text "Einstein and Cubism: Science and Art" has been edited by Dr. Joseph Masheck, editor of *Artforum* from 1977 to 1980 and Professor of Art History at Hofstra University, from a great mass of competing draft sheets, revisions, supplements, and notes that had grown out of a lecture delivered in 1979 at the Hebrew University of Jerusalem symposium commemorating the centenary of Albert Einstein's birth.

The lecture on Picasso's *Guernica* was given at the Carpenter Design Center, Harvard University, on December 15, 1966.

—Lillian Milgram Schapiro, Editor

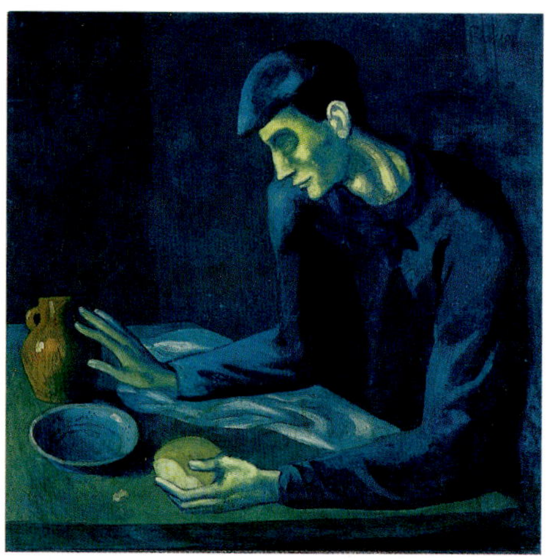

Figure 1. *The Blind Man's Meal*, autumn 1903, oil on canvas, 37½ x 37¼" (95.3 x 94.6 cm), The Metropolitan Museum of Art, New York, Gift of Mr. and Mrs. Ira Haupt, 1950 (50.188).

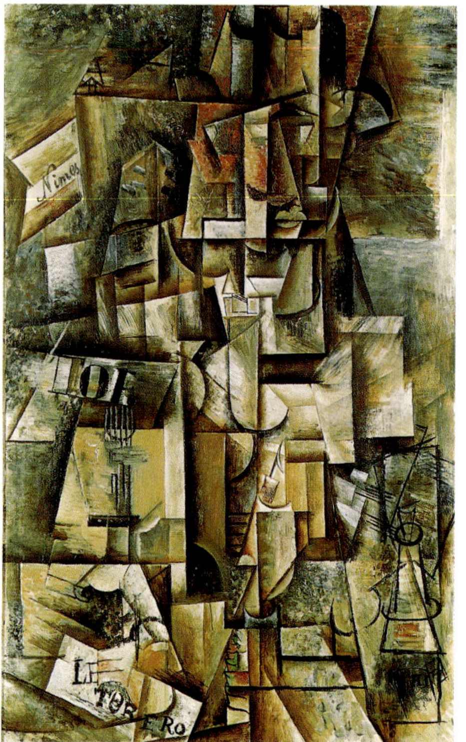

Figure 2. *The Aficionado*, summer– autumn 1912, oil on canvas, 53⅛ x 32¼" (135 x 82 cm), Kunstmuseum, Basel. Gift of Raoul La Roche, 1952.

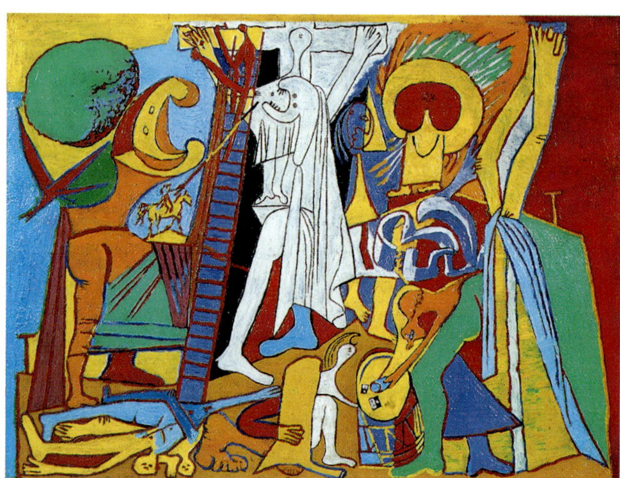

Figure 3. *The Crucifixion*, February 7, 1930, oil on plywood, 19¾ x 25⅞" (51.5 x 65.5 cm), Musée Picasso, Paris.

THE UNITY OF PICASSO'S ART

Picasso's art presents itself to us today as an example of a lifework that one cannot describe in terms of any single set of characteristics. If the works of Pablo Picasso were not identified directly with his name, if they were shown together in a big exhibition, it would be rather difficult to say that they were the work of one man. And yet, one of the most important characteristics of a true artist is that his work has a unified character, that it has a style that belongs to him. In the nineteenth century it was customary to say that the Western civilization of that century was inferior because it had not succeeded in creating a unified architectural style. Architects were able to design a building in a Moorish style, in a classic style, in a Gothic style, in a Baroque style, in a modern one. This fact of stylelessness, associated with the ability to work in all styles, was a sign of some inherent cultural defect. The lack of a particular, ripened, unique style belonging to the time itself was the outcome of some failure of integration or of common conviction in the society. We think of that as all the more true of an individual who is unable to find his way to a clear purpose and conception of his own goals and who therefore moves from one way of working to another, follows every impulse where it leads him, and in the end produces a great array of objects that are without a center, a core of meaning. And yet we look

Figs. 1-3

upon Picasso not as an eclectic artist, not as an artist who is entirely
Fig. 4 derivative, nor as an artist who is an ape of art rather than an ape of nature as was said in the older times, but as a man of extraordinary originality and power. There is no example in all history of another painter who has been able to create such a diversity of works and to give them the power of successful art. How are we to think of his unity then? Where shall we find it? Were we perhaps mistaken in posing the question of the relation between the unity of style and the character of an artist or of a culture in the terms to which we are accustomed when speaking of the nineteenth century? Shall we distinguish between two kinds of unity in the work of an artist: first, the unity of the individual work, which we sense without thinking of any other works that the artist has created; then unity of style, which is a characteristic of a whole series of works in which appears a consistency in the forms used by the artist? I have read the recent writings of a psychiatrist who argues that our ability to recognize an artist's work by his style is a sign of some difficulty, of a neurosis, which the artist has. The artist is forced to repeat himself constantly—he cannot break through some limiting habits. But in that case, all of us who have a handwriting of our own, or the familiar characteristics that permit one to recognize our voices and our speech, would therefore be neurotic. And every great artist who is immediately identifiable through his work would have to be regarded as neurotic. That is hardly an acceptable account of the unity or the consistency of a style.

Now besides, these conceptions of style or of unity of style as given in the single work and which of course are themselves partly conjectural—since we start from some idea of what consistency entails or what kinds of forms are consistent—besides *that* conception of unity of the single work and the consistency of an artist who holds to a particular set of forms through his life, one can approach the question of unity by looking into the character of the development of an artist. An artist may work differently at one moment of his life from the way he works at another moment. But one may observe not just a continuity between the different styles, one may observe also a growth, a process of unfolding in which a goal emerges gradually, or in which we sense

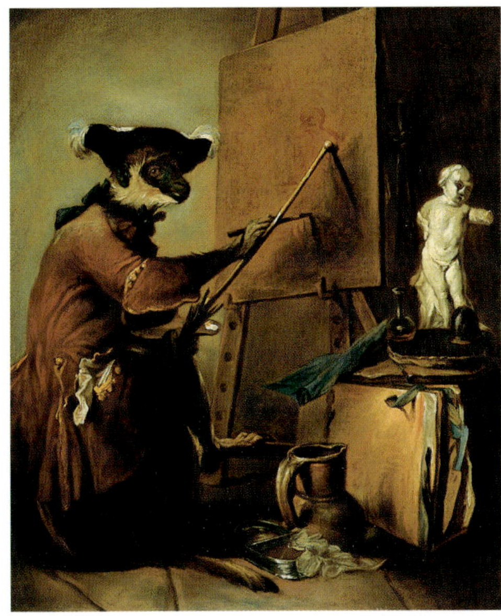

Figure 4. Jean-Baptiste Siméon Chardin, *The Monkey as Painter*, c. 1740, oil on canvas, 28¾ x 23⅞" (73 x 59.5 cm), Musée du Louvre, Paris.

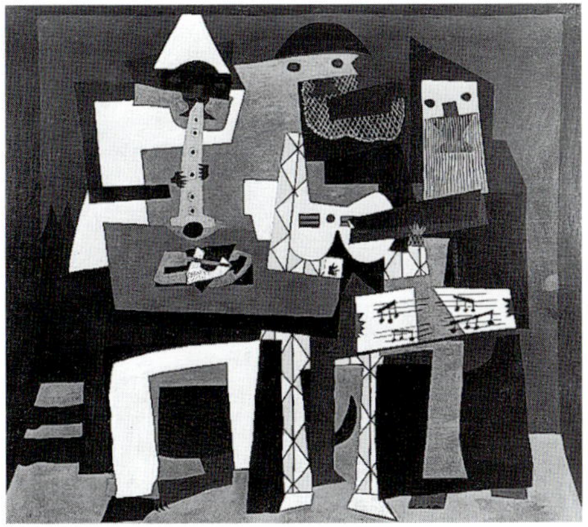

Figure 5. *Three Musicians*, summer 1921, oil on canvas, 79 x 87¾" (200.7 x 222.9 cm), The Museum of Modern Art, New York, Mrs. Simon Guggenheim Fund.

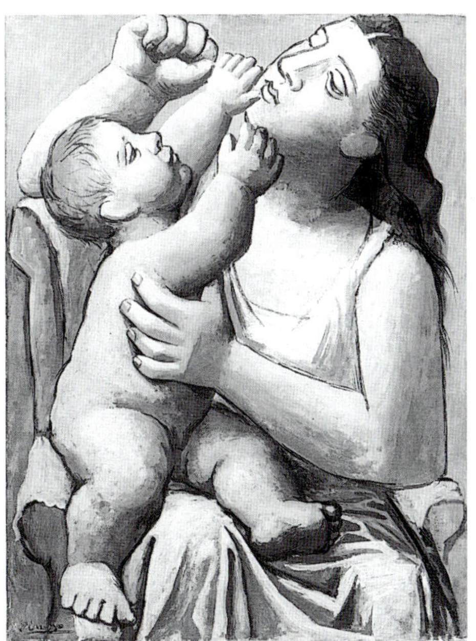

Figure 6. *Mother and Child*, summer 1921, oil on canvas, 38 x 28" (97 x 71 cm), Private collection.

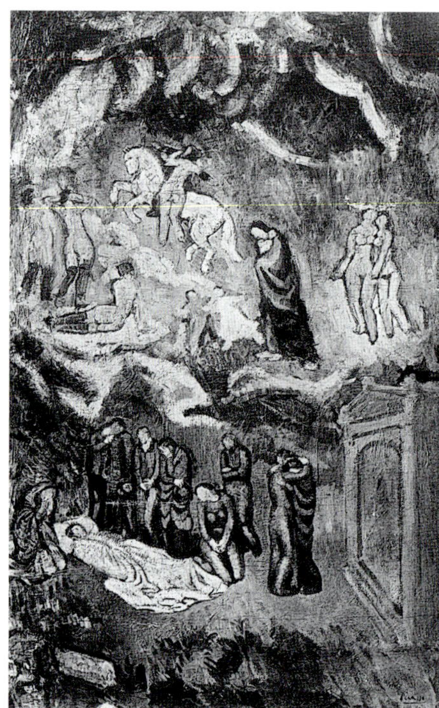

Figure 7. *Evocation* (*The Burial of Casagemas*), summer 1901, oil on canvas, 59⅛ x 35½" (150 x 90 cm), Musée d'Art Moderne de la Ville de Paris.

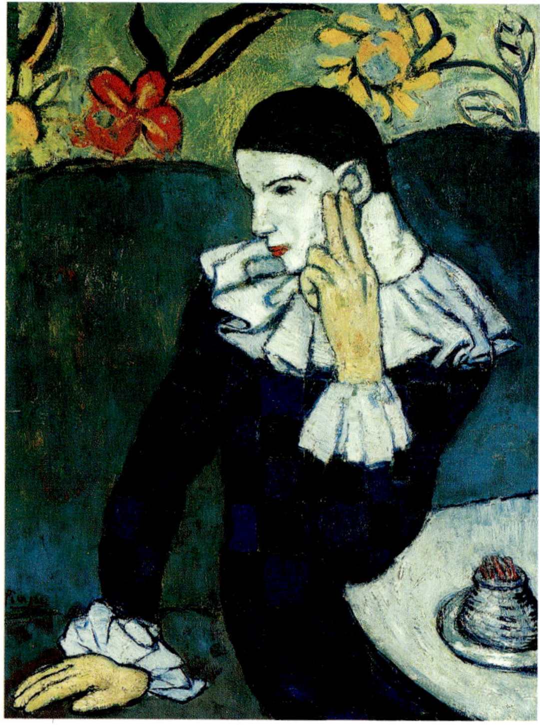

Figure 8. *Harlequin*, autumn 1901, oil on canvas, 32⅝ x 24⅛" (80 x 60.3), The Metropolitan Museum of Art, New York, Gift of Mr. and Mrs. John L. Loeb, 1960 (60.87).

the rightness and the development from the point of view of the realization of an individual's qualities in the successive works, only because we have the whole series and are therefore able to see relationships that would not be evident otherwise. Can one, then, looking at the work of Picasso as a totality—that is, in the seventy to seventy-five years during which he had been a painter and draftsman—can one discern in the immense production of his work certain features that relate to his growth, to his development, to his very diversity that will give us an idea of a unified personality as an achievement that depends precisely upon that unfolding? That insight would still not dispose of the criticism that has been made many times of the disunity of Picasso's work; for one cannot help but notice also in Picasso's work that at the very same moment he is able to paint and to draw in several different styles, he is not bound to a particular way of working at a moment. There exists in his practice a radical change with respect to the very concept of working, of production. Working involves, at least within our tradition, the commitment to a necessary way of working. If you can work in any other way you please, then no one way has a necessity; there is an element of caprice or arbitrariness of choice, but one that does not exclude alternatives that also characterize Picasso's way of working.

Figs. 5-6

Picasso enters the scene of European painting with an astonishing diversity of practice. At the occasion of his first show in Paris around 1901, a French poet, Félicien Fagus, reviewing that exhibition, said: This young man of twenty is able to paint in every manner of the day. We do not know what his own style is. In every one of these ways he is gifted. Will he succeed in finding *a* style? Will he become an artist with a commitment to something that belongs to himself alone? And the answer of Picasso was to create a whole series of individual styles, but more than that, to produce parallel unique styles of his own and then, at a later point in his life, to draw upon many styles he had created before. Where is the unity of the individual? Where is the consistent point of view? Can one speak of style in his work as a set of forms and a mode of combining, of ordering, of realizing expressive wholes that we sense belong to him uniquely? It is not easy to answer these questions; as I

Figs. 7-8

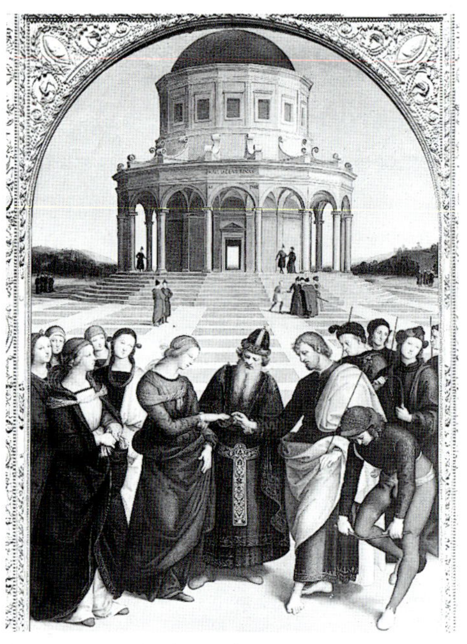

Figure 9. Raphael, *The Betrothal of the Virgin ('Sposalizio')*, 1504, oil on panel, 66$\frac{15}{16}$ x 46$\frac{7}{16}$" (170 x 118 cm), Pinacoteca di Brera, Milan.

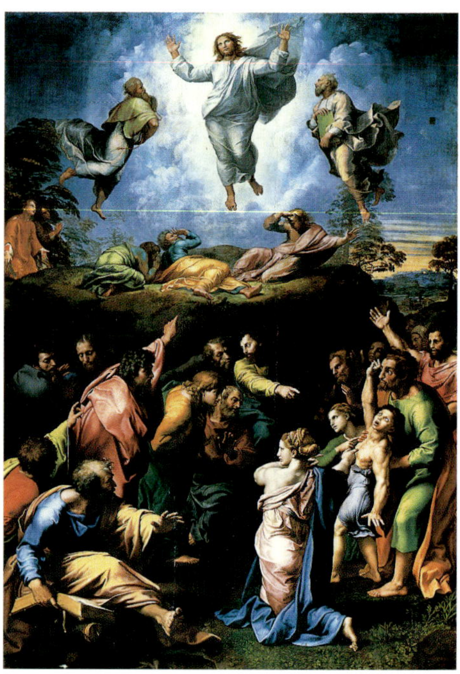

Figure 10. Raphael, *Transfiguration*, 1517-20, oil on panel, 13'3$\frac{7}{16}$" x 9'1$\frac{7}{16}$" (4.05 x 2.78 m), Musei Vaticani, Pinacoteca, Rome.

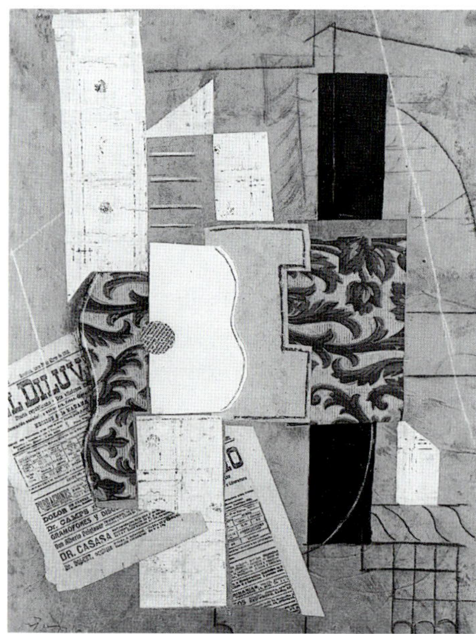

Figure 11. *Guitar*, spring 1913, pasted papers, charcoal, chalk, and India ink on blue paper mounted on ragboard, 26$\frac{1}{8}$ x 19$\frac{1}{2}$" (66.4 x 49.6 cm), The Museum of Modern Art, New York. Nelson A. Rockefeller Bequest.

said before, our ideas of what constitutes a consistent and ordered mode depend to a great extent upon the models of style that we have learned to recognize in older works. In the 1880s an English writer could say that Raphael is an extraordinary artist who had very different styles, so that one could not say if one were confronted by the *Betrothal* (the *Sposalizio)*, by the *Transfiguration*, and by a Madonna and Child that Figs. 9-10
they were the works of one painter. Raphael appeared to have that variety to an observer, and a very sensitive observer, in the 1880s. We also note that the conception of the accord of one aspect of the work with another aspect of the work depends partly upon a taste of a moment that is limited by goals and norms that have emerged recently and that will lead the observer to reject as somehow un-unified forms that, at a later time, will be accepted as thoroughly consistent. As an example, I may cite the practice of artists in the fifteenth and sixteenth centuries of painting a gold background in a picture that has highly realistic figures and deep landscape. Since gold is a conventional means and a highly luminous color with occasional spiritualistic implications that have been opposed to the idea of realistic painting of deep space and landscape, such works appear at first shocking to us. In time, we come to accept them; we find that this disparity has some kind of secret sense that we do not have to justify in any logical way; we simply begin to feel that these features work together to achieve some qualities that could not have been achieved in any other way, and these are qualities of high value. In a corresponding sense, Picasso at a certain moment placed on a canvas, which had been the customary field for paint alone, bits of paper and cloth, and cigar bands, rope, and wood—various textures Fig. 11
that were not produced by the painter but imported from outside. These alien elements were then brought into contact with quite other elements. One would assume in advance that could not work; they did not belong together; there was a kind of falsity, or conflict of styles and of means, that excluded real unity or harmony. Yet the artist was able finally to convince us, to make us accept this, to regard this as a happy invention. It was possible for a whole generation of artists afterward to live by further manipulation of the same forms, and of the principle

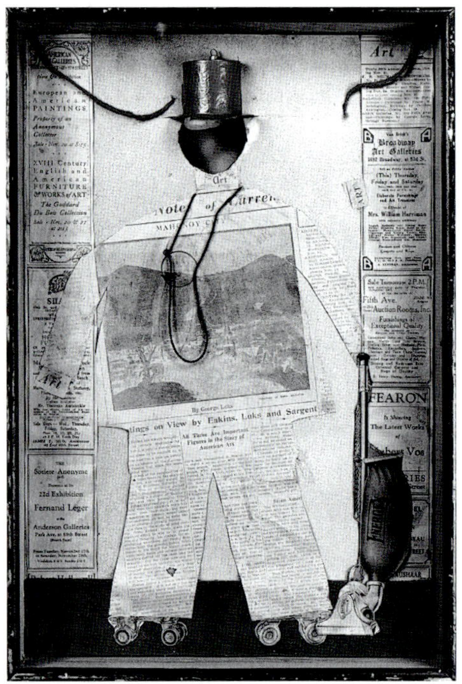

Figure 12. Arthur G. Dove, *The Critic*, 1925, collage of paper, newspaper, fabric, cord, and broken glass, 19¾ x 13¼ x 4¾" (50.2 x 33.7 x 12.1 cm), Collection of Whitney Museum of American Art, New York. Purchase, with funds from the Historic Art Association of the Whitney Museum of American Art, Mr. and Mrs. Morton L. Janklow, the Howard and Jean Lipman Foundation, Inc., and Hannelore Schulhof, 76.9.

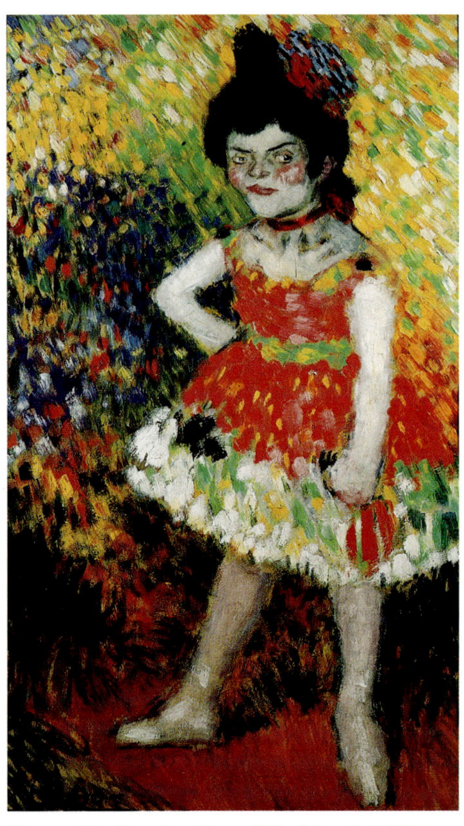

Figure 13. *Dancing Dwarf (La Nana)*, 1901, oil on cardboard, 41⅛ x 24" (104.5 x 61 cm), Museu Picasso, Barcelona.

underlying them, and even beyond that, to recognize that there was some deeper relationship to our own world, to our own interests, to the texture of our social and physical environment in such inventions. The judgment of unity is not an easy or obvious one, and we should allow for the fact that certain modes of form that appear to be on the whole discrepant, to involve a break with a consistent attitude, may ultimately disclose a deeper consistency or a consistency on another level. Fig. 12

To approach this question, I propose to show in sequence works of Picasso from about 1900 on and to look at these works from the point of view not so much of the inner consistency of each work as a painting—I believe that these works, or almost all those I am going to show you, have the unity of a work of art—but I shall ask you to consider rather the shifting characteristics from work to work and to ask yourself, What sort of sense has the passage? Does the artist expand his world? Does he make discoveries? Does he enrich your sense of his own being and of the possibilities of art through that succession? In other words, does the course or career of the successive styles and even the occasion of working in several styles at the same time introduce an element of enrichment, of value, or do these fail to emerge from that succession? And finally we can ask, How does the career as a whole, as observed through the variety of works and the unfolding of certain characteristics, speak to us as human beings who share with the artist within our own culture certain broad aims with reference to self-development, to self-realization as good human beings? I shall begin with the work of Picasso around 1900 to 1903.

The first example of his work in that 1901 exhibition that I described is the *Dwarf Dancer*. He painted, as I said, in a manner that recalls a number of Parisian artists of the time, but generally Parisian artists who are fairly new, original, and active—those in the circle of Henri Toulouse-Lautrec, for example, or of the Nabi painters and some of the new Symbolist painters, also of Paul Gauguin. Here you see a painting of a theme from the Parisian world that, coming from Spain for the first time, he seems to delight in. The streets, the cafés, the amusements, the varied human types all attract him by their picturesqueness, Fig. 13

their colorfulness, their activity, their air of freedom. He paints with a vigorous brushstroke, with many little touches in a quasi-Impressionist see Fig. 8 manner. In the *Harlequin*, you see how at the very same time or nearly the same time he also is able to work in a more obviously outlined, patterned manner with big, flat areas and with themes that are not vivacious themes but more contemplative ones that relate to reverie. He places great importance on features of ornament, on deliberate patterning, and on a pronounced simplicity of the large form in contrast to the broken, all-over, scattered quality of the other work. And the colors, as you can see, are again of a rather different kind, a limited palette with one or two dominant hues.

This is followed by the first stage in which he seems to shape a style that is recognizably his and that is still valued today by many who find it difficult to accept the work that he did as a Cubist painter and in more recent times. It is called the Blue Period not because the color of every Fig. 14 painting is blue—there are some that tend toward violet and green but on the whole the blue is so striking. It is suffused in the work; it is the color of both the figure and the surroundings of the figure, so the figure is immersed in the color blue. And the normal associations of bluishness with depression are intensified by the line drawing and by the gesture, the posture of the single figure represented. These are essentially figures of pathos.

The paintings of this Blue Period are usually of homeless, impoverished figures in postures of self-constraint, of self-enclosure, figures who often turn away from the world either through blindness, or dimmed eyes, or through the lowering and shutting of the eyes while the figure listens rather than looks. The entanglement of the body within itself, the arrangement of the limbs so that they form knots, closed forms, a suggestion of introverted, medieval types, and, above Fig. 15 all, the emptiness and sparseness of the environment and concentration of color on one mood give these pictures their particular sentiment, or sentimentality. Important, with respect to the previous work, is the study of the modeling and the interlaced arabesques that are the carriers of a movement—a melody of sorrow, if you wish.

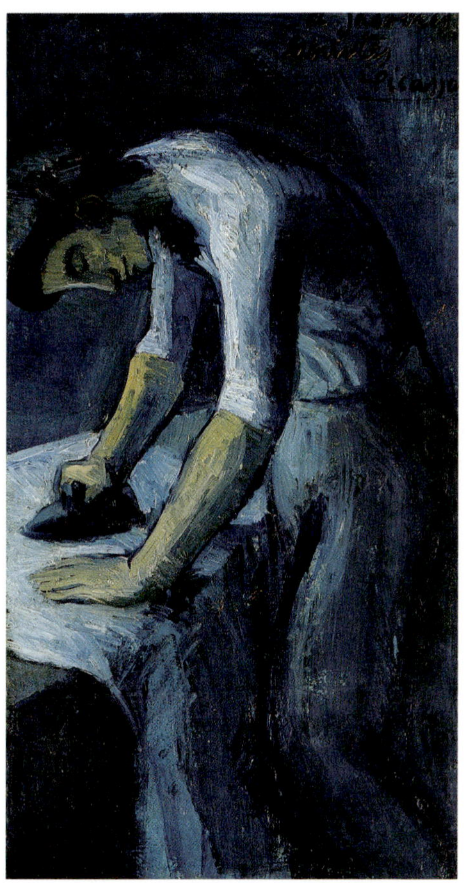

Figure 14. *A Woman Ironing*, 1901, oil on canvas mounted on cardboard, 19½ x 10⅛" (49.5 x 25.7 cm), The Metropolitan Museum of Art, New York, Alfred Stieglitz Collection, 1949 (49.70.2).

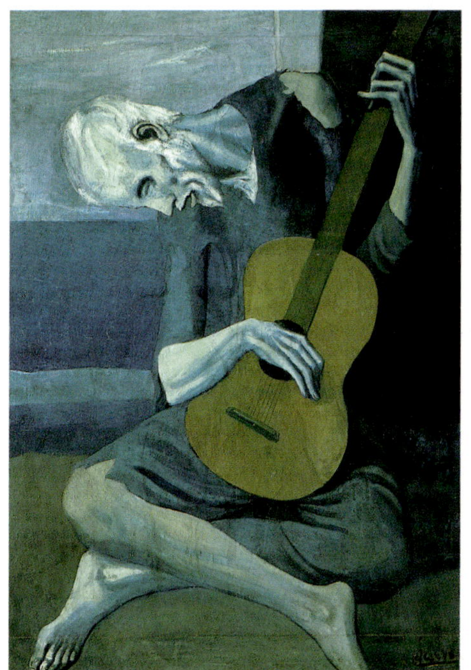

Figure 15. *The Old Guitarist*, autumn 1903, oil on panel, 47¾ x 32½" (122.9 x 82.6 cm), The Art Institute of Chicago. Helen Birch Bartlett Memorial Collection, 1926.253.

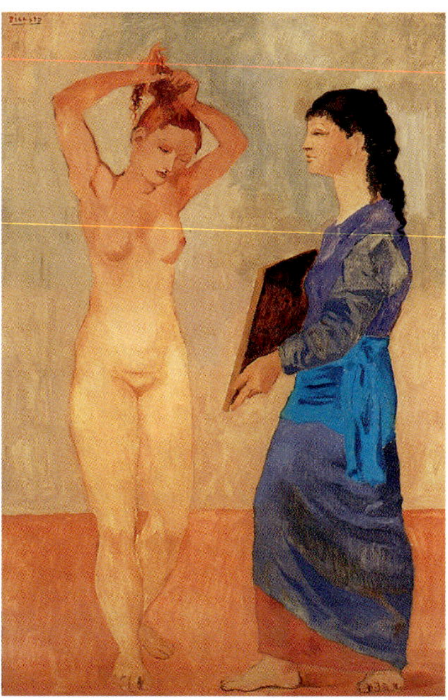

Figure 16. *La Toilette*, early summer 1906, oil on canvas, 59½ x 39" (151 x 99 cm), Albright-Knox Art Gallery, Buffalo, New York. Fellows for Life Fund, 1926.

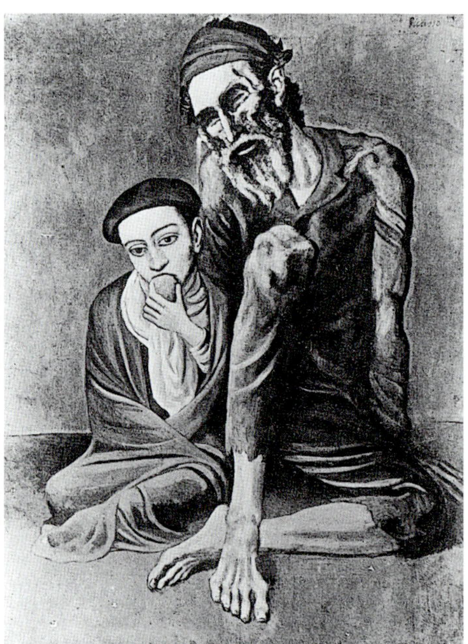

Figure 17. *The Old Jew ("The Old Man")*, 1903, oil on canvas, 49¼ x 36¼" (125 x 92 cm), Pushkin Museum, Moscow.

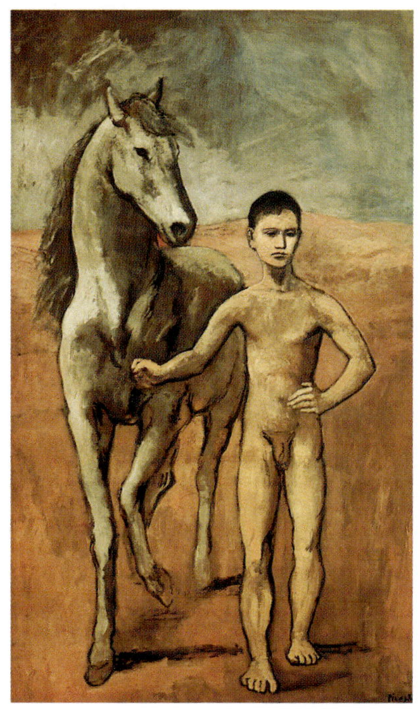

Figure 18. *Boy Leading a Horse*, early 1906, oil on canvas, 7' 2⅞" x 51⅛" (220.6 x 131.2 cm), The Museum of Modern Art, New York, The William S. Paley Collection, 575.64.

This phase is followed in 1905 by the Rose or Pink Period. The figures become more serene. They are shown in postures of self-enlargement and elongation. They raise their hands above their heads instead Fig. 16 of entwining the limbs within each other. They admire themselves, or are shown as objects of respect that are beautiful within themselves rather than broken down. The previous figures belong to a moment of Picasso's youth when he pities himself as a homeless immigrant in Paris Fig. 17 and identifies with the bohemian and the blind and the poor, the outcast, as in Charles Baudelaire's beautiful prose-poem *The Old Acrobat*, in whom Baudelaire finds an image of the old artist, the old poet, who is forgotten, who lives in a corner and to whom no one listens any longer and who has to feed his own sorrow with his self-pitying poetry. That phase, which corresponds, as I said, to a thought of the painter about himself—the painter occupied with his position within his immediate surrounding world as an outsider and as almost an outcast, homeless and unknown—is followed by the Rose Period. The blue remains, but the totality is more luminous in color, and the pink and rose and red tones begin to prevail with the theme of the glorification of the beautiful, and with the woman holding the mirror to the beautiful nude as if herself an artist who reflects the beauty that is admired.

But it is in a whole series of other paintings that we can see the continuity and the importance of this change of attitude. Many large paintings show a small figure—and that figure represents Picasso's sense of Fig. 18 his own smallness physically—leading a great horse, elegant in posture, noble, reminiscent of classical and Renaissance conceptions of the hero who guides the horse, one of the Dioscuri. In the choice of colors, the relations of the gray and the bluish tones are somewhat austere, but they do not have that oneness of suffused color of a single, predominant sentiment. Instead, there is a balance, an opposition of forces, and a searching of the outline for strength and elegance rather than for a melodic, recurrent, emotional undulation of the line.

There is a painting in which we are able to observe how Picasso at this moment transforms himself and his object in painting. In a drawing of a dancer in the Oberlin museum—and it is significant how many of the figures that he paints at this time belong to art—he represents a Fig. 19 girl in profile with a fan in her hand and the other hand thrown over the arm. In the painting of *Woman with a Fan* the hand holding the fan Fig. 20 is retained but the other hand is raised in a commanding posture. He converts what appears to be a retired, recessive figure—one almost weakened by the drawing in tentative strokes and possessing an expression that relates to musing, to reverie—into a strong, commanding figure, like a priestess conducting a ritual with an instrument in one hand and a commanding gesture in the other. The figure in *Woman with a Fan* is inspired, I believe, by a painting by Dominique Ingres, in the Fig. 21 Brussels museum, of Augustus calling upon Virgil to stop when he reads from his poem a prediction about the family of Augustus. The great emperor is shown with his right hand raised; in the lower hand he holds the woman who has fainted in his lap. His profile is the immediate model for the conception of *Woman with a Fan.* From the the original drawing of the figure, with her relaxed and recessive posture, he has constructed in the painting *Woman with a Fan* a figure of command, authority, and power, with a precedent of imperial authority.[1]

At this time there are also many paintings in which Picasso represents a youth with a laurel wreath on his head, or in a posture of adulation by others, or a figure standing on a great horse as a bareback rider, or with gestures of acrobatic skill in powerful movement. The main theme, then, is of the artist figure, the performer, as triumphant, laureate, admired, in contrast to what appeared in the Blue Period, and with that an important change in the means of painting, both in the lines and the colors, but also in the conception of the whole field of the work.

He becomes more concerned at this time with the artist not only as an acclaimed performer or a man of achievement but also as one who is attentive to his own art, who is studying, investigating the processes of art. He shows two acrobats: one who is seated on a great block of Fig. 22 stone—massive, sculptural, vertical and horizontal in his limbs, like the block of stone; and the other, the youthful acrobat, girlish, labile, balancing herself, asymmetrical, on a spherical stone. Two different modes of balance in art, belonging to the world of the acrobat as well as to the

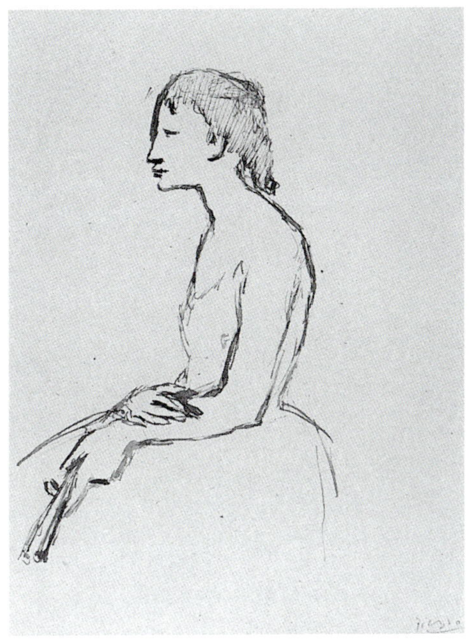

Figure 19. *Woman with a Fan*, early 1905, pen and black ink on paper, pasted on white cardboard, 12¾ x 8⅞" (32.7 x 22.5 cm), Allen Memorial Art Museum, Oberlin College, Oberlin, Ohio, Charles F. Olney Fund, 1949.

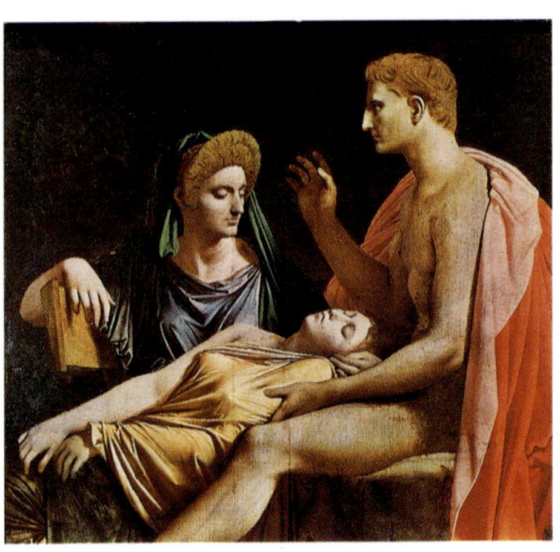

Figure 21. Jean-Auguste-Dominique Ingres, *Tu Marcellus eris*, fragment cut from a version of *Virgil's Reading from the 'Aeneid' before Augustus and Livia*, 1813–14, oil on canvas, 54¼ x 55⅞" (138 x 142 cm), Musées Royaux d'Art et d'Histoire, Brussels.

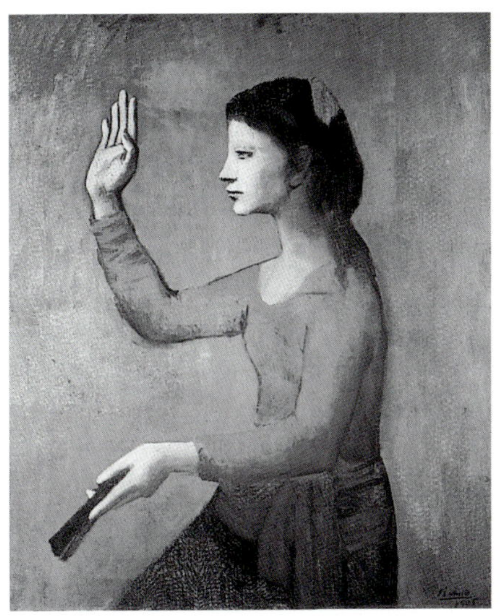

Figure 20. *Woman with a Fan*, late 1905, oil on linen, 39½ x 32" (100.3 x 81.3 cm), National Gallery of Art, Washington, D.C. Gift of the W. Averell Harriman Foundation in memory of Marie N. Harriman.

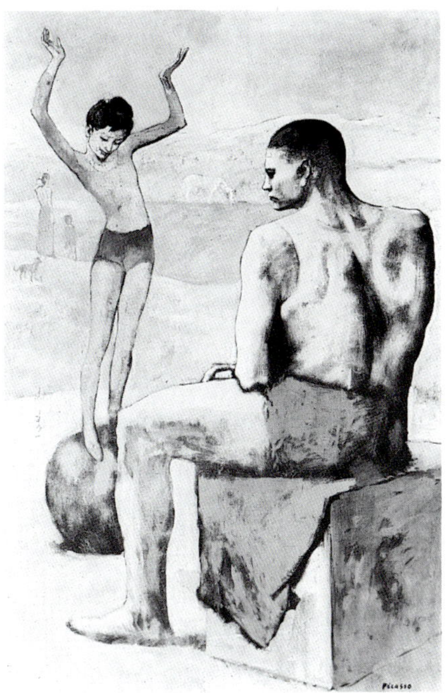

Figure 22. *Acrobat on a Ball*, 1905, oil on canvas, 57⅞ x 37⅜" (147 x 95 cm), Pushkin Museum, Moscow.

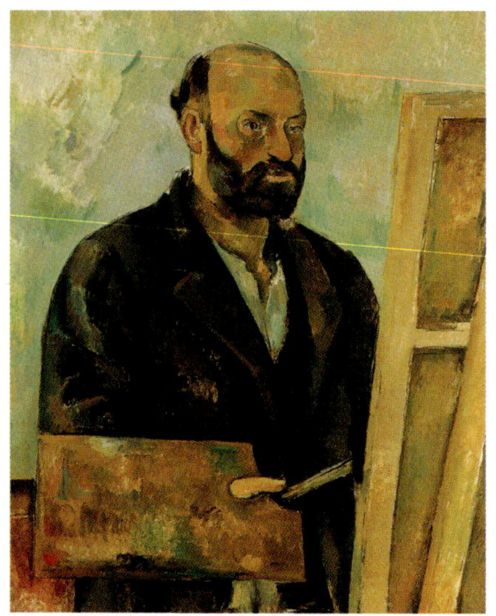

Figure 23. Paul Cézanne, *Self-Portrait with Palette*, 1885-87, oil on canvas, 36¼ x 28¾" (92 x 73 cm), Foundation E. G. Bührle Collection, Zurich.

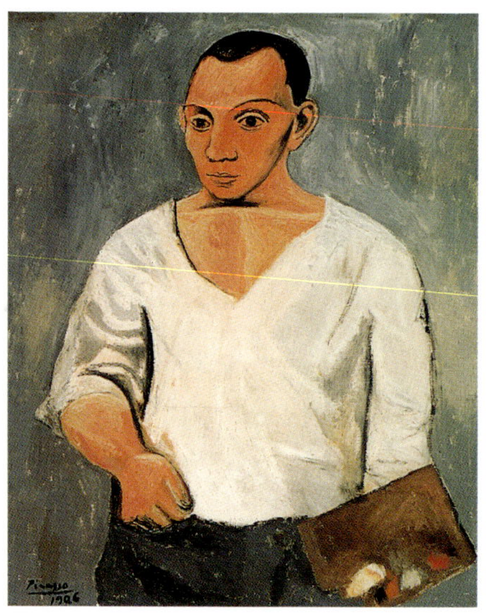

Figure 24. *Self-Portrait with Palette*, autumn 1906, oil on canvas, 36¼ x 28¾" (92 x 73 cm), Philadelphia Museum of Art. A. E. Gallatin Collection.

painter, are presented together. It is a theme of the consciousness of art as a skilled activity of manipulating the instruments, which here is the human body itself, and adjusting them in relation to ideal forms of stone, to forms in nature, against a background that is vague and relates to wandering Gypsies or bohemians. You can see in this work a new attitude toward both the theme and the mode of painting. However, it is still a story-picture rather than a fully realized conception if we approach it in terms of what is to follow. He is telling you about the practice of art, about the conditions of balance, about the opposed possibilities of such balancing, the relationships to the vertical and horizontal coordinates and the plane surface and modeling in the one case and to the curvilinear, asymmetrical, and unstable in the other.

From this point he moves to a new approach partly through the discovery of the work of Paul Cézanne, who had just died and was to have a great exhibition in Paris that was enormously impressive to artists and that influenced them in various ways. Picasso paints this self-portrait as
Figs. 23-24 Cézanne had painted a self-portrait. The color is no longer blue or rose,

but even though it has some delicate tints of green and pink, it is mainly in white, gray, sand, beige, and stone colors, that is, the colors of materials of construction, of workmanship, and with a characteristic dryness and weight. And he uses them with fine intervals between them. He represents himself in a stylized way that minimizes the expressive character of a face, or becomes a mask by minimizing the normal expression of a face. It becomes a masklike face with geometrically drawn features, with very distinct shapes that relate to each other rhythmically and as characteristic forms. He gives an immense strength to the right arm that paints. It is that of an artisan-worker with confidence in his manipulation. He identifies the silhouette of the palette, from which he derives his colors, with the outline of his arm and with the edge of his smock. There is an enormous cohesiveness of the shapes and also closeness of the tones to one another and a greater legibility of the parts in the whole, and a search for variation that you can see in the drawing of the eyes and the two lines of the V of the opening of the smock: one more convex, the other more concave. There are many finesses of form, but they are kept within a large, strong, simple effect. This, we may say, is the first work in which Picasso shows himself as a painter for whom the will to a strong, classiclike, finely knit, and necessary relatedness of the parts to each other, yielding an effect of strength and purposiveness of design in the work, appear without reference to a particular sentiment about the person rendered, unless we admit also that this is an attitude toward oneself. He is determined now to be an artist in a newer sense than before, not an artist who projects his dreams and passions, fantasies, yearnings, self-pity, and sorrows into the picture, but one who wants to show his true strength as that of an artist who can build, manipulate, apportion, who knows the rightness of every element within the whole in an architectural sense. He is inspired to it by the example of Cézanne without following Cézanne's color or brushwork. The painting of Picasso is a much thicker, more material kind of painting. It has more abrupt, clear contrasts of color, unlike Cézanne's subtle modeling and searching of colors throughout, but he takes from Cézanne that idea of the palette, which is a flat plane right in front of the picture, which continues into the silhouette of the figure, or the fine

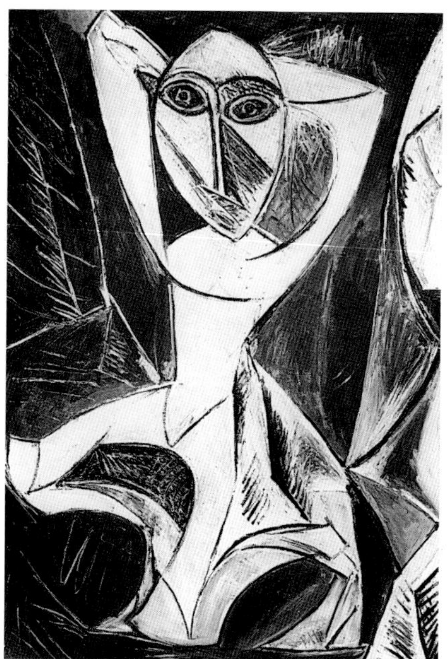

Figure 25. *Nude with Raised Arms*, spring–summer 1907, oil on canvas, 59⅛ x 39½" (150 x 100 cm), Private collection.

cutting of the collar and the precise determination of the angle of the brushes against the diagonals of the figure, and of the easel and the canvas. But there are hundreds of elements within it that could come to your eye at once if you saw the original. We are not concerned now with that so much as with the new decision, new direction, of the young Picasso at the age of twenty-five to move away from the colored periods, so to speak, toward austerity, construction, precision, and control.

Within a year that style gives way to a search for intensity of expression without the use of the normal signs. The signs are not those of a sorrowing or joyful face, of a posture that either celebrates or detaches oneself, but it is the angularities and the abrupt, strong contrasts that become expressive, and also the energy of production of the lines, the shapes, the spots in the work. Noteworthy now, more than in the preceding work, is the connectedness of the shapes in the figure and the shapes in the ground. The simplest illustration in the *Nude with Raised* Fig. 25 *Arms* is the big shadow along the nose, as a triangle in black, and the black triangle between the face and the raised right arm. They belong together, and with them also goes the white triangle, which is complementary or conjugate to it. These three work together in a rhythmical manner but also in a surprising manner. They do not belong to nature; they belong to art, but they have a powerful effect within the work. We can see further developments of the same idea in the hanging curtain with the swinging triangles, or in the rounded shape between the legs and at the breast and also in the drapery in the lower right. Wherever you turn, you discover examples of a spontaneous, purposive energy of shaping; at the same time there is an aspect of savagery, of intense, wild expression in the physiognomic. There are also differences in the drawing of the eyes and the limbs that relate to that. So here we have the notion of the artistic process as primitive and yet rational, well-ordered, cohesive, and surprisingly connected to parts that you don't notice at first because they don't belong to objects but function as part of an object or part of the empty space around and between the object; the parts are all of the same order of necessity and make similar contributions to the whole. In that way the canvas at last has become completely his own.

Now there is an intervening period between this *Nude* and Cubist painting in which he explores the solidity, the convexity, and the concavity of objects and their cast shadows, their existence in three dimensions, (Figs. 26-27) as if he is trying to recover the elemental conditions of the presence of things within our space and especially their tangibility, their tactility. But I pass over that phase to turn to what was called Cubist painting.

The name Cubist painting arose from that first study of the effort to restore weightiness and solidity in an elementary sense to the objects represented. But very soon the component surfaces, the planes in these objects, began to be detached from the object, so in painting a head there is no longer a bounding outline of the head. At the edge of the head there are plane surfaces that seem to advance from the side of the head and behind the head; likewise the neck and shoulders have become shuffled (Fig. 28) into bits of segments of modeling and passages of light to dark and overlapping planes. We no longer have what was called Cubist or Cubistic in the year 1908. By 1909 and 1910, the trend was away from it.

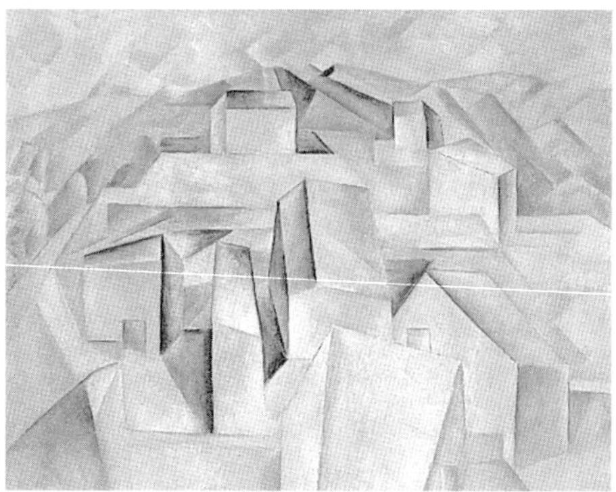

Figure 26. *Houses on the Hill, Horta de Ebro*, summer 1909, oil on canvas, 25⅝ x 31⅞" (65 x 81 cm), The Museum of Modern Art, New York. Nelson A. Rockefeller Bequest.

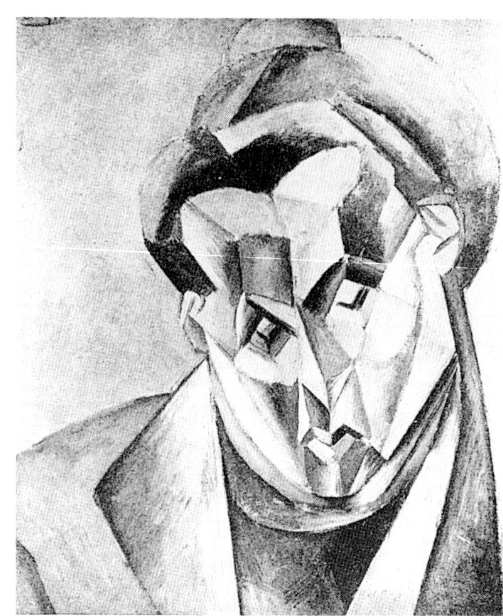

Figure 27. *Head of a Woman (Fernande)*, summer 1909, oil on canvas, 25⅝ x 21¼" (65 x 54 cm), Museu de Arte Moderna, Rio de Janeiro.

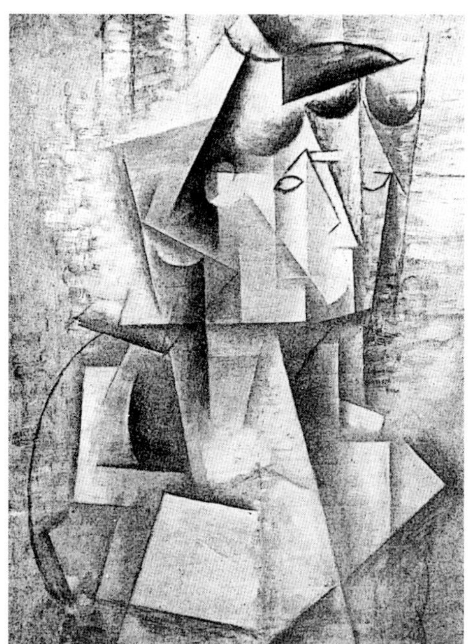

Figure 28. *Girl from Arles*, summer 1912, oil on canvas, 28¾ x 21¼" (73 x 54 cm), Private collection.

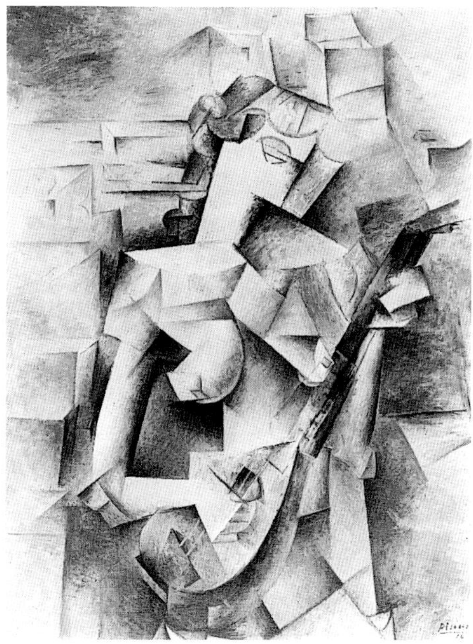

Figure 29. *Girl with a Mandolin (Fanny Tellier)*, late spring 1910, oil on canvas, 39½ x 29" (100.3 x 73.6 cm), The Museum of Modern Art, New York. Nelson A. Rockefeller Bequest.

Cubist painting is in itself so complex—it has so many aspects—that it would be impossible for me in a few minutes to give you an adequate idea of the underlying notions or approaches. I can simply point to a few features that are important as a new development, as an enlargement of Picasso's sense of art. It has to do with the exploration of possibilities that he envisages one by one without anticipating what would come out of them. Neither he nor Georges Braque, who was his fellow inventor of Cubism in the years 1908 to 1914, could have known in 1909 what the 1910 art would be. Nor in 1910 what the 1911 art would be. They were themselves taken by surprise. It was a process of extraordinary fertility of new forms that seemed to emerge with each new stroke or new step, so that a picture had to be either scrapped or had to be the starting point of another picture the very next time he painted, but an entirely new one with reference to certain features. Fig. 29

Now in Cubist painting there is no attempt at simulation of physics, no influence of modern mathematics; it has nothing to do with non-Euclidean geometry or the fourth dimension. A German astronomer, Johann Karl Friedrich Zöllner, in Leipzig, wrote a book on the fourth dimension as a space in which spirits were concealed, from which they came forth into the three-dimensional world. That was an old idea of seventeenth-century metaphysicians, that there is a fourth dimension that is the abode of spiritual beings. And that idea was applied to Cubism because it looked so abstruse and the normal relationships of planes, of surfaces in three dimensions, were continually violated by it.

In these Cubist paintings it is very hard to recognize—to see—that a given plane is in front of another plane and behind a third plane. Fig. 30 There is a shuffling and overlapping and transparency and paradoxical discontinuity and then renewed continuity that is not in accord with our normal perception of the order of layers in a three-dimensional space or the positions of things in an overlapping series. But that type of free composition with a new approach to continuity and discontinuity is inspired by the conviction that painting is a process of forming lines and strokes in a free manner so that they have a high degree of orderliness through the correspondences of tones, of balance, of direc-

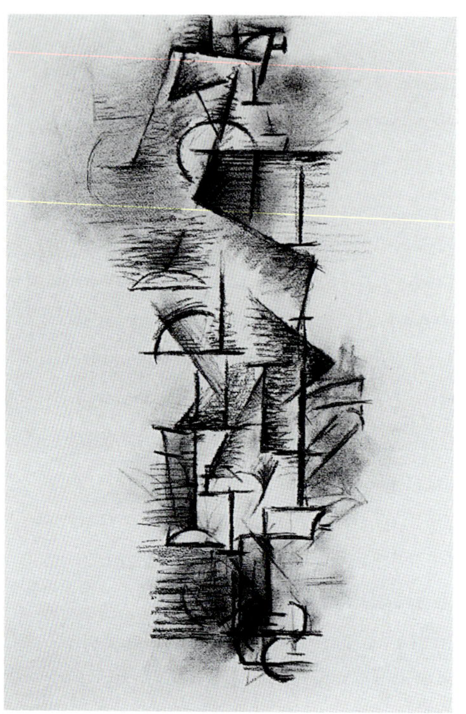

Figure 30. *Standing Female Nude*, summer 1910, charcoal, 19 x 12⅜" (48.3 x 31.2 cm), The Metropolitan Museum of Art, New York, The Alfred Stieglitz Collection, 1949 (49.70.34).

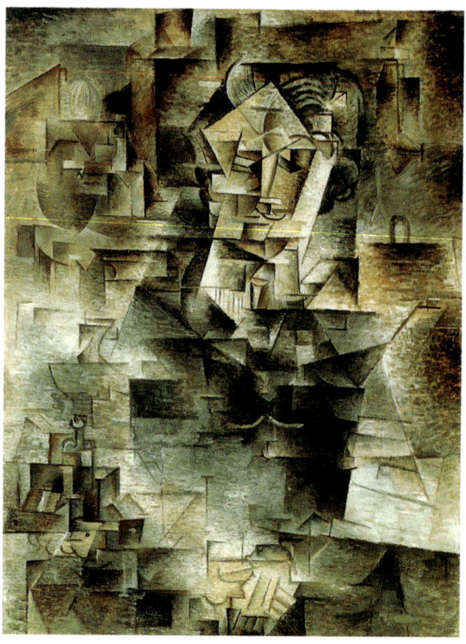

Figure 31. *Portrait of Daniel-Henry Kahnweiler*, autumn 1910, oil on canvas, 39⅝ x 25⅝" (101.1 x 73.3 cm), The Art Institute of Chicago. Gift of Mrs. Gilbert W. Chapman in memory of Charles B. Goodspeed, 1948.561.

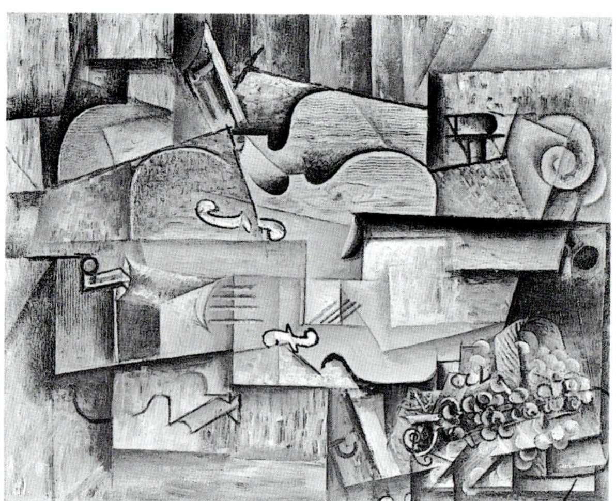

Figure 32. *Violin and Grapes*, spring–early autumn 1912, oil on canvas, 20 x 24" (50.6 x 61 cm), The Museum of Modern Art, New York. Mrs. David M. Levy Bequest.

tions, but also a high appearance of openness, randomness, a continual changing and shuffling of forms.

There was satisfied a new norm of creativeness as a process of perpetual innovation, not only from canvas to canvas, but within each canvas. But the work itself was done in an austere way with a limited tonality, usually of grays, beiges, and browns, colors that seem unemotional—we may call them colors of thought—and with a search both for elements that come out of a known object, like a human head, and for elements that are introduced to connect parts, which are arbitrary constructions for the sake of unity and which represent nothing. One can make an analogy by taking as a model the characteristics of sentences about things, sentences about words, and sentences about the signs, or the marks through which words are written or the sounds produced. For example, if I say, "I am Meyer Schapiro," I am talking about myself. If I say, "I am a pronoun," I'm not speaking correct English; I have to say, "*I* is a pronoun." I am not talking about myself but about the word for myself. If I say, "*I* is a vertical line," I am referring to the stroke through which I make the word *I* on a sheet of paper. There are three different senses of the word *I*. In the Cubist painting all three senses exist. There are recognizable signs for eyes, nose, and so on; there are lines that belong to the category of lines out of which noses and eyes are made; and finally, there are strokes through which such lines are built up, and also strokes that build up planes. Perhaps that would be a rough account of this phase of Cubism. I say "this phase" because a year later it was altogether different.

Fig. 31

In the next phase, around 1912–13, a new series of paintings is dominated by the theme of musical instruments, especially hand instruments—mandolins, guitars, violins—and also by objects of the table—smoking things, books, papers—various elements that belong to a sphere of manipulation, but especially musical instruments. They are constructed from straight and curved lines. They are a means for producing music through separate, discrete notes, and possess a great charm that is not easily analyzable and that we respond to as a whole and not only in terms of isolated parts.

Fig. 32

This phase also includes the introduction of writing and of objects, collage, whereby the painting, which has become an object in itself constructed by the painter with elements that he has discovered through analysis of the procedures and means of painting the marks and strokes Fig. 33 that build up the signs, becomes a field of free invention and construction but with some guiding feelings or moods and the sense of poetic analogy with the musical and with the printed matter, since printing and writing are instrumentalities for the production of meaning, formed of a small number of standardized unit shapes—straight lines, curved lines, letters, periods, brackets, parentheses, and so on. Since the painting of Cubism has become an object of its own kind, as it were, for itself, and no longer through the values of representation while preserving certain features of representation as a starting point or as a point for reflection and elaboration, so we see in 1912 the development of the idea of applying to the painting, which is a thing in the world, objects from the world on the same level of "thing" character.

So Picasso and Braque apply bits of newspaper and in this case a tablecloth, but that tablecloth is itself stamped, printed, has on it a stamped or printed ornament. That ornament is a highly realistic, almost photographic representation of caning, of a network, and that Fig. 34 network produces a pattern of lights and darks in a rhythmical fashion. Not only is this a painting, but it is a painting on which there is something from the real world that has been pasted onto the same canvas; but that object from the real world is itself decorated with a painting, but a painting that is absolutely regular, but that regularity is intricate, and not only is it intricate but it has an ambiguity of light-dark pattern. Then once having set that, he writes "JOU," which is perhaps from the word *journal;* he paints a cigarette over it with a cast shadow; he produces in this free Cubist constructed manner various vessels; and he also paints the edge of the table with a perspective suggestion. So the boundaries between the simulated and the real are now removed. It is a quasi-metaphysical, or epistemological, painting in which the painter enjoys the reflections and his own power of manipulating different stages of what we call reality: the real object, the simulated object, the

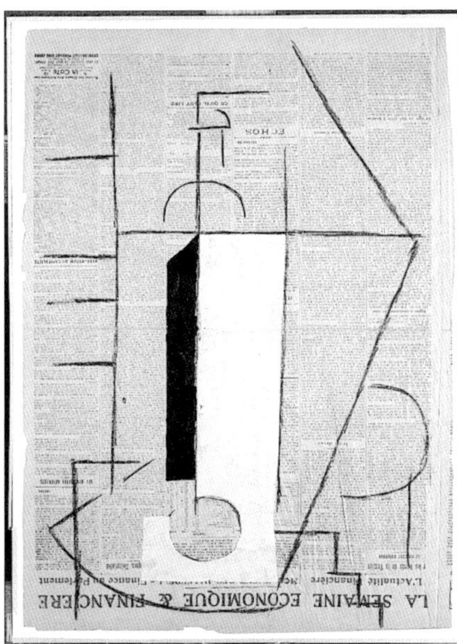

Figure 33. *Bottle on a Table*, winter 1912-13, pasted papers, charcoal, and pencil on newsprint, 24⅜ x 17⅜" (62.5 x 44 cm), Musée Picasso, Paris.

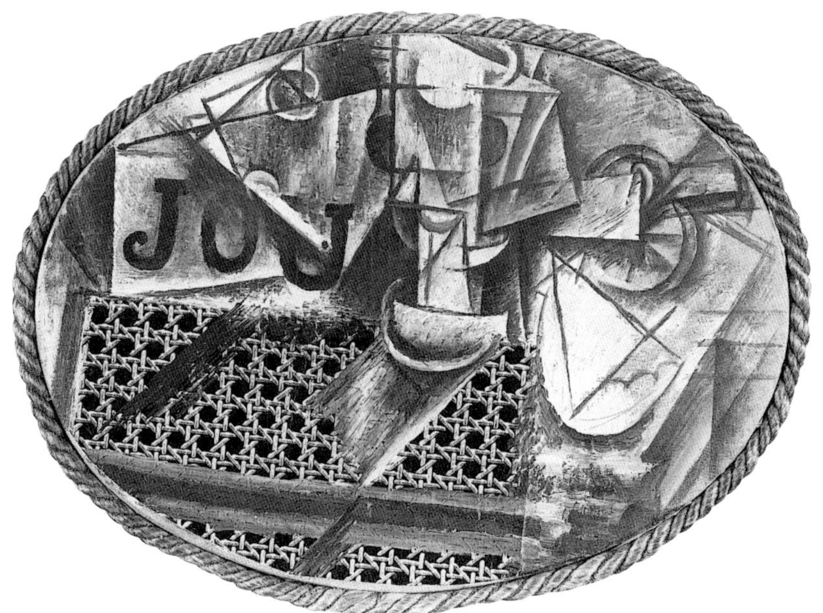

Figure 34. *Still Life with Chair Caning*, spring 1912, oil and oilcloth stuck on oval canvas framed with rope, 10⅝ x 13¾" (27 x 35 cm), Musée Picasso, Paris.

conjunction of these, and various arbitrary constructions that bind them. And finally around the whole he puts a rope, which is a frame formed by twisting two strands and you cannot tell precisely how the two strands are fitted to each other. Hence, something of the ambiguity of the painting appears in the frame, which is a real object and belongs to the world just as much as it belongs to the painting. This is an example of the passage of Picasso from an early stage of art in which he worries deeply and sighs about the state of the artist, his poverty and estrangement in the world, to a state where he is a sovereign inventor and manipulator of what belongs to the innermost procedures of his art, but with a great daring and imaginativeness as to the fundamental underlying relationships within painting, not in order to generalize it as a philosopher would but to make a whole that has its own attractiveness and intensity and incites our exploration and admiration for all these colors and tones and ingenious play of elements.

Having broken up the world in terms of the mode of conceiving and representing it through marks, signs, diagrammatic structures, and so on, and having integrated them with real objects, so that what we say about the world is itself a part of the world—speech is just as truly as existent a thing as molecules and atoms—Picasso follows this sense of the material reality, of the processing of the canvas, with a trend toward reconstituting the world that has been decomposed. And in the period 1914 to 1920, in a series of works, the artist subjects come back, not the instruments of manipulation but the personality, the man who makes the work of art. So there are Harlequins, musicians, dancers, artists, figures who, when they are represented, are nevertheless composed of segments, of pieces, that is, of units that have arisen through a process of segmentation, of analysis, but they are now used to reconstitute a bounded form, a whole, a statuesque presence. In one example, the figure of a musician holds with one hand a sheet of music inscribed "SI TU VEUX," the name of a popular song; in the other, he holds his instrument, his mandolin or guitar, but he is not personal; he is not emotional; he wears a mask for a face. The background is formed of large panels or segments arbitrarily put together but finally composing a rectangle just as the

see Frontispiece

components of the figure, these little segments of color and patterned ornament, constitute what we recognize as a Harlequin or a musician.

And the great picture *Three Musicians* is based upon a similar reconstitution of a band. At this point there is a return to the objects in the world that stimulate the artist; these artists face us more directly and express joy in their mobility, their anonymous presence, and their intensity as performers, as shown through the vehemence of contrast, the sharpness of angles, the abruptness of details, and the surprising variations of every part that reappears, like eyes, nose, hands, instruments, and legs. Each one has its own character, but together they form one band. There is some analogy to jazz music, which was fashionable in Paris at that moment. see Fig. 5

While he is reconstituting objects through segments that previously had functioned as collage, as bits that had been attached to a decomposed structure, he begins to draw again from nature, but he does not return to the drawing style of 1904, 1905, and 1906. He represents people of his world—the dealer Ambrose Vollard, the composer Igor Stravinsky, the director of the ballet Serge Diaghilev—very much his immediate world, people whom he admires, who admire him, and who have a particular strength or authority through their daring and originality as promoters of art or as artists, as composers, as writers. He draws them carefully, with great scruple as to the fullness of the body, but he often connects lines in ways that recall details of Cubism, for example, in the drawing of Vollard, the little curve of the furniture between his sleeve and his jacket at the right or the crossing of hands and even the crossing of legs and the perspective of the legs, or the setting of the head against the framework of the paneling of the wall. There are many features in the folds and elsewhere that remind us of his Cubist experience. Also, the dosage of little shadow points throughout the work, the passage to light in them, depend upon the experience in Cubism of producing planes that are open rather than bounded by outlines. Figs. 35-36

He then undertakes to paint monumentally after so many years of the tendency toward flattening out, though with great density of layers

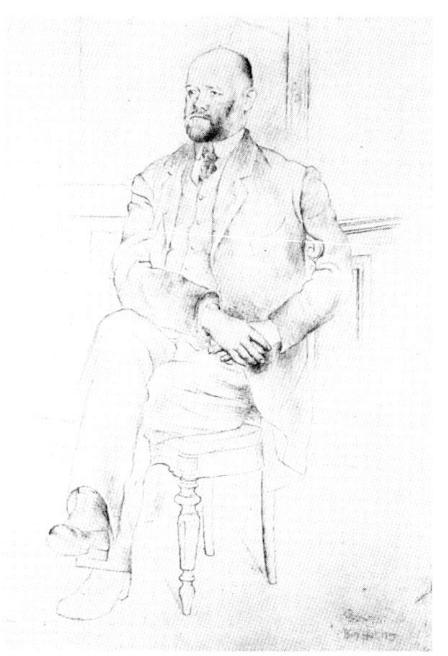

Figure 35. *Portrait of Ambrose Vollard*, 1915, pencil, 18⅜ x 12⅝" (46.7 x 32 cm), The Metropolitan Museum of Art, New York, The Elisha Whittelsey Collection, The Elisha Whittelsey Fund, 1947.

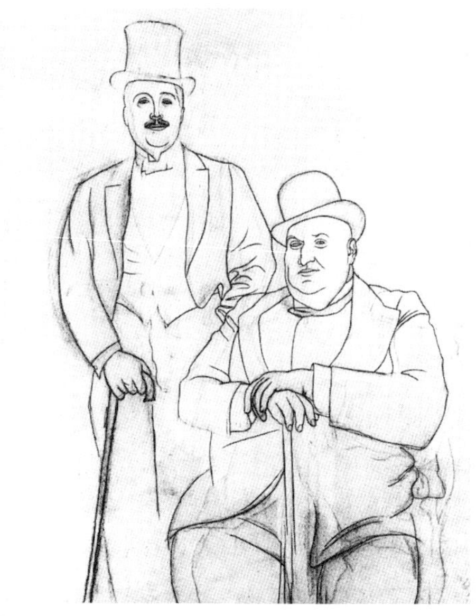

Figure 36. *Sergei Diaghilev and Alfred Seligsberg* (after a photograph), summer 1919, charcoal and black pencil on paper, 25½ x 19⅝" (65 x 50 cm), Musée Picasso, Paris.

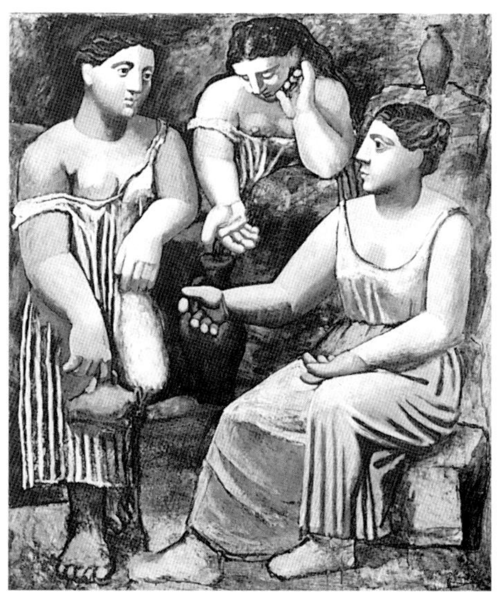

Figure 37. *Three Women at the Spring*, summer 1921, oil on canvas, 80¼ x 68½" (203.8 x 174 cm), The Museum of Modern Art, New York, Gift of Mr. and Mrs. Allan D. Emil.

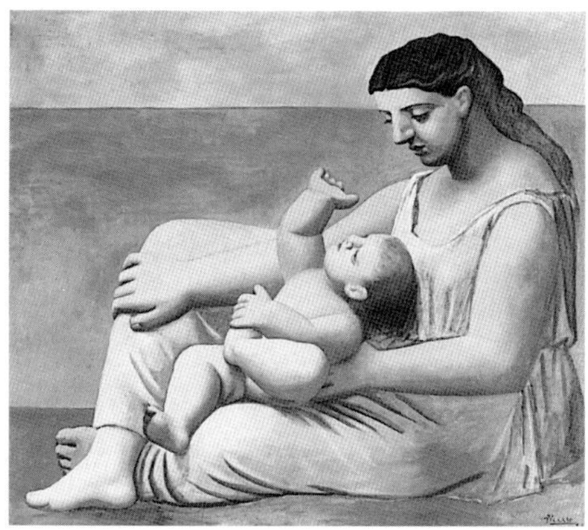

Figure 38. *Mother and Child*, 1921, oil on canvas, 56½ x 64" (143.5 x 162.5 cm), The Art Institute of Chicago.

within a shallow space on the canvas. He undertakes gigantic figures, very often women, in highly formalized sculptural groupings. There is (Fig. 37) a constant search for this connectedness that I have mentioned, which you can see in the way in which one figure relates to the other.

The great paragon, the model of such unity, gives us also a clue to a human content, to an interest that is of his own life since he has married and has a beautiful child and has become deeply attracted by the family world. In his *Mother and Child*, the woman clasps her own knee; the child clasps its foot and raises a hand to the mother; the mother clasps (Fig. 38) the back of the child. So we have a high degree of monumentalized compactness, strength, and stability. It is an idealization of the security and permanence of the maternal-child relationship or of the relationships of friendship, of some kind of communicativeness of a pair of individuals. We have moved far away from the earlier interest in the work of art as a realization of ideas connected with the instrumentalities of art and the powers of invention of art toward the expression of large meanings. And this turn is parallel to the reconstituting activity going on at the same time in Cubist paintings. While he was doing these paintings he was still making paintings like the *Three Musicians*. In the morning he made Cubist paintings; in the afternoon he made Neoclassical paintings. So that for him the two styles were both available and provided problems that he solved in different ways and belonged to two different aspects of his personality. This is a most extraordinary phenomenon in the whole story of art in the last few hundred years.

Within the phase of this monumentalized Neoclassical painting—which perhaps was connected with experiences during World War I and shortly after and is paralleled by the turn toward classicism and old normative types and toward the search for stability of forms (we see that in the writings of Paul Valery, of T. S. Eliot, in the new music of Stravinsky after the war period and may even have been a response to the feelings of these men during the war and shortly after)—the Cubist paintings become more luxurious, show clearer, larger forms, present an air of luxury and fullness. An immense melon that is cut, a classical head in black, great sheets of music, ornamented drapes, decorated windows and

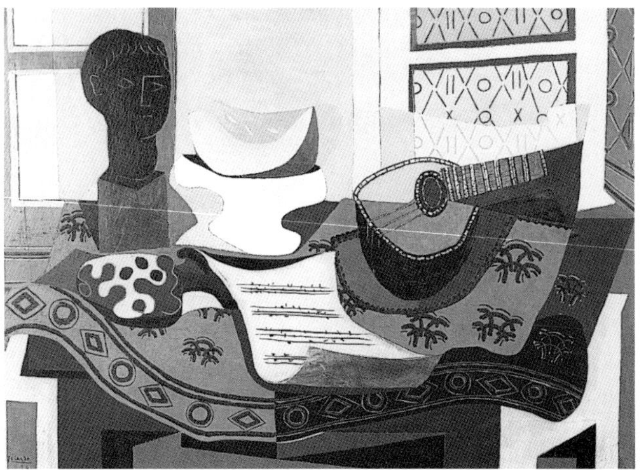

Figure 39. *The Red Tablecloth*, 1924, oil on canvas, 38¾ x 51¾" (98.4 x 131.4 cm), Private collection, New York.

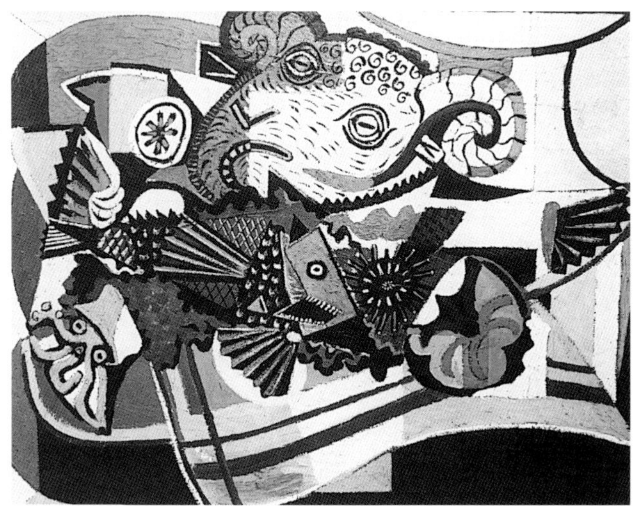

Figure 40. *The Ram's Head*, summer 1925, oil on canvas, 30½ x 39⅛" (77.5 x 99.4 cm), Norton Simon Museum, Pasadena, California. Gift of Alexandre P. Rosenberg.

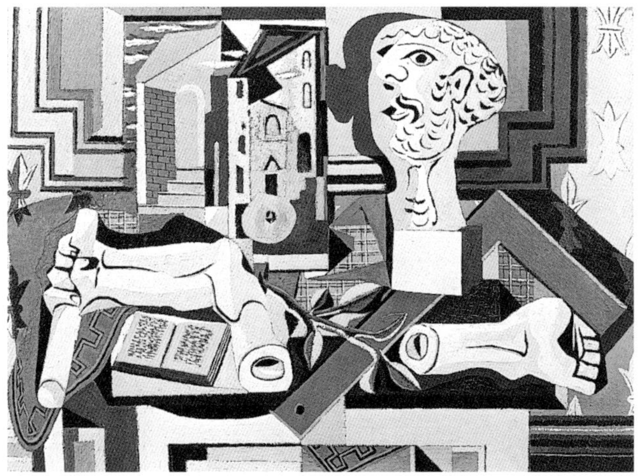

Figure 41. *Studio with Plaster Head*, summer 1925, oil on canvas, 38⅝ x 51⅝" (98 x 130 cm), The Museum of Modern Art, New York. Purchase, 1964, Inv. no. 116.64.

curtains, and then through the windows a deep blue sky, these belong to a world of serenity, enjoyment, luxury, and stability, and also largeness of effect. They depend upon the Cubist analysis of the components of painting but now are applied in an entirely different way, and through that application many of their features disappear from his painting. Fig. 39

Within a few years, on the very table on which he has painted this luscious melon and this sheet of music and the beautiful drapes and given you the view of this serene sky and placed a classical sculpture, he introduces themes of violence and of shattering brutality. A severed head of a ram is placed on a table next to a bit of fruit and various marine forms, with especially prickly, irregular, broken, dangerous edges and with saw-tooth ends, especially in the head of the ram, and also many abrupt contrasts of dark and light color and a particular thickness of the pigment, or, in another image, severed limbs. They are, of course, bloodless distortions. Formerly the distortions were purely artistic, now they appear to belong to reality but are not fully so. You can see that what has been severed is not a real leg or hand but a plaster cast, which again is part of the studio equipment. The head, a classical head, is given a tense and somewhat distorted expression. The T square for drawing is set in an unstable position. The many elements are so dense and close that there is an effect of clatter, a noise in these pictures, a very powerful, stimulating one, full of great dissonances, but held together through the staging of the tones and their circulation in the work. Fig. 40 Fig. 41

This new phase is a discovery that this magnificent monumental body, this humanity that he has reintroduced, has its side of terror and pain and anguish and is also associated with a rising feeling expressed in sadistic operations: That is, instead of distortions, we see real, bloody dissections in the pictures. It is accompanied also by the shift from the sense of the body as the external statuesque body to the inner body as felt, the body that the neurologists call the body image and the body schema, and that is constantly reshaped and distorted by various emotions or instabilities or sufferings of the individual. When he paints *The Dance* at this time, he introduces—and I'm sure without benefit of reading any works of neurologists or psychiatrists—a figure of whom

the head at the right is a phantom profile and whose heart is shown by
Fig. 42 transparency; the figure and the movements of the figure are not at all those of muscles but a strange, abrupt motion. At the left is a dancer with head thrown back, a head formed of three heads: a shadow head, a profile head, a frontal head, and that suggests to us the actual sensations in loss of balance with giddiness, what may be called vestibular sensations in the painting of the outer head. And that reference to the inner body, the body that you know when you have a toothache or you are very tired and your limbs feel different from the way they look—your mouth feels much bigger, or when you have a headache it seems something is going on that is not visible but is much more important than the visible head—that aspect of inner experience of the body is now discovered by Picasso as a ground of representation of the human being. He advances, then, from the externality of the traditional body in art to the rendering of the internal body sensations, the somatic sensations. Observe also how in representing the breast of the woman dancing, there is a phantom breast with a pronounced nipple in black; then there is a breast that has the form of a human eye with a pupil; and then in the blue space under it there is an analog of a breast with a red-and-white striped central point. So there is a redundancy or perseveration of some feeling of the body through multiplying that organ or that part throughout the body. This is something familiar to psychiatrists and neurologists, but it doesn't belong to the seen body, only to the felt and reported bodily sensations. How Picasso came to that I have no idea at all. But it is infused in a series of works at this time and realized in paintings through which these features become real constituents of the structure and of the expression.

Fig. 43 From that also comes the well-known painting *Girl before a Mirror* with the profile head and the full head and the inner body with the rib structure, not anatomically conceived but as a set of repeated forms, and also the inner body, the womb. And with that doubling of the body—the outer and the inner body—there is a third body, the body that we contemplate in the mirror, which reverses our own, which belongs to us, and which nevertheless has only a phantom existence. The arm is

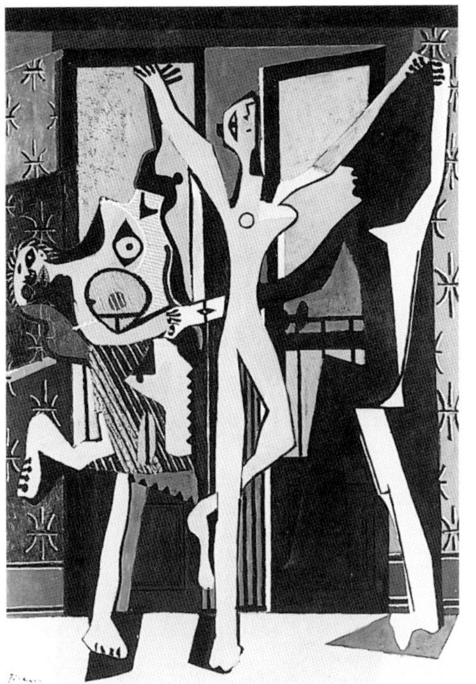

Figure 42. *The Dance*, June 1925, oil on canvas, 84⅝ x 55⅞" (215 x 142 cm), The Tate Gallery, London.

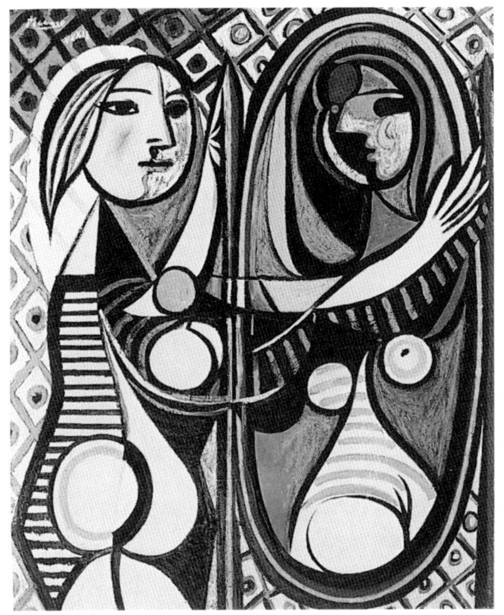

Figure 43. *Girl before a Mirror*, March 14, 1932, oil on canvas, 64 x 51¼" (162.3 x 130.2 cm), The Museum of Modern Art, New York. Gift of Mrs. Simon Guggenheim.

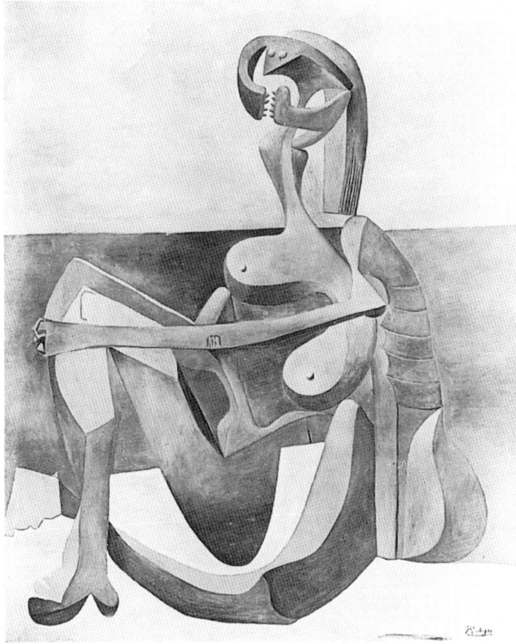

Figure 44. *Seated Bather*, early 1930, oil on canvas, 64¼ x 51" (163.2 x 129.5 cm), The Museum of Modern Art, New York. Mrs. Simon Guggenheim Fund.

raised toward it. We are reminded of the woman who admires herself in the mirror and the woman who holds the mirror up to her, that theme—and also the *Woman with a Fan* and the raised arm—that is a recurrent theme in his work, which we will see again at a later period.

Fig. 44 I have said that there are also feelings of violent aggression, hatred, a frequent fantasizing of destructiveness of the human body. He produces gigantic blown-up bone structures. They look like outer bodies, monuments, sculptures against the sky, but they are essentially extrusions of the inner body, the bones as a model, with great emphasis upon the teeth and the pointed, dangerous parts, the clutching parts, and the aggressive elements of the body.

If he is able then to represent the Crucifixion, it is not from religious feeling alone nor only from admiration of medieval paintings that he had seen, but from the discovery that in classical art and in other arts in the past the representation of mythology and of religious themes must be understood in human and in material terms as expressions of powerful passions, impulses, instincts. But I think that Picasso came to it not so much from a reading of scientific books or their popularizations but rather from the poetry and stories written in the 1920s and 1930s in French and Spanish. In the *Crucifixion* he represents a figure with
see Fig. 3 immense bonelike jaws, organs. He enlarges limbs, shortens them, twists them. He builds up a scene in which the figure of Christ himself is practically obscured or lost within the momentousness of signs of great violence and passions in the figures attending the scene, whether of suffering, sorrow, or apocalyptic imagination.

He became interested in mythology then, and especially Greek mythology. As perhaps one of the first modern artists who read Greek myths—he was called upon by the publisher Skira to illustrate Ovid's *Metamorphoses*—he found in them not the sweetness of ordinary academic classicism but rather themes of instinct, of primordial violence, cruelty, and sacrifice, and the clash and wildness of passions. The Greeks were for him great primitives, who also possessed philosophy and science. But in these myths he tried to give to the erotic and to the destructive, sadistic sense and the themes of death their fullest value, in contrast to the ordinary celebration of the aesthetic or beauty within the myths. The great etching *Minotaurmachy*, done around the 1930s, is an example. He represents that Cretan monster at the right as a looming, ominous figure with his hand stretched out—a very important theme for Picasso. A little girl holds a light up to him and bears flowers; then a suffering horse, which is in rictus, and a dying or dead woman toreador fallen over the back of the horse, Christ climbing a ladder, two girls with pigeons looking out of a window. The whole emanates from a personal world of reminiscences of his childhood but also of fantasies that are connected with his life at the moment. It is done now without any Cubist intricacy or abstruseness and instead by direct rendering of the separate figures. But that clarity of representation here is the bearer of the most mysterious, most indecipherable personal projections, as in a dream. You might hit upon a correct interpretation of a few details but only with great difficulty. In the distance, we see the boat with white sail as in the story of the Minotaur and Theseus.

Figs. 45

While making these prints of Greek stories and weaving into them his own elaboration of personal life and memories, he also loves to represent the bullfight with the agonizing horse and the tremendous, destructive bull. I include this image particularly because the view of *Guernica* will follow.

Fig. 46

In *Guernica*, which was the first canvas that he painted in connection with a political occasion, we see the continuity with what he had been doing before, of a completely nonpolitical, personal, imaginative kind and in relation to mythology. The theme of *Guernica* has been studied, deciphered with respect to partisanship and the occasion of the image; but I believe that those decipherments are not justified by the actual history of the painting, the way in which it came into its present form through numerous stages of which we possess photographs made while the work was in progress, nor is the political interpretation borne out by the relationship to previous and subsequent paintings in which the same figures appear. We are able to understand these better in connection with that series of a nonpolitical kind: the severed arm, for

Fig. 47

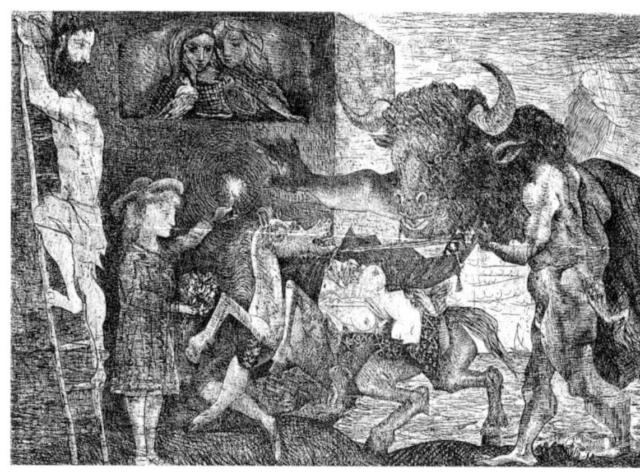

Figure 45. *Minotaurmachy*, spring 1935, etching and scraper, 19½ x 27⁷⁄₁₆" (49.5 x 69.7 cm), state V, The Museum of Modern Art, New York. Purchase Fund.

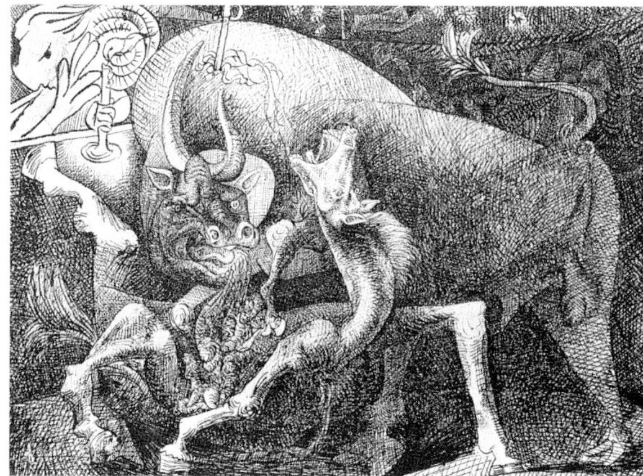

Figure 46. *Woman with a Candle, Fight between Bull and Horse*, July 24, 1934, pen and India ink, brown crayon on cloth pasted on plywood, 12⅜ x 16" (31.5 x 40.5 cm), Musée Picasso, Paris.

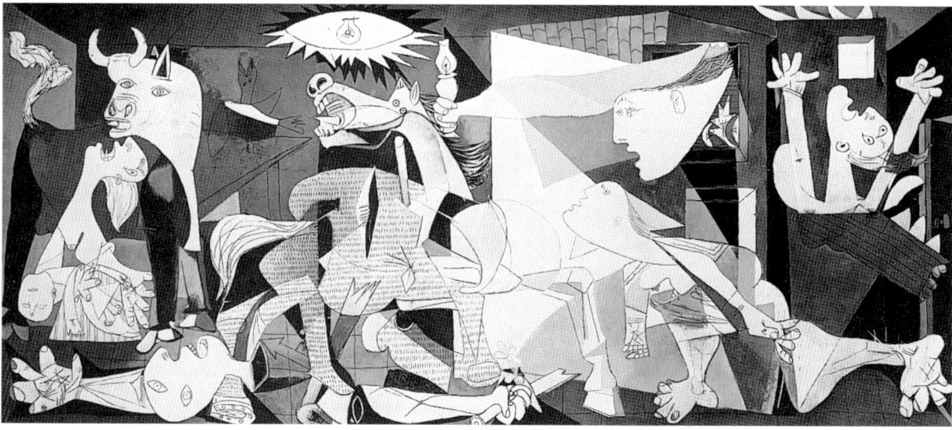

Figure 47. *Guernica*, May 1–June 4, 1937, oil on canvas, 11'5⅜" x 25'5½" (349 x 776 cm), Museo Nacional Centro de Arte Reina Sofía, Madrid.

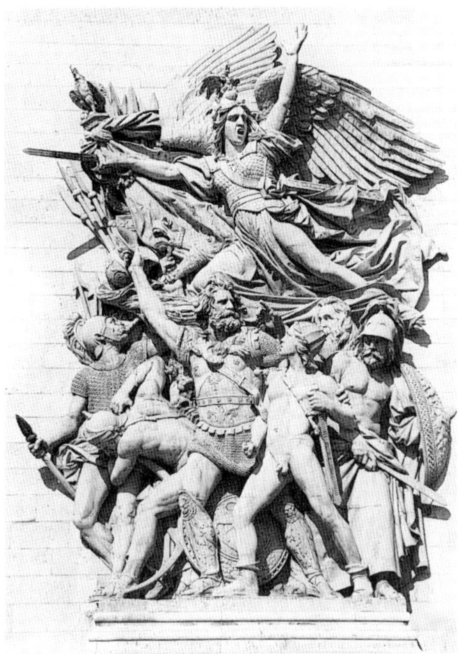

Figure 48. François Rude, *"La Marseillaise" (Departure of the Volunteers in 1792)*, 1833–36, stone relief, c. 42 x 26' (12.80 x 7.92 m), Arc de Triomphe, Paris.

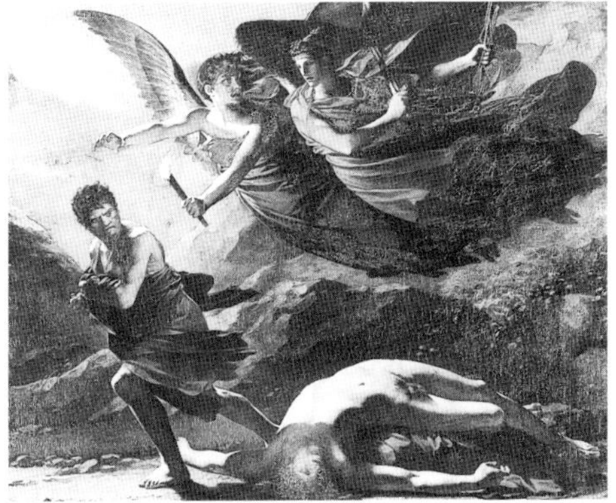

Figure 49. Pierre-Paul Prud'hon, *Justice and Divine Vengeance Pursuing Crime*, 1808, oil on canvas, 7'11⅝" x 9'7" (2.34 x 2.92 m), Musée du Louvre, Paris, Département des Peintures (INV 7340).

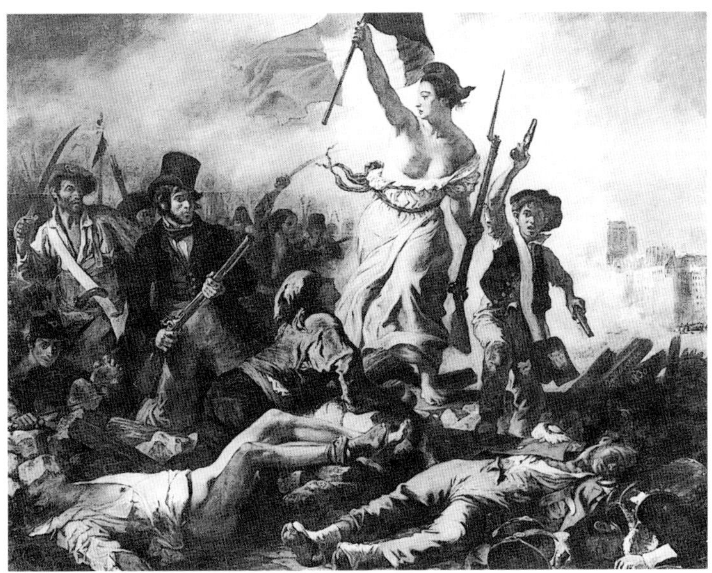

Figure 50. Eugène Delacroix, *Liberty Leading the People*, 1830, oil on canvas, 8'6⅜" x 10'7 15/16" (2.60 x 3.25 m), Musée du Louvre, Paris.

example, at the lower left, or the woman with arm stretched out holding a light, or the figure of the agonizing horse. Many other details of this work can be shown to have been resuscitated from preceding works for this occasion.

Moreover, other elements in it do show a relationship to great monuments of French political history, like the Arc de Triomphe's *Departure* Fig. 48-50 *of the Volunteers in 1792*, or Pierre-Paul Prud'hon's picture of *Justice and Divine Vengeance Pursuing Crime*, or Eugène Delacroix's *Liberty Leading the People.* They provided certain vague models of great masses of figures in movement advancing, extending their limbs, gesturing, but the specific form and the associated meanings in the preceding works show that they did not originate in a political image, though they were made for a political occasion.

However, after having finished it, he made a series of works that were comments or reflective versions on what he had done for the *Guernica*, and some of them are even more striking and more fully realized. For Fig. 51 instance, the painting *Horse in Agony* is much more powerful and much stronger in its expression and contrast and has more refinement in the execution than in the big canvas of *Guernica.* Observe here the rendering of the open jaw as an interior of the animal and not only the outside. You see the gums and the palate; you see the teeth and the rigid, paralyzed tongue of the animal in its agony, attempting to cry out. You observe also the twisting of the nostrils and the reshaping of the teeth. Finally, observe how the lower part, with the contrast of triangles and see Fig. 25 wavy forms, brings us back to that *Nude with Raised Arms* of 1907.

Fig. 52 Similarly in drawing the *Weeping Woman* afterward, he draws the eyes with little arrowlike shapes piercing the eyes, and from the eyes issue lines that cross each other and come right up to the mouth. Those lines, I believe, are an attempt or a suggestion from a diagram he might have seen as an art student of the optic chiasma, the crossing of the nerve path, the nerves from the two eyes, but he uses them in order to show the eyes not as seeing eyes, but eyes that are suffering internally; it is a picture of the derangement of the senses in anguish, in pain. The ears are turned backward, but not to listen. The whole surface of the face

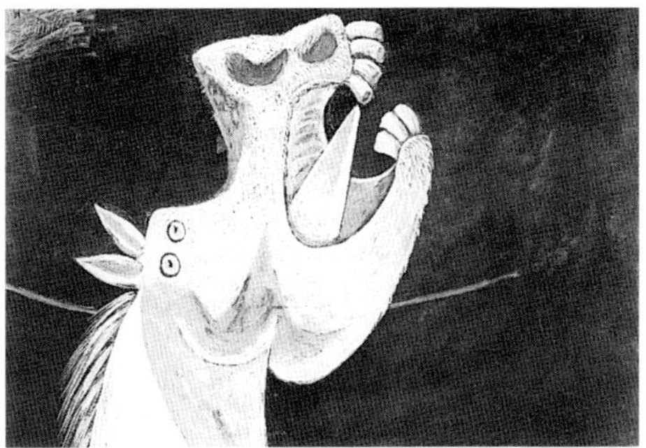

Figure 51. *Horse in Agony*, May 2, 1937, oil on canvas, 25½ x 36¼" (65 x 92.1 cm), Museo del Prado, Madrid.

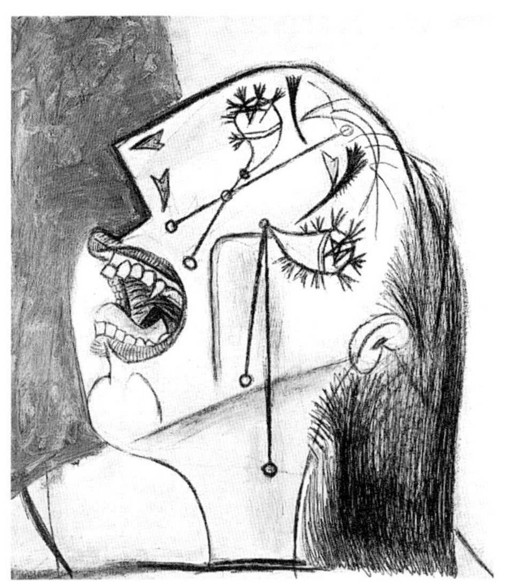

Figure 52. *Weeping Woman*, June 26, 1937, gouache and colored crayon on canvas, 21⅝ x 18⅛" (55 x 46 cm), The Museum of Modern Art, New York.

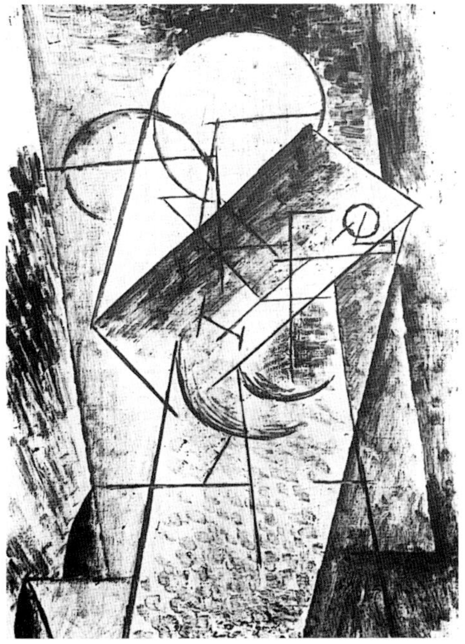

Figure 53. *Head*, late 1912 or early 1913, oil on canvas, 21⅝" x 15" (55 x 38 cm), Private collection, Westport, Eire.

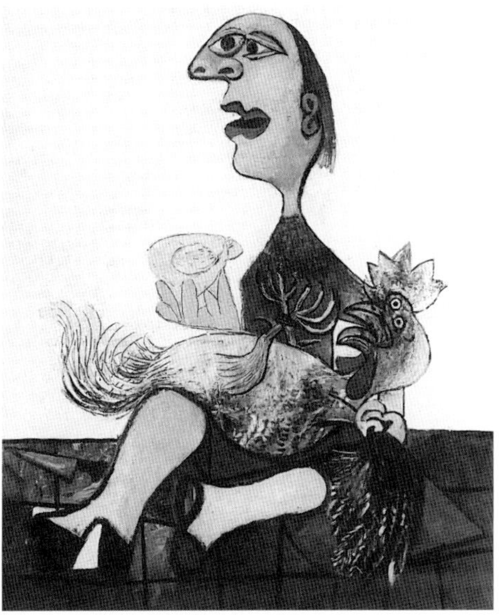

Figure 54. *Woman with a Cockerel*, 1938, oil on canvas, 57¼ x 47⅝" (145.5 x 121 cm), Baltimore Museum of Art.

seems to be filled with broken and disordered nerve paths. He opens the mouth and gives much more importance to the mouth as a revelation of the inside of the body, the actual suffering body; he strengthens that by the play of black and white and streaking in the whole. He could not have treated the face in that free manner had he not almost thirty years before made in his Cubist paintings drawings from a human head
Fig. 53 in which he isolated shapes, reconstructed them, and applied touches freely to define planes or layers within it but without clear definition of the boundary of a head. But the Cubist one does not have an emotional charge of suffering or a concentration upon parts or features belonging to regions of sensitivity; while when he returns to the human head in the *Weeping Woman*, the freedom of drawing acquired in one context becomes the basis of an organic representation, not the head as seen but as he imagined—the feeling of a head that is in suffering, that is splitting apart. It is the interiorizing of expression in contrast to the elimination of the physiognomic in the Cubist phase.

The last outcome of the series with the *Guernica* motif is called the
Fig. 54 *Woman with a Cockerel;* but the head has been recognized by his friends as his own—distorted, of course, treated very freely. The cock is clutched with one hand and is prepared for sacrifice. There is a knife on the floor at the left. The legs of the cock are tied together and the claws are held up like a menorah, a brilliant succession of prongs. The figure holds a shell. The cock's comb forms a zigzag, which is a favorite theme of aggressive drawing on his part. You see that the heels of the woman are cut out to form a triangle, like the shape of the knife. There are also wonderful delicacies of painting in gray and white: the body of the animal with the featheriness and weighted heavy masses and the more taut surfaces, and the feathers held in the hand against a sharp, harsh, dry whiteness of the background, which we cannot help but feel in this work to be a cruel white against the grays and blues and flesh colors.

Now I would like to make a brief summary of certain constancies within this large development. One can say that this is the course of growth of a man who has continuously discovered and transformed himself; who has passed from a stage in which he paints pathetically or tries to glorify himself, to the discovery of the artist as an achiever, to the discovery, finally, of the work of art as an objective field with its own problems and necessities; and who discovered his freedom and power of invention and manipulation within them, and he has passed from that into the rediscovery of the human in various forms, which I have not tried to interpret or explain in relation to beliefs and values of the moment or to his own experiences. In each case we see a continuity based upon enlargement of the objects of art and the field of experience, but depending upon the discoveries made in the preceding stages. Now through all of them he has acquired a conviction about the nature of art that has remained a strong component of his later work, and that is the confidence in art as a process of radical transformation; the artist, confronting some objects or entertaining some ideas, in starting to order them, to picture them somehow, to build with them, is impelled to steps of a drastic character to bring them into a new form or to shape them so that their coherence has a power and value of its own equal to that or beyond that of the elements that went into it or that serve as a means of intensifying the expression of those particular themes or contents that led him to undertake the work in the first place.

He has made two works in which he expresses his ideas about transformation as a radical means of the artist, as a program of the artist. He illustrates the beautiful story by Honoré de Balzac called *The Unknown Masterpiece* (Fig. 55) about an artist who dreams of reconciling the opposite claims of the style of the classics—which is that of line, sculptural beauty, precision, definite form—and the style of the Romantics—which is that of color, of suggestiveness, of vagueness, of fusion, and of openness. He works on one canvas, again and again, and finally destroys the whole in the impossibility of achieving a reconciliation. But other artists with a similar program did manage to fuse or synthesize these two supposedly inherent antagonists or opposite poles of artistic invention. Picasso shows the artist drawing the model. A woman is knitting; she is making a stocking. She is taking threads that have one form and through them is creating a three-dimensional concave whole that has a

quite different character. And as the artist looks at the woman and transfers the form to the canvas, he projects a tangle, something utterly different from the woman—not a perspective drawing but a free projection. On the other hand, the same Picasso has created the *Painter and*
Fig. 56 *Model.* The artist, you see at the right, is an abstract-looking contrivance. He holds up a brush in his hand, looks at the model, who is again an abstract Cubistic contrivance, and the product on the canvas is a pure classic silhouette of a woman. It is as if he is saying that what you call reality, the evident physical beauty of things, is itself a product of our invention, construction, power of ideas, power of giving coherence, wholeness to something that in actual life is always changing, uncertain, and full of different aspects seen in various perspectives.

So there are two kinds of transformation: from the reality to an abstraction; from an abstraction into a reality. But both are given to him; he possesses them fully; he is able to explore them and produce a thousand different kinds of paintings through this discovery of the reversibility of transformational processes in art.

But that process is available to him because he has transformed himself as well. When he did these last works, this is how he was photo-
Fig. 57 graphed by an American painter and brilliant photographer, Man Ray, with powerful, keen, absorbing eyes, irresistible, unforgettable eyes, and in that photograph, he holds his head in one hand and holds the arm of that hand in the other. That posture of the body is the posture
Fig. 58 in the early work of the sad acrobats and circus people in Paris of 1905: the mother with her hand on her head, her eyes looking down; the boy turned away in profile with his arms enveloping his body. What is the difference? He has retained to the end his self-closure and self-preoccupation; but he has acquired at the same time a tremendous power of vision, of perception, and a great power of manipulation with his hands. He has become strong in the processes of art, and that strength is the outcome, the sign, of this perpetual transforming process. He has then a unity in his art in so far as a direction and a set of powers have been developed and fulfilled through many stages in each of which he has had to turn to a different side of his experience. He has been able to

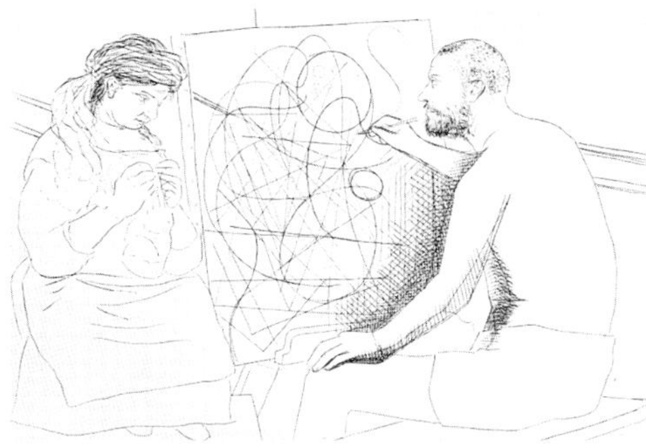

Figure 55. *Painter with a Model Knitting*, 1927, Plate IV from *Le Chef d'oeuvre inconnu* by Honoré de Balzac (Paris: Ambrose Vollard, Editeur, 1931), etching, 7 9/16 x 10 7/8" (19.2 x 27.7 cm), The Museum of Modern Art, New York, The Louis E. Stern Collection.

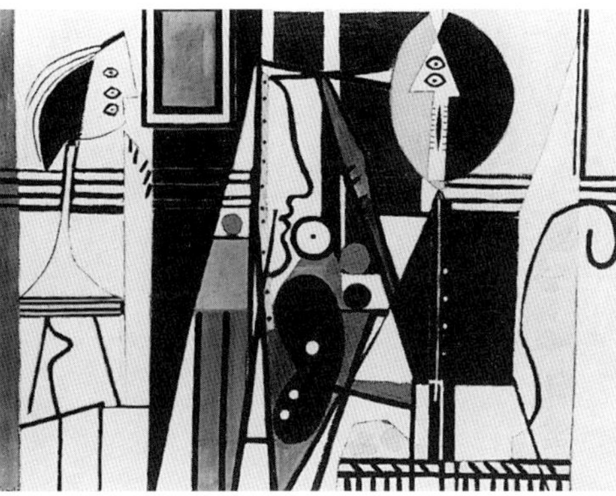

Figure 56. *Painter and Model*, 1928, oil on canvas, 51 1/8 x 64 1/4" (129.8 x 163 cm), The Museum of Modern Art, New York. The Sidney and Harriet Janis Collection.

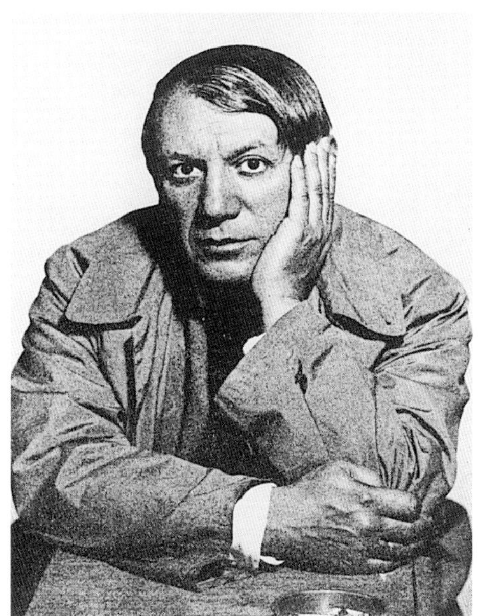

Figure 57. Man Ray, *Pablo Picasso*, 1932, photograph, *Les cahiers d'art*, Nos. 7–10, 1935.

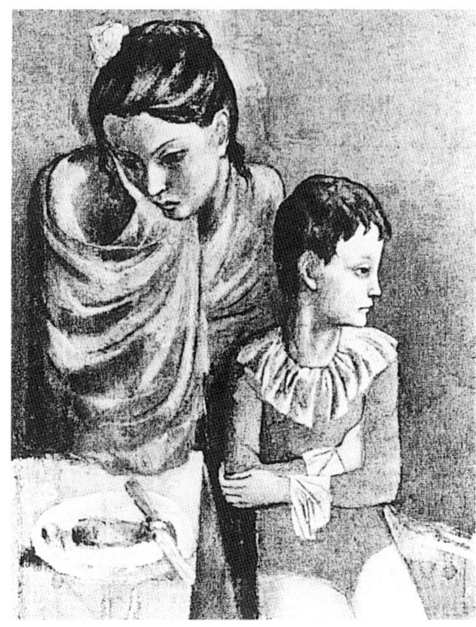

Figure 58. *Mother and Child*, 1905, gouache on canvas, 34 5/8 x 27 3/8" (88 x 69.5 cm), Staatsgalerie, Stuttgart.

Figure 59. *Seated Woman*, 1931, wood, 22 x ¾ x 2" (55.7 x 2 x 5 cm), Musée Picasso, Paris.

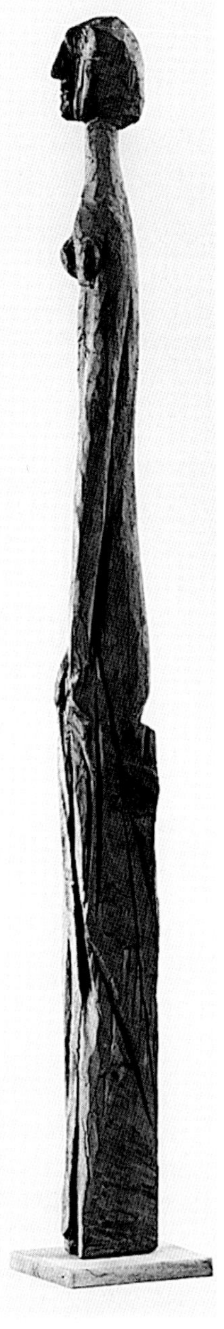

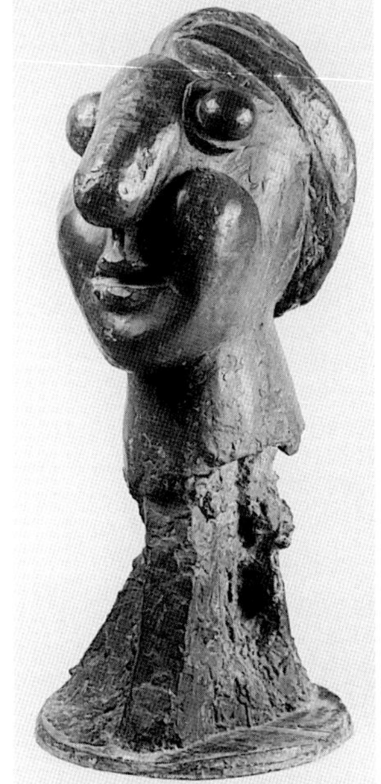

Figure 60. *Head of a Woman*, 1931–32, bronze, 33½ x 14½ x 17⅞" (85 x 37 x 45.5 cm), Galerie Louise Leiris, Paris.

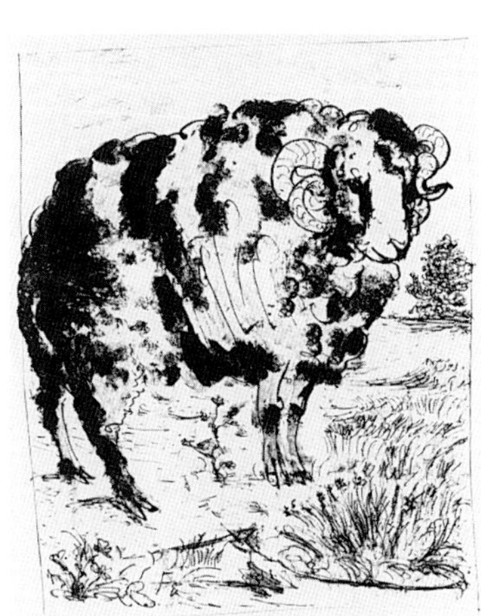

Figure 61. *Le Belier* [The Ram], 1942, lift-ground acquatint, etching, and drypoint, 16 5/16 x 12 7/16" (41.5 x 31.5 cm), pl. 5 from *Histoire Naturelle (Textes de Buffon)*.

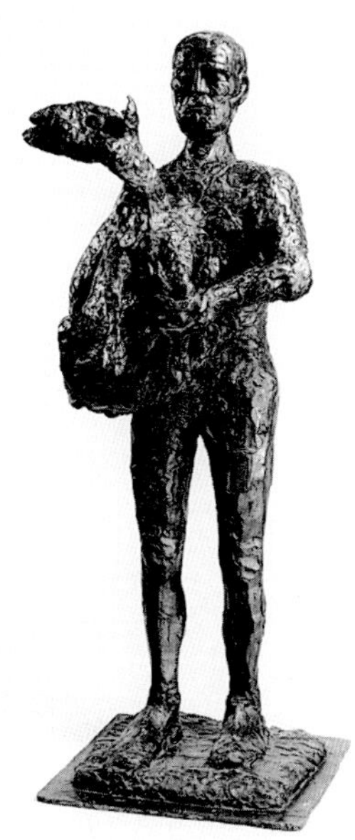

Figure 62. *Man with Sheep*, 1944, bronze, 86⅝ x 30¾ x 28⅜" (220 x 78 x 72 cm), Philadelphia Museum of Art, Gift of R. Sturgis and Marion B. F. Ingersoll.

assimilate altogether new experiences, but they depend finally upon the power of the eye and the power of the hand, in a mind, in a body, that itself is highly sensitive, reactive, responsive, and that feels every moment and every object immediately.

That, however, is not the complete story of Picasso. While it is true that after 1940 most of his works fall into fairly familiar modes of painting, though among them are splendid works and unique works, they do not yield any large discovery of form, any core idea, that can be likened to Cubism, of the two kinds, or to his classicism, or to the approach to the body image, to the internality of the body in relation to emotion, of the 1920s and 1930s. Nevertheless, in his last twenty years he has produced important sculpture, works of an astounding character, with an entirely different sentiment. In the 1930s, his sculpture is much within the range of the forms seen before, as in the long figure illustrated here, in the slenderness and delicacy of form, of which we may find parallels in primitive art, but still retains much of the known figure within our own tradition, or in the great head suggestive of certain phases of Matisse. Fig. 59 Fig. 60

But in the 1940s and 1950s, he produces monumental bronze sculptures in which an animal is a primary figure. This is indeed a great turn within his art, although he had made beautiful drawings of animals all through his life—of monkeys, of bulls, and of horses—and in the late 1930s he had produced these magnificent drawings and lithographs to illustrate Buffon's *Natural History*. In the sculpture, however, of the 1940s and 1950s, a new theme appeared: the human figure who holds an animal tenderly, who warms himself with the animal, who shows care and intimacy, and who draws a heat of the animal to himself and gives it support. The figure is straightforward; it has very little stylization or artificial adjustment, posture, or elegance, and the animal has apparently greater articulation and freedom of movement when held by the man. Fig. 61 Fig. 62

Another animal is his great goat, which at first seems as strange and arbitrary as any construction in his Cubist or post-Cubist phase. The sense in this is the artist's great love of the organic—not the organic in

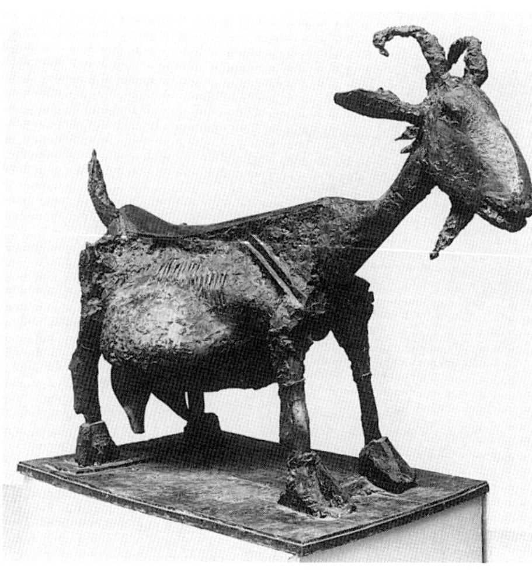

Figure 63. *She-Goat*, 1950, bronze (after assemblage of palm leaf, ceramic flowerpots, wicker basket, metal elements, and plaster), 46⅜ x 56⅜ x 28½" (117.7 x 143.1 x 71.4 cm), The Museum of Modern Art, New York, Mrs. Simon Guggenheim Fund.

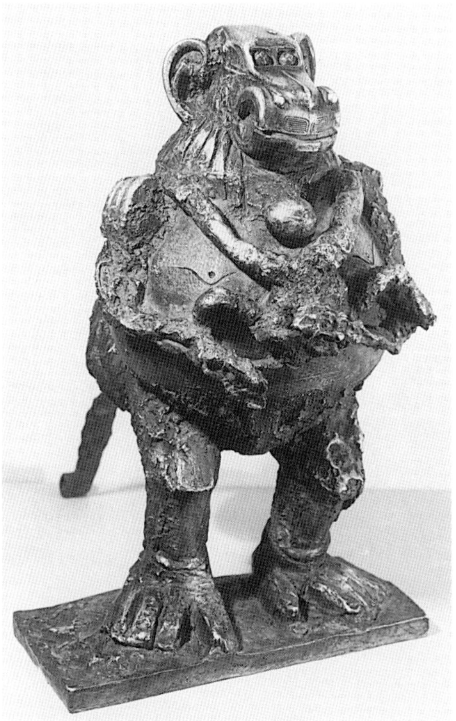

Figure 64. *Baboon and Young*, 1951, bronze (after original plaster with metal, ceramic elements, and two toy cars), 21 x 13¼ x 20¾" (53.3 x 33.3 x 52.7 cm), The Museum of Modern Art, New York, Mrs. Simon Guggenheim Fund.

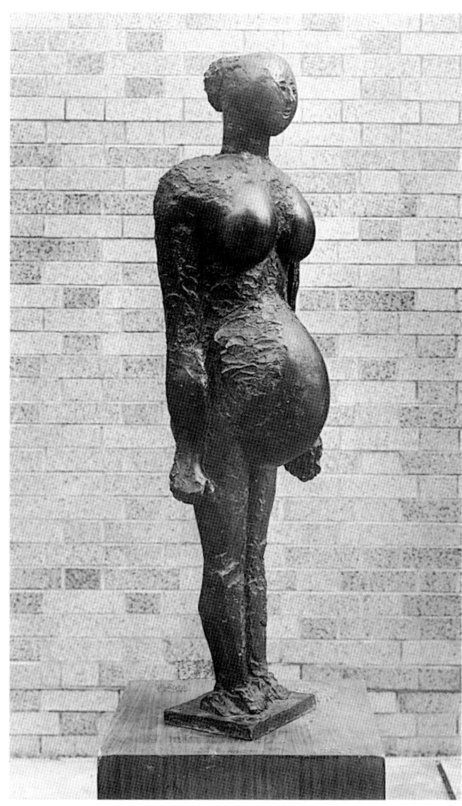

Figure 65. *Pregnant Woman*, 1950, bronze, 41¼" (104.8 cm) high; at base 7⅝ x 6¼" (19.3 x 15.8 cm), The Museum of Modern Art, New York, Gift of Mrs. Bertram Smith.

the sense of the total harmony and functioning but of the many organs, the parts, of the animal: the teets of the goat, the fleshiness, the hairiness, the horn-character, the stiff tail, the hoofs—all these parts are attached to one another, made into a loving whole that is at the same time very strange, very familiar, and individual, and arises from a real joy in the animal's presence. Fig. 63

And, similarly, the *Baboon and Young*, in which all that would have appeared to be shapeless and ugly in sculpture here appears to be right and to have a remarkable, intuitive justness and reality, and the fact that he chooses the moment of the immense mother and the clinging child and attaches one to the other like a relief upon its ground gives to this a quality of a fundamental, natural, and of all the promise of vitality and the existence of vitality in this otherwise ungainly and strangely proportioned natural being. Fig. 64

This continues to the image of the pregnant woman. Here, distortion is natural. Not only is it natural but necessary and good; it is part of the process of creation and of growing. You see then how Picasso in his old age, not in painting but in sculpture, has arrived at an extraordinary realism through a feeling for life—life not as something to be pitied or as an object of hatred or of cruel impulse or destructiveness, not as an object for rearrangement into a work of art, not as something subject to fantasy and whim, but something in a marvelous way given immediately to our feeling of the living as a necessary and a good in existence. This is a most extraordinary phenomenon in an artist and was reached in old age—and perhaps could not have been reached without old age, or without that long passage from the earliest work that you have seen until this recent work. Fig. 65

1 [For further discussion of this connection, see Schapiro's esssay, "Picasso's Woman with a Fan: On Transformation and Self-Transformation," *Modern Art: 19th & 20th Centuries, Selected Papers, Vol. II* (New York: George Braziller, Inc., 1979): 111–20.—Ed.]

overcome the backwardness of their culture by engaging modernity as time and motion—and at that, uniform, mechanical motion (often in association with newly rapid forms of mechanized travel)—the time evoked by their paintings and sculptures was, as they themselves declared, Henri Bergson's *durée*, rather than the measurable time of the physicist's clock. Therefore they championed the abrupt, unique, and instantaneous in the shock of a violent event within a small indoor or outdoor space—small by the scale of the distances and velocities of the bodies to which Einstein's ideas of relativity and simultaneity were applied—with some drastic break in an ordered series marking an interruption, an arrest, a closure, an extreme moment.[15]

In admitting the independence of the two fields, Giedion leaves it a mystery how the same revolution in the concepts of space and time was achieved independently by feeling and thought; yet he cannot refrain from describing the unconsciously produced structure of forms in painting with the specific terms of mathematical reasoning in physics:

> Concurrently the arts were concerned with the same problems. Artistic movements with inherent constituent facts, such as cubism and futurism, tried to enlarge our optical vision by introducing the new unit of space-time into the language of art. It is one of the indications of a common culture that the same problems should have arisen simultaneously and independently in both the methods of thinking and the methods of feeling.

Can Giedion have meant that the painters, in determining the still life of the table in their small canvases, applied the physicists' metric of space-time, with its unit of 186,000 miles per second (the distance traversed by light in one second)? At times he writes as if he wished the reader to believe that it was indeed the new discoveries of the physicists that were in question in those paintings. A paragraph on the Italian Futurist Umberto Boccioni exemplifies Giedion's oscillation between the languages of "thought" and "feeling":

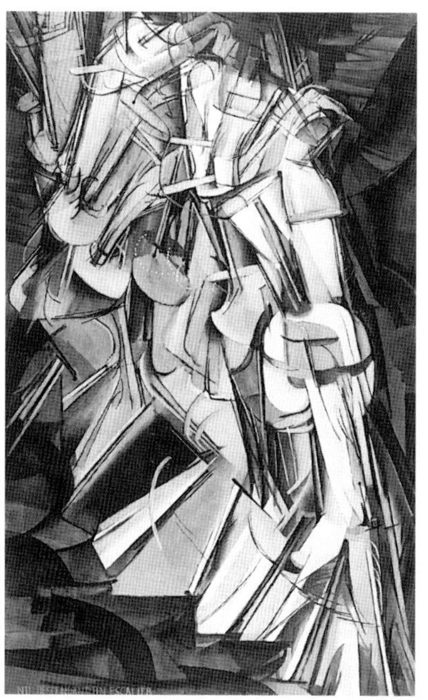

Figure 1. Marcel Duchamp, *Nude Descending the Staircase, No. 2*, 1912, 58 x 35" (147.3 x 89 cm), The Philadelphia Museum of Art (Louise and Walter Arensberg Collection).

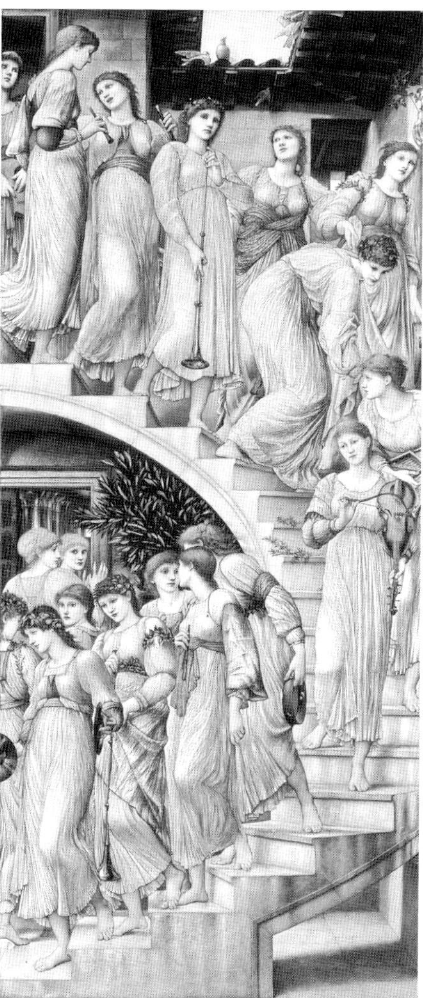

Figure 2. Edward Burne-Jones, *The Golden Stairs*, 1876–80, oil on canvas, 9' 1" x 3' 10" (2.69 x 117 m), Tate Gallery, London (NO4005).

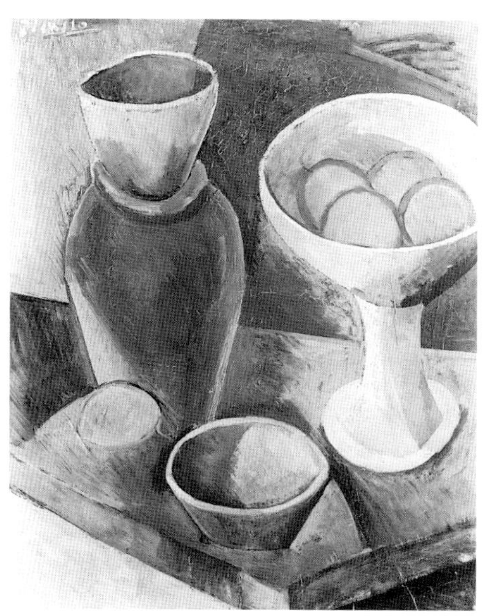

Figure 3. *Pitcher, Bowl, and Fruit Bowl*, spring–summer 1908, oil on canvas, 31⅞ x 25⅝" (81 x 65 cm), Philadelphia Museum of Art, A. E. Gallatin Collection.

> The productions of futurist painting, sculpture, and architecture are based on the representation of movement and its correlates: interpenetration and simultaneity. One of the futurists' best minds and without any doubt their best sculptor, . . . has most clearly defined their purposes. In an effort to penetrate more deeply into the very essence of painting, he sought terms for his art, terms which, now obscurely felt, now shining clear and immediate in his increasing creative experience, anticipated those that later appeared in the atomic theory. "We should start," he said, "from the central nucleus of the object wanting to create itself, in order to discover those new forms which connect the object invisibly with the infinite of the apparent plasticity and the infinite of the inner plasticity."[16]

Perhaps the reader who is acquainted with the philosophical literature of the time will recognize here more of Henri Bergson than of atomic physics.

One can find in paintings and relief sculptures of ancient, medieval, Renaissance, and more recent art countless representations of actions, especially figural postures in legible motion, successive in time and space in a small or shallow visual field close to the viewer.[17] Read from left to right (or the reverse), the episodes form a narrative or processional whole in which the sequence of occurrences in space corresponds to and is grasped by the viewer as an order of positions in time and implies a causal connection in the continuity of movement between neighboring figures or scenes. More interesting as a device that fuses the spatial and temporal in the closed field of the plane is the practice of painters, common from the fifteenth to the sixteenth century in western Europe, of depicting in the deep perspective background of a dominant action in the foreground several progressively smaller episodes that narratively precede or follow the major one. In an image of the Nativity of Christ we will see in the distance the smaller figures of the Annunciation to the Shepherds and, not far off, the Magi on the road to Bethlehem guided by the star; or the Annunciation to Mary, the Visitation, and Mary and Joseph on the way to Bethlehem. The order of episodes in time and the distance between them not only correspond broadly to an order in space: Within the system of perspective representation the diminishing or increasing sizes of the figures roughly correspond to the intervals of time among the depicted events.

Indeed, classic Greek and Renaissance artists had already conjoined space and time in paintings and even sculptures of ongoing actions, rendering different moments of a single episode by distinguishing its successive stages in the postures of figures who appear to be engaged simultaneously in the same action. Johann Wolfgang von Goethe, in his analysis of the Hellenistic statue of the Laocoön (in his first *Propyläen* essay), isolated in the seemingly simultaneous states of the three victims the different stages of the event: the progressive entanglement and constriction of the father and his two sons by giant serpents. This conception of an imagined action as embodying a series of consecutive moments had been formulated by Gotthold Ephraim Lessing in his *Laokoon* (1766), in which he distinguishes in principle between the successiveness inherent in literary narration and the simultaneous aspects of the sculptural or the pictorial. With the latter, however, the artist can bring to view the emergent or developing and climactic stages of an event by proper choice of the pregnant instant. Lessing recognized that an artist could bring to view the artist's desire for "movement."

Giedion would have us believe that in drawing the mouth of a vessel as seen from above and its base as a straight horizontal line seen at eye level, a Cubist painter wished to represent as simultaneous and in space-time his or her successive sightings of the object from different points of view. In the arbitrary perspective of a Picasso still life of 1908, for
Fig. 3 example *Pitcher, Bowl, and Fruit*, the treatment of ellipses and bases of objects is as if the painter had stooped and rose and lowered his head, shifting from one viewpoint to another—quite differently from the perceived unity of a pre-twentieth-century composition, felt in regard to the pattern of the shapes in relation to each other and to the whole as a set of consistent relationships. But that these separately conceived

aspects of parts of a bottle or glass are presented together on the same canvas as if they had been beheld in the same instant is no ground for connecting the artist's conception with Einstein's acute demonstration of the impossibility of establishing the absolute simultaneity of two events distant from one another according to his 1905 theory of Special Relativity. The forms of the fractioned parts of the represented still-life object, incompatible with a perspective view of the whole object from a single viewpoint, render the separate parts in their broadest and clearest aspect as known rather than as projected in a momentary sighting. In one such painting Picasso has extended a printed label as a detached vertical plane, tangent to its cylindrical bottle and shown in its "real" rectangular planar form, unaffected by perspective foreshortening on the curved surface of the bottle—in accord with an aim often expressed by the Cubist painters to represent the object as it is, in departure from the Impressionist rendering of a simple, momentary aspect in which its form was absent or lost.

It was not by moving around an object before him in the studio and thereby shifting his glance that the Cubist painter discovered such shapes in objects. He had encountered them in older art in the museums and in the work of contemporary self-taught painters, and he understood them as "objective" renderings that supported his own desire to give to figuration a stronger effect of stable, composite reality, in contrast to the ephemeral, Impressionistic semblance. (But like the Impressionists he made his process of conception and execution evident by the distinctiveness of the surface of the painting as a field of operation with marked brushstrokes, flecking, and arbitrary continuities that could be read more as decisions of the painter than as simulations of objects.) This goal was often affirmed in statements of the inventors of Cubist painting, who were aware of primitive art from which they derived a model of strength and intensity of expression through simpler, more freely drawn and arbitrarily composed rhythmic, elementary forms. The difference between their works and those of the tribal artist lies in the features of modeling with light and dark and of distinct brushwork persisting from their previous art. In the shaping of objects they soon gave up the continuity of closed contours in those admired archaic images in favor of a unity and balanced structure of discontinuous, fractioned lines and planes, in asymmetrical though rhythmically grouped forms.

In Giedion's account the time-space interval supposedly represented or evoked by the painting is inferred from the multiple viewpoints in the spectator's perspectives of the different parts of an object in a Cubist work: by a circle as the opening of a cup or bottle, and a horizontal line as its base, by the unforeshortened label of a cylindrical bottle as a plane rectangle with a uniformly lettered name—all conceptual forms. This method of representation, called "conceptual" in distinction from the "perceptual" or perspective method—whereby the fractioned parts of an object are separate forms, independent of a fixed sighting point for the object as a whole—was a familiar feature in many works of ancient archaic and medieval art. At the beginning of the twentieth century, modern painters often spoke of their art as a rediscovery of the primitive's approach to depicting objects as *known* rather than as directly *seen*;[18] and Cubist painters in particular depicted objects piecemeal, in distinct parts, as known by their enduring primary qualities, rather than as they would appear in a consistent perspective view that deforms and obscures their parts (a building in such a picture shows perspective convergences or diminutions, but with the predominance of such primary qualities as strong volumes and sharp light-dark distinction, without atmospheric perspective). In Egyptian painting and relief the single eye of a profile head is shown *en face*, the shoulders presented in their full breadth, the waist, legs, and feet in profile, with no functioning of parts, which are united by a continuous outline; and in a corresponding way Georges Braque and Picasso, who admired those ancient and primitive works, sometimes pictured a near-profile head with an eye in front view and a nose in pronounced profile. These artists were aware of such precedent and often drew a simple object in that precise, didactic style as a composite of its discrete parts (see, for example, drawings by Jacques Villon).[19] The method survives in some scientific illustration and in the drawings of architects and engineers presenting together on a single sheet of paper the plan, elevations, and cross sections of a building or machine.

In many Cubist works, Renaissance perspectival drawing—ordering a scene as if viewed from a certain viewpoint—is deployed with great liberty in the choice of viewpoints: parts of the same building may be shown as if seen from several points in separate pictures, each in "correct" perspective, together on the single sheet or canvas. In the Baroque period, Leibniz had referred to the multiple perspectives of a town when viewed from different sides *(Monadology,* §§ 57–58) to illustrate his idea that because of the infinite number of simple substances, it is as if we know the world more fully through perception of an object from different positions. For Leibniz, time is a property of objects, indeed, relative to objects in space—here, the city, which has a temporal existence through features of change in its static aspect. Note that this does not introduce time as a property of the picture and its represented objects, and surely not as space-time: Measurement of the latter is performed adequately with respect to the coordinates of a single observer's position.

On the other hand, artists of the past have indeed taken account of time in their rendering of action or the changing state of objects, and have found means of evoking the experience of duration, of succession, and of the instantaneous as a point in the flow of time in a pictorial composition that is viewed also as a simultaneously visible whole, enclosed in a frame and with a balanced, ordered arrangement, a stable structure of its parts. Time has been suggested even in ancient painting and relief by devices of which one may say broadly that they fuse the irreversible order of objects in space and moments in time through a binding horizontal axis. In ancient and medieval narrative imagery, in which there is no fixed perspective viewpoint, though a unified visual field presents itself within the framed field (as of a printed page), the irreversible sequence of episodes is often read in one direction, from left to right (or the reverse), so that the position of a scene within a narrative series corresponds to its place in time between a preceding and a succeeding action. When in later art a perspective view coordinates the parts of a deep space in a consistent projective system, the convergence and diminution of lines in depth produce an order of the apparently near and far. This effect is also exploited, as previously mentioned, for narrative order and dramatic effect and the depiction of movement in depth, toward and away from us, where artists of the fifteenth and sixteenth centuries place in a distant landscape, behind their major foreground scene, episodes that came before or after, in a progressive enlargement or diminution of its apparent size, like a railway train first seemingly enlarging on approach and then contracting in recession.[20]

To return to an earlier point, by invoking *simultaneity*—a term used often by the Futurists and certain Cubists of the second line, though not in fact by the originators Braque and Picasso—Giedion shows he has misunderstood Einstein's analysis of the concept. In the article of 1905 Einstein actually demonstrated that the simultaneity of events distant from one another in space is impossible to establish. Objects and events are located in the space-time of the mathematician Hermann Minkowski by means of a coordinate system in which time is measured in seconds and space by a unit of distance traversed by light in one second, the two units together proving a symmetrical frame for locating an event and also an absolute measure of the interval between events in both time and space for any object with respect to an observer, whether at rest or in motion. For objects and events in our proximate earthly space, and with our low velocities of motion, this metric yields results hardly different from measures by the classic Galilean coordinates. For the small, intimate space framed in a Cubist still life painting or even for the larger field of a Futurist scene of the city street, measurement by Minkowski's space-time metric, adapted to an utterly astronomical scale of 186,000-mile units, would make no significant difference. The features of the new art pertain to vastly different scales of time and space than do the phenomena and theoretical assumptions scrutinized by Einstein: the scale of movements of the observer and earth and planets and stars, with relative distance measured in terms of the velocity of light by tiny fractions of a second.

Common to both Giedion and Panofsky is the notion of a Cubist break with Renaissance geometrical perspective as replaced by a fourth dimension as the dimension of time. Panofsky's remark on Picasso's "opening up the fourth dimension of time" recalls a note in his earlier essay "Perspective as 'Symbolic Form.'" There he summarizes an article then just recently published (in 1925) by the Russian constructivist painter El Lissitzky. In Panofsky's account, Lissitzky contrasts the new conditions of the most modern painting with the rigid three-dimensionality of the Euclidean space of Renaissance perspective—bounded, finite, and closed. The new art has tried to break the former constraints by splintering the visual center, just as Futurism no longer represents intervals in depth through foreshortening but, in accord with the most modern insights of psychology, creates an illusionary space by contrasts of variously placed and toned spatial values of the colored surfaces. But Lissitzky proposes a third solution: the conquest of an "imaginary space" by means of mechanically moved bodies that, rotating or oscillating, kinetically describe figures—a turning rod, for example, generates an apparent circle or cylinder. Art, according to Lissitzky, is thereby raised to the standpoint of non-Euclidean geometry, although the space of the "imaginary" rotating body remains Euclidean like any other empirical space. Here, Panofsky found Lissitzky's thinking "disputable" but "instructive."[21]

Yet small as they are, even if Cubist table objects, Futurist isolated figures in motion, or moving machines, or street scenes were regarded as attempts to symbolize relativity space-time relations (contradicting both the works and the statements of Braque and Picasso), one would still have to question the argument of Giedion and Panofsky built on the principle of multiple viewpoints; for it would be difficult to find a single painting by Picasso or Braque in which that principle is carried out consistently and offers a legible order of succession. It is instructive to describe these relations precisely, for they will bear on the validity of the intuitive, generalizing methods so habitual in large-scale historical analogizing of ideas.

In earlier Cubist painting, if parts of a figure are rendered separately as if from different viewpoints and eye levels, these supposedly varying

positions of the painter or fixations of the shifting eye are not discernible in the painting as a distinct order in time. The supposedly temporal in that art is not clearly discernible in the artist's process as a sighting of the parts in a succession of discrete positions that could be matched with the moments in time, but it appears as a random or unspecifiable collection of moments in time. There is no clue to the order in which the artist viewed and painted those parts of a figure or still-life object. To speak of them as examples of Minkowskian space-time (or of a classical space-and-time) is entirely arbitrary; here the concept of the simultaneous is applied malapropos. The separate views implicit in the fractioning of parts and their rendering from different viewpoints may be compared, again, with the ancient Egyptian paintings and reliefs—Henri Rousseau could speak of Picasso's style as "Egyptian," in contrast to his own (pre-Cubist, about 1908) as "modern"—of which the style is of course not Cubist. In certain Cubist paintings from about 1910–11 to about 1913–14 multiple viewpoints are inferred from such details as an eye *en face* in a profile or near-profile head, a bottle with a label on one plane while its opening is a circle and its base a straight line, a mandolin with some parts seen in profile and others *en face*, and so forth. Picasso has often drawn *both eyes* as frontal in a profile head, but even this effect, rare in ancient art, is found in the early medieval art of his native Spain, in so-called Mozarabic art (especially manuscripts) of the tenth century, as in a drawing in which two nostrils appear in a nose in profile.[22] The difference between the Cubist and archaic fractioned representation concerns the greater freedom of Cubists in combining different views of parts of an object but also, specifically, the open Cubist form without continuous bounding
Figs. 4-5 contour for the object as a whole. By these means a contrast obtains between the distinctness of the simple, partial form, often closed, and the broken, indefinite outline of the object constituted by such parts, which is fundamental for the phase of Cubism in question, though by 1913–14 Picasso and Braque represent objects with closed contours.

Again, these are modes of representation familiar to ancient and
Fig. 6 primitive art, particularly to Egyptian representations of the human

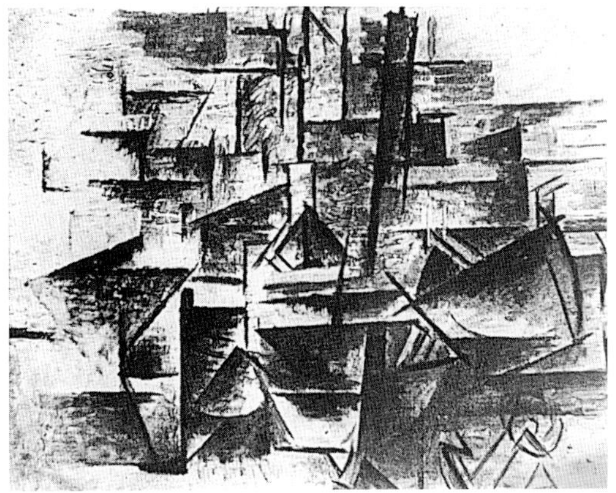

Figure 4. *The Harbor at Cadaqués*, summer 1910, oil on canvas, 15 x 17⅞" (38 x 45.5 cm), National Gallery, Prague.

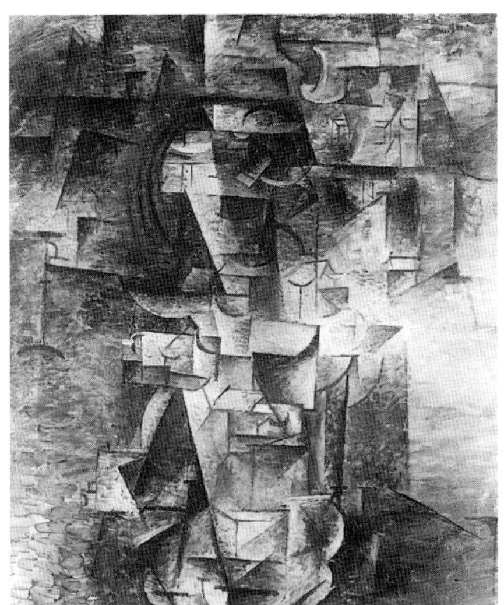

Figure 5. *Woman*, autumn 1910, oil on canvas, 39⅜ x 31⅞" (100 x 81 cm), Museum of Fine Arts, Boston. Charles H. Bayley Fund and partial gift of Mrs. Gilbert W. Chapman.

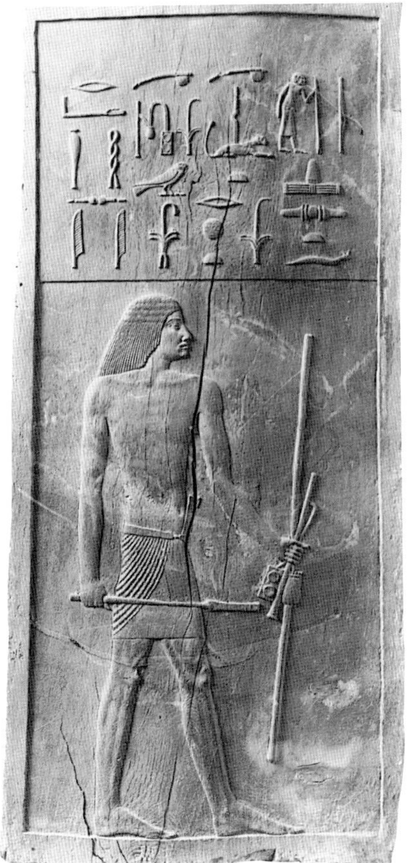

Figure 6. *Wooden Panel of Hesy-Ra*, from the northern edge of the Saqqara Cemetery, mid-Third Dynasty (c. 2686-2613 B.C.), wood, height: 45¼" (115 cm), The Cairo Museum.

figure with a frontal eye and profile nose, mouth, chin, and jaw, with frontal shoulders and breast but profile legs, and to the so-called "conceptual" method of constructing an image of a three-dimensional object in the drawings of children, where, as in the ancient Egyptian works, there are no implications of a sequence of sightings in time. In the Cubist rendering of a cylindrical glass on a table, with its different perspectives of the upper opening of a vessel and its slightly flat horizontal base, we find every kind of projective form of the circle, ellipse, and straight line; an instrument that recorded a viewer's successive fixations on details of a picture would not reconstitute the order in which these details were seen or painted. Shall we imagine the artist rising on tiptoe or a ladder to see the circular opening and kneeling to sight the flat horizontal base? The theories of Giedion and Panofsky suggest a cinematic art in which successive shots are constituted in a set of temporally overlapping frames, usually representing movement in one direction, as in the drawings of Rodolphe Töppfer and Wilhelm Busch, nineteenth-century originators of the "strip cartoon."[23]

Let us examine in more detail just how artists of earlier centuries treated time and space. In the fourteenth century, painters had begun to expand the setting of narrative scenes to a distant horizon and sky, and to organize the figures and landscape objects to accord with the observed or calculated perspective diminution and convergences. The apparent deepening (and heightening) of the pictured space provided not only a rich landscape or architectural background for a major episode in the foreground but also places for successive events that preceded or followed the main one. As previously noted, progressively smaller figures in the distance make up a series of consecutive actions in which an order of size of the figures is matched with an order of positions and postures in both time and space. In depicting the Fig. 8 *Adoration of the Magi*, in 1423, Gentile da Fabriano shows within one frame the journey of the three kings from different lands, their meeting on the way to Jerusalem, their sighting and following the course of the star in the distant sky. They converse with Herod in Jerusalem and, advancing to the foreground, arrive finally—close to the picture plane—at the manger in Bethlehem, with an immense retinue of horsemen still behind them. In some versions of the subject the Annunciation to the Shepherds is shown occurring on a remote hilltop, with a herd of sheep in the landscape. The shepherds receive the message of the Savior's birth from an angel in the sky near the horizon: They sometimes reappear, enlarged, in the foreground, adoring the Child. What was once a series of isolated, often closed scenes, ordered Fig. 7 from left to right or from above downward, virtually close to the spectator and the plane of the picture surface, is transformed into a sequence in a deep and high space. The change is linked with the painter's new interest in the third dimension as a field of movement—significantly, of travel and traffic—and with the conception of events as displacements of participants in motion within an environment, in an extended time as well as space. The moving star, the journey of the Magi, and the meeting with the Holy Family (likewise in other cases, such as Passion cycles) are actualized in the picture as successive events through that coordination of a perspective of space and a "perspective" of time (not unlike the correlation of distance and time in railway or airline timetables). Besides those of the Magi, scenes of Christ's Entry into Jerusalem and of the Road to Calvary were enlarged to admit lengthy processions across the full extent of the pictured setting in both the foreground and deep space. What one could have seen only from many different viewpoints and at different moments is made visible and intelligible in the picture through the ordered fusing of space in a single summating perception, unified by the perspective laws and by the cohesive patterning of shapes, lines, and colors, and by adaptations to the boundaries of the field and to the larger elements of nature and buildings.

This conception is of particular interest as an example of artists' practical thinking about motion in the imaging of time and space. It intuitively connects events consecutive in both time and distant space, fusing them with each other by representing in perspective the successive positions of bodies in motion within a single frame. This double perspective of time and space becomes concrete in art when painters are

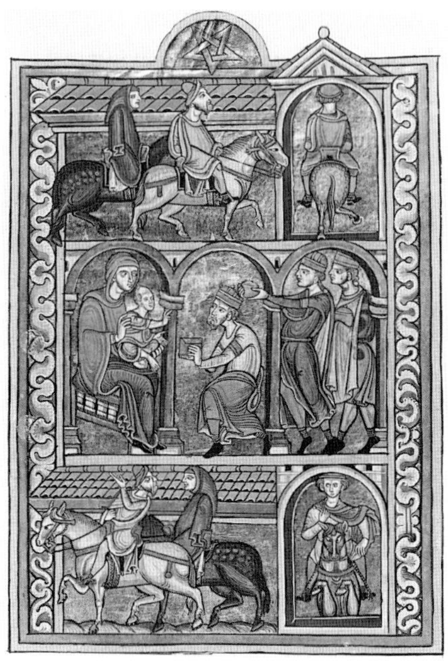

Figure 7. *Adoration of the Magi: Their Arrival and Departure*, The Pierpont Morgan Library, New York, PML 710, fol. 19V.

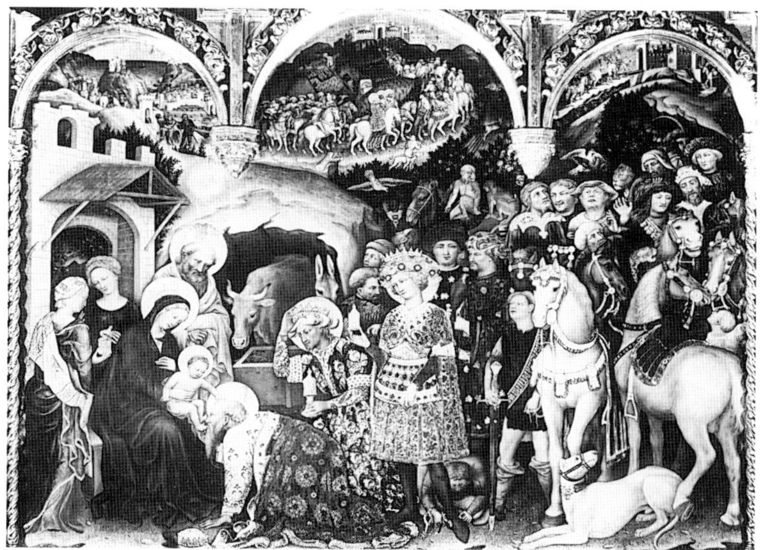

Figure 8. Gentile da Fabriano, *Adoration of the Magi*, 1423, commissioned by Palla Strozzi for the Strozzi Chapel, Santa Trinità, Florence, tempera on panel, 9'10" x 9'3" (3 x 2.82 m), Galleria degli Uffizi, Florence.

more attentive not only to the forms of moving objects but also to the continuity of events and the surroundings of human action, in their changing but law-bound appearance according to their distance from the observer in an imagined space and time. The combination of one-point, focused perspective, which implies a fixed viewpoint and a static observer, with a succession of scenes in depth, is common in paintings of the fifteenth and sixteenth centuries. In the background of a religious or mythological image one often sees various episodes that preceded or followed the major scene. Nicolas Poussin and other seventeenth-century painters used a perspective without a distant vanishing point or constant sequence in the diminutional relations of objects of the same natural class—human figures, trees, and clouds in a large three-dimensional space—a great, impressive example being his *Blind Orion Seeking the Rising Sun* (1658). In such series of events unfolding in time the figures ordinarily become larger or smaller according to their location in space and their order in time; the perspectives of space and the succession of observations in time are therefore inseparable. And sometimes as they approach the horizon, distant scenes are not only smaller but also less active, less energetic—a diminution that may be compared to the changes in the length of fast-moving objects in physical space-time (but perhaps, too, with reversal of the respective values of mass, energy, and velocity in Einstein's system?).

Intimations of time in Cubist painting are not sensed as qualities of the three-dimensional form that Picasso, Braque, Fernand Léger, and other originating Cubist painters so often declared to be their primary concern. The different viewpoints from which the parts of a bottle or face are supposedly drawn do not produce an unequivocal order in time—not as in music or in drama where the action has structure in time, a rhythm, and tempo of successive events. In music the order and duration of the hearer's perceptions correspond to the duration of the tones and intervals of the music and to the order of the consecutive sound events. Nothing of that legible sequential pattern in time appears in the Cubist paintings, as it does in the old narrative paintings.

Other modern painters also used the term *simultaneity.* To some it meant, as with Robert Delaunay, the appearance of intense contrast induced by strong differences between adjacent spectral hues on the canvas—a phenomenon that had been investigated methodically early in the nineteenth century by the chemist Michel Eugène Chevreul *(De la loi du contraste simultané des couleurs,* 1839)—such contrast being regarded by Delaunay as the carrier of light in painting.[24] To others, as with the Futurists, simultaneity meant a dynamic integrating force and cosmic principle, the pictured totality of varied events, their interactions, impacts, and collisions, within a local field at one point in time, for which the term *instantaneity* would perhaps have been more apt. In addition, what the Futurists attempted to depict was what they called the simultaneity of "dynamic sensations" in representing a moving figure, a machine, or the buildings and traffic of a city street by a series of sucessive overlapping, partly transparent positions on one canvas, like the appearance of a moving object in a photograph made with rapid consecutive shots on the same frame of film. None of these effects, however, is illuminated by aligning the principle of representation to Einstein and Minkowski. The concept of simultaneity, in the sense of both Futurist painting and the immediacy of impact in earlier Impressionist works—for example, Édouard Manet's *Races at Longchamp* (c. 1867) or his *A Bar at the Folies-Bergère* (1882), Edgar Degas's dancers and racehorses, as well as Pissarro's city streets[25]—is better understood through a text of the poet-physicist-inventor Charles Cros (1842–1888), a friend of the Impressionist painters. Cros's treatise *Principes de méchanique cérébrale* (conceived by 1874; published, 1879) defines "form" as

> a simultaneity of several specific elementary impressions, some alike, some different. . . . An ensemble of different impressions, considered as affecting simultaneously the seats of consciousness, is classified under the category of forms. For example: at a ball, the lights, the invited guests, the music, the sound of voices, the flavor and taste of the ices that you enjoy and a thousand other impressions, taken together

> yet at any instant un-decomposable by the self, constitute a form, whether experienced in reality or evoked in memory or imagination.[26]

Before there appeared in writings on art explicit allusions to Einstein and to space-time, writers described the "fourth dimension" in modern painting as a directly sensed quality of space, without reference to time. The American painter Max Weber, who was attracted in Paris by the first works of the Cubists, and for a few years practiced the new mode, explained the connection in an article titled "The Fourth Dimension from a Plastic Point of View," published in July 1910 in Alfred Stieglitz's New York avant-garde journal *Camera Work:*

> In plastic art, I believe, there is a fourth dimension which may be described as the consciousness of a great and overwhelming sense of space-magnitude in all directions at one time, and is brought into existence through the three known measurements. It is not a physical entity or a mathematical hypothesis, nor an optical illusion. It is real, and can be perceived and felt. . . . It . . . is the space that envelops a tree, a mountain, or any solid; or the intervals between objects or volumes of matter if receptively beheld. . . . It is the immensity of all things. . . .
>
> Two objects may be of like measurements, yet not appear to be of the same size, not because of some optical illusion, but because of a greater or lesser perception of this so-called fourth dimension, the dimension of infinity. Archaic and the best of Assyrian, Egyptian, or Greek sculpture, as well as paintings by El Greco and Cézanne and other masters, are splendid examples of plastic art possessing this rare quality.[27]

Better known than Weber's text are the statements of the poet and art critic Guillaume Apollinaire, an intimate friend of Picasso. In a lecture of 1911 on the Cubists published in 1913 in his book *The Cubist*

Painters; Aesthetic Meditations, he added the analogy to science while holding to the aesthetic concept:

> Today, scientists no longer limit themselves to the three dimensions of Euclid. The painters have been led quite naturally, one might say by intuition, to preoccupy themselves with the new possibilities of spatial measurement which, in the language of the modern studios, are designated by the term: the fourth dimension. Regarded from the plastic point of view, the fourth dimension appears to spring from the three known dimensions: it represents the immensity of space eternalizing itself in all directions at any given moment. It is space itself, the dimension of the infinite; the fourth dimension endows objects with plasticity. It gives the object its right proportions on the whole, whereas in Greek art, for instance, a somewhat mechanical rhythm, constantly destroys the proportions. . . .
>
> Finally, I must point out that the fourth dimension—this utopian expression should be analyzed and explained, so that nothing more than historical interest may be attached to it—has come to stand for the aspirations and premonitions of the many young artists who contemplate Egyptian, negro, and oceanic sculptures, meditate on various scientific works, and live in the anticipation of a sublime art.[28]

One wonders if Apollinaire might have been influenced by the thinking in Weber's article, so close are the two texts in language and in the concept of the quality of expansive energy in the new art, identified as a fourth dimension.[29]

Weber affirmed his sense of that added dimension as a material reality and a feature of all great art in the past and present; but where Apollinaire brings to his enthusiastic support of the new art and its space as a fourth dimension some ties with current widespread beliefs of spiritists and Theosophists, Weber had firmly dissociated himself from occultism. Behind the use of the term *fourth dimension* by Weber and Apollinaire we do sense something of the vogue of Theosophy and occult spiritism during this time. These beliefs had adherents among artists and eminent men of science: Theosophists were quick to claim in contemporary physics points of support for their doctrines and often alluded to a fourth dimension. In 1908 a leading mathematician, Felix Klein, found it necessary to dissociate his science from the contagion of that impressively abstruse term. According to Klein, the "fourth dimension" was initially popularized before 1873 with "experiments of the spiritualist Slate," which the astronomer Johann Zöllner actually sought to affirm on the principle that a medium attuned to four rather than merely three dimensions would be able to make things disappear and reappear as if by extrapolation from the known relation of two and three dimensions—in the manner of Edwin Abbott Abbott's *Flatland: A Romance of Many Dimensions* (1884), known to Klein as an anonymous work.[30]

At the same time as, or soon after, Apollinaire's text, the two Cubist painters Gleizes and Metzinger, whose book I have already quoted, spoke explicitly of the mathematician Riemann: "If we wished to relate the space of the painters to geometry, we should have to refer it to the non-Euclidean mathematicians;[31] we should have to study at some length certain of Reimann's [sic] theorems." Although both Picasso and Braque denied dependence of their work on mathematics, and Gleizes and Metzinger insisted that painting is an art, intuitive and personal, and not a science or philosophy, the discussion of Cubism as the expression of a new worldview shared by scientists continued. Much later, the French critic Maurice Raynal, who had been an early defender of Cubism, remarked, in recalling its history, that the Cubist painters had ardently discussed the fourth dimension and non-Euclidean geometry, of which he himself had first learned as a youth at the Lycée Louis le Grand, in Paris.[32] In 1914, however, Georg Riemann is invoked together with Janos Bolyai, N. I. Lobachevsky, Eugenio Beltrami, and, earlier, Joseph-Marie de Tilly, as the creators of non-Euclidean geometry, in the preface to the catalogue of an exhibition of Cubist art in

Prague early in 1914, written by the organizer, Alexandre Mercereau, who was most active in bringing Cubist art to Prague, Budapest, and Moscow. "In harmony with the innovations of science," Mercereau writes, "today's art seeks to discover ultimate laws more profound than those of yesterday." Here the "postulated principles" of the named mathematicians "have not destroyed those of Euclid but merely relegated them to their true status as one postulate among many."[33]

Well before painters and writers on art referred to Einstein, Cubism had been described as a style that evoked or imaged a fourth dimension. In the circle of the avant-garde this beguiling esoteric term had connoted at first a mysterious, exalting space, extremely suggestive to devotees of occultism and theosophy. It was followed by explications of the strange and, to some observers, paradoxical aspect of the illusory layered and modelled space in the Cubist paintings as in accord with new scientific concepts of time as a fourth dimension and of non-Euclidean geometry. Later, when relativity theory became more familiar through popularized accounts, that penchant for abstruse analogies in writings on the arts survived in grandiose analogies and glib assertions about the history of both science and art, embracing Einstein, Minkowski, and occult spiritism alike. For instance, the novelist Vladimir Nabokov ascribed to Alexandr Pushkin's prose a fullness of three dimensions, but Nikolay Gogol was "fourth-dimensional at least": "He may be compared to his contemporary, the mathematician Lobachevsky, who blasted Euclid and discovered a century ago many of the theories which Einstein later developed." To characterize further the mysterious, irrational world of Gogol's stories Nabokov likened it to "such conceptions of modern astrophysics as the 'Concertina Universe' or the 'Explosion Universe'. . . . There is a curvature in literary style as there is a curvature in space."[34]

The explanation of Cubist painting as having a basis in treating time as fourth dimension has even been extended to Marcel Proust: "The painter tries to give at one and the same time all those aspects of an object which one could ordinarily discover in it only by viewing it in turn from different angles. . . . Time then is like the fourth dimension which, in combining with the other three, perfects space. . . . Seen though the perspective of time, space is set free, transcended."[35] A more recent example comes from the engineer and architect Buckminster Fuller's rather wildly indulgent commemorative tribute to the abstract painter Joseph Albers (1888–1976): "Albers' sensitivity gave him access to nuances of the physical Universe's most powerful secrets. It opened, for instance, a whole field of mathematically brilliant insights into the positive and negative foldability of papers and other crisp films or metal sheets with results as multi-dimensionally beautiful as they were scientifically surprising, for some of them physically anticipated electromagnetic waves as well as Einstein, Reiman [sic], curved space, wave propagations."[36]

From a scanning of articles, books, and reviews by artists and their friendly critics who in the years before the end of World War I wrote of Cubist painting in France, it appears that Einstein and Minkowski were really unknown to the authors. This is all the more likely since there are mentions of several other mathematicians and physicists in the same artistic literature. In France, Einstein's Special Relativity had already been discussed by the physicist Paul Langevin in the *Revue de Métaphysique*, a leading philosophical journal, in 1911; and in the book of Émile Meyerson, *Identité et réalité* (1912) are several pages on the ideas of both Minkowski and Einstein.[37] Yet the first direct reference by a painter to Einstein that I have been able to find is in a letter of January 1922 addressed by the Spanish Cubist painter of the inner Parisian circle, Juan Gris, to his friend the critic Raynal, who as early as 1912 had written of scientific affinities of the space and time of Cubist painting. Gris had just read Charles Nordmann's *Einstein et l'univers* (1921), a popular exposition of relativity, and filled with admiration for Einstein, he requested anything available "by him or about him" to read.[38] Furthermore, Eugeni d'Ors, the Spanish writer and friend of Picasso since their youth in Barcelona, in his brilliant work on the painter *(Pablo Picasso*, 1930), a book rich in comparisons of art styles to mathematical concepts and operations, to political forms, and to the morphology of cultures, nowhere alludes to Einstein, even though as early as 1908 d'Ors had attended Langevin's lectures at the Sorbonne on the theory of relativity (and after World War I, he had occasion to take part in the meetings of the Committee on Intellectual Cooperation of the League of Nations, at which Einstein was present).[39]

The Futurists did not speak of time in the sense of Gleizes and Metzinger when they referred to science as a source of modern mobility and dynamism. Unlike the originators of Cubism in France, whose art they criticized as static, they found in dynamic movement the key principle of modernity and strove to express in painting and sculpture their perception of moving objects. In expounding these ideas, they referred to Bergson, in philosophy, although their concepts of dynamism and motion are so often linked in their imagery and manifestos to the mechanical and to a militant ideology of modernism as technical progress. Their spokesman, the poet Filippo Marinetti, wished to affirm the revolutionary importance of science for modern life and thought. He cites as the sign of its paramount influence "man multiplied by the machine . . . a fusion of instincts with the efficiency of motors and conquered forces."[40] In the First Manifesto of Futurism (February 20, 1909), Marinetti wrote, "Time and space died yesterday. Already we live in the absolute, since we have already created speed, eternal and ever-present." Signing the next, "Technical Manifesto" a year later, Umberto Boccioni, Carlo Carrà, Luigi Russolo, Giacomo Balla, and Gino Severini celebrated "the dynamic sensation itself":

> Indeed, all things move, all things run, all things are rapidly changing. A profile is never motionless before our eyes but it constantly appears and disappears.
>
> On account of the persistency of an image upon the retina, moving objects constantly multiply themselves. . . . Thus a running horse has not four legs but twenty, and their movements are triangular.

And in an exhibition manifesto of February 1912, the same five artists condemned Picasso, Braque, André Derain, Metzinger, Gleizes, Léger, and others, for, notwithstanding their "laudable" initial radicalism, "obstinately continu[ing] to paint objects motionless, frozen, and all the static aspects of Nature. . . . We, on the contrary, . . . seek for a style of motion."[41]

One wonders if Marinetti, author of the initial manifesto, could possibly have known of a talk given by Minkowski in September of 1908, or even read its publication in German, before composing the initial manifesto, dated five months later. For Minkowski (who died in 1909), had said, "Henceforth space by itself, and time by itself, are doomed to fade away into mere shadows, and only a kind of union of the two will preserve an independent reality." He projected: "We should have in the world no longer space, but an infinite number of spaces, analogously as there are in three-dimensional space an infinite number of planes. Three-dimensional geometry becomes a chapter in four-dimensional physics."[42]

In Russia, where Futurism was welcomed together with Cubism by young artists, it was explained by some defenders in a mixed language of terms from Theosophy, mathematics, and the new physics.[43] As a revolution in art, Futurism was attractive also to some political revolutionaries, who saw in the daring liberty of artists a stimulus to radical social change. The poet Vladimir Mayakovsky could speak of "Einstein's Futuristic brain."[44] Braque and Picasso, however, the inventors of Cubism, while conscious of the modernity of their work, were unpolitical in the years just before 1914 and asserted the independence of the new art as a product of free imagination engaged with new aesthetic possibilities and with problems of form construction and expression that they had established themselves. Their relation to contemporary mathematics was in their conviction that their art was a free construction without "dependence" on "reality" and subject, thus, to exacting requirements of a "plastic" order and consistency.

The various stages of Cubist painting give another ground for doubting the seriousness of the analogy with physics and its worldview, as if both expressed the same outlook or spirit of the age. For the interpretation of the new art as an effort to realize space-time in painting ignores the varying structures of form in Cubist art and the different qualities of the objects discernible in the images. Apart from the mistaken account of both Cubist and Futurist art as analogous to relativity theory in the conception of space-time and simultaneity, the history of these styles, the individual variations at any moment, and the change of forms from year to year make one doubt the justness or even the heuristic value of the analogy. It would be difficult, if at all possible, to characterize one type of new space, so much do these structures vary. In the few years of Cubism's vogue from 1908 to 1920 several different styles are called Cubist, with the style of the originators themselves, Braque and Picasso, undergoing far-reaching changes from year to year. I shall first describe briefly the successive stages of Cubist painting between 1908 (considering Picasso's *Demoiselles d'Avignon*, of 1907, as not yet a Cubist, but rather a Fauve, work, with its compact, distinctly outlined figures, empirical perspective, and neoprimitive details) and 1914. I shall then comment on Cubism in the immediate postwar years.

The course of Cubist art itself shows that if the painters were ever occupied with multiple viewpoints in depicting the parts of an object on the same canvas it was for a brief period. Between 1908, when the name *Cubism* was first applied to Braque's paintings in view of their strikingly regular, massive forms, and the late 1910s and early 1920s, when some of the advanced painters returned to a "classic" figurative style even as others turned toward abstraction, there was a rapid development of several short-lived phases during which compact voluminous shapes, inspired in part by Cézanne's example, were progressively thinned and flattened, and the strongly marked enclosing outlines were broken and dissociated from the volumes of the objects, so that it becomes quite impossible to speak any longer of different sides of an object, or "moving around" it to render its form.

The new abstruse-looking style, which induced comparison with science, was practiced by Picasso and Braque for only the few years between about 1909 or 1910 and 1913, while it was works of 1908 and 1909 that had provoked the name *Cubism* for their art. The first works, with distinct, compact, bulky elements—often buildings of simple geometric forms and trees closely grouped as massive units in definite planes in a landscape depth—do remind us of certain paintings by Cézanne, which were admired models of a grave constructive art of rigorous composition. The forms of the objects rendered appear modeled and voluminous, as in Picasso's landscapes with buildings at Horta de Ebro, which were inspired by certain paintings of Cézanne and suggested to skeptical and hostile viewers in their solid geometric forms the name *Cubism* (see, for example, Paul Cézanne's *Turning Road at Montgeroult* of 1898).[45] The architectural themes and order were a significant choice for young painters reacting against Impressionism, who aimed at cohesive composition of pronounced elementary forms. The painters and their followers often spoke of their desire to represent the enduring or essential forms of objects as known and conceived by the mind and to surmount thereby the flux and vagueness of appearances. Fig. 9

By 1910, depicted depth was reduced to a shallowness like low relief, with the formerly closed contours of objects disengaged as brusque, discontinuous strokes or segments of lines that, together with small repeated flecks of neutralized tones of color, suggest increasingly open planes. These overlap and intersect one another, fade or end abruptly, appear suspended, intricate, abstruse, incomplete, forming and deforming their objects. Many of these elements are now unintelligible as representations or conventional signs, yet they are purposive as a coherent visual structure of elementary geometric forms, straight and curved lines, plane surfaces, and flecked touches. We understand them better if we take them as freely chosen and freely grouped constructive marks limited to a few elementary types: the straight line, the segment of a circle or ellipse, the unit stroke in a visible constructed whole of discrete units, however unclear they appear in the fusion of figure and ground.

A change took place in 1910–12 to less modeled forms with greater discontinuity of lines and flecks: slender scaffoldings, straight with a few curved, rhythmical lines. Everything came out of the wonderfully fertile collaboration between Picasso and Braque. Some forms are recognizable as schematized parts of objects, others are freely associated marks for rhythmical and contrasting effect yet all consist of the same Figs. 10-11

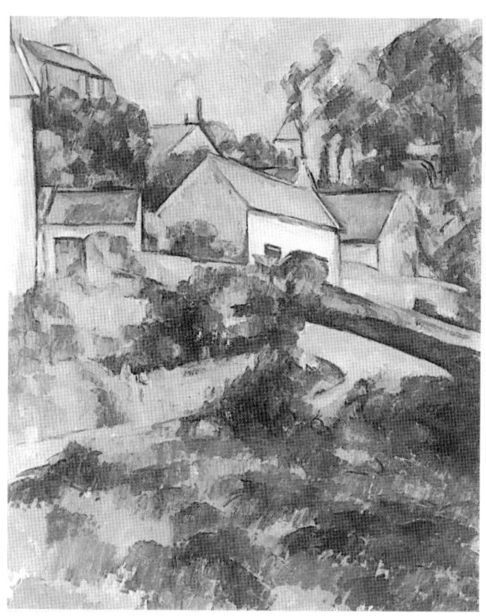

Figure 9. Paul Cézanne, *La Route Tournante à Montgeroult*, 1898, oil on canvas, 32 x 26" (81.2 x 66 cm), The Museum of Modern Art, New York, Bequest of Mrs. John Hay Whitney.

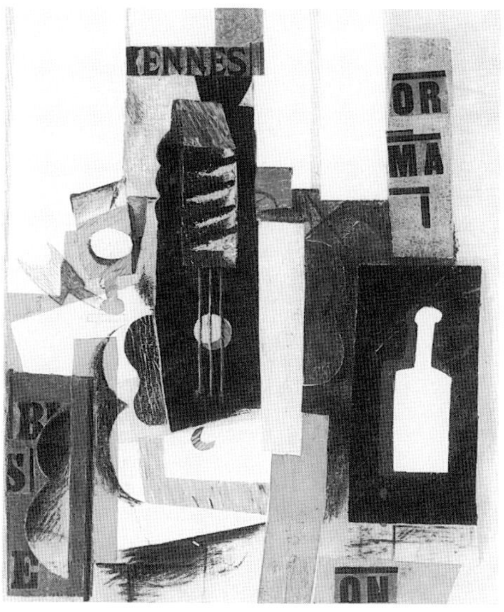

Figure 10. *Still-life with Guitar (Glass, Guitar, and Bottle)*, early 1913, oil, pasted papers, lead white, and pencil on canvas, 25¾ x 21⅛" (65.4 x 53.6 cm), The Museum of Modern Art, New York, Gift of the Sidney and Harriet Janis Collection, 1967.

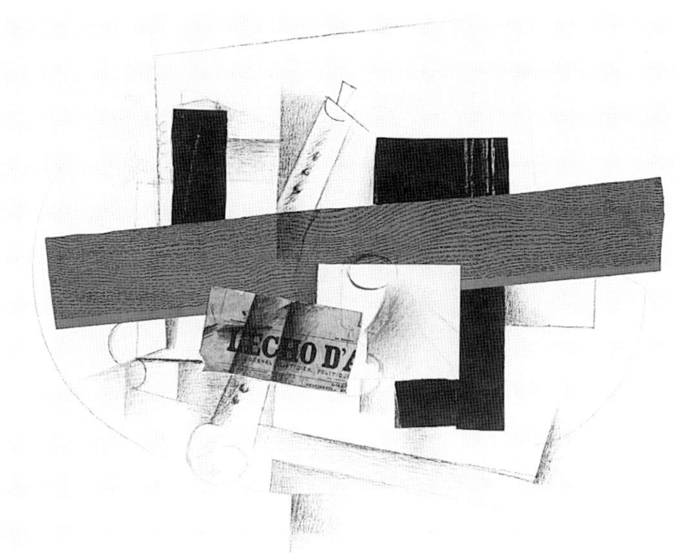

Figure 11. Georges Braque, *Clarinet*, 1913, pasted papers, charcoal, chalk, and oil on canvas, 37½ x 47⅜" (95.3 x 120.3 cm), The Museum of Modern Art, New York. The Nelson A. Rockefeller Bequest.

or closely related substance, as if in musical accompaniment, development, or variation on the object forms. From about 1911–13, the elements of modeling and the discontinuity and merging of planes, which had been characterized as four-dimensional and suggestive of time in the simultaneous effect of different sightings of the same object, gave way to flattened forms as a layered overlapping of intersecting planes in a shallow space close to the surface of the canvas. One came, indeed, to speak of the two-dimensionality of the painting as true to the essence or nature of the art. Painters who called their art "abstract" or "nonobjective" drew from this later phase of Cubism the principle of an art of the free construction of regular geometric forms with a strict and legible system of form on the corresponding flat surface of the rectangular canvas.

Also in 1912 and 1913, bits of written words or musical notations, segments of printed and ornamented papers applied to the surface beside the painted and drawn parts signaled a further departure from the original modeling and relief-depth of the Cubist picture. One passed from the mysterious, fancied fourth dimension to an art of two dimensions quite without modeling or depth, as is readily apparent in works of Picasso and Braque from 1913. After 1915 or 1916, but especially during the 1920s, Picasso and other Cubists, as well as ex-Futurists, would turn to a classicizing or veristic style of representation, sharp and clear, in picturing large natural forms, sometimes monumental, massive figures, in apparent three-dimensional space, with allusions to classic and sculptural styles. The development of this style may in part be traced to the influence of World War I, including Picasso's feelings as an alien in a warring country, and to the French conservative *Rappel á l'Ordre* (Call to Order) for postwar industrial recovery, with its appeal to maintain the French classical tradition. Yet the early phase left its mark in persistent features of composition in both abstract and mimetic painting, for we detect in details traces of the preceding practice in arbitrary breaks and continuities of line or form and structure.

In 1918–20 modeling, light and shadow, and perspective were essentially rejected. The preference for flatness decreed an inherent necessity or demand for truth to the more tangible reality of the canvas surface and the brush marks upon it, just as architects insisted then on truth to the nature of materials and to the technique of construction in the new functionalist buildings and preferred thin planes to modeled and articulated solid form. The same Gleizes who in 1912 had written of the bases of Cubism in non-Euclidean geometry and the fourth dimension of time could in 1919 state the following as axioms of the new postwar Cubism:

> Painting is the art of giving life to a flat surface.
> The plane surface is a two-dimensional world.
> Through these two dimensions it has truth.
> To enrich it with a third dimension means to wish to change its nature, its real essence.[46]

So one passed from the alleged fourth dimension, with its abstruse connotations, to a new orthodoxy of the exclusive two-dimensional form as a truth to the material nature of painting, a painted assembly of elementary geometric forms on the plane surface of the canvas, freed from the illusory appearance of depth as simulated by means of light and shade and perspective.

By then, in 1919, the name *Cubism* was understood and accepted by artists and critics as a purely conventional term that no more reflected the character of the style than the term *Gothic* gives a clue to the origin or nature of the medieval art designated as such. Cubism was recognized as a historic style, already distant and an ancestor of the new styles of abstraction (and an encouraging sign of vital, communal revolutionary spirit of reform among artists and poets). Only after the decisive change of style during the war, then, did one begin to associate Cubism with Einstein. His theory began to reach the lay public in popular expositions in 1919, after the spectacular confirmations of General Relativity, whereas before World War I, Special Relativity had been discussed only in a few philosophical publications that seem not to have reached artists or critics.

Another theme in the analogy drawn between modern painting and relativity theory has been the concept of the equivalence and convertibility of matter and energy. In the reduction of solid forms of objects to planes of color, and in the elimination of the modeling with light and shadow that generated the appearance of volume and spatial depth, Wassily Kandinsky as well as the Suprematists saw a resemblance to the physicists' (and philosophers') replacement of the old notion of matter by new concepts of substance, force, energy, and field. Even the belief in the existence of atoms as ultimate units had been questioned earlier as a superfluous survival of ancient materialism in science, though one continued to classify different kinds of atoms and atomic particles by mass as well as by charge. The supposed vanishing of matter had already been invoked in terms of the Impressionist painting of the nineteenth century, in which outlines of objects were blurred or dissolved in light and air. But an essential feature of Impressionism and the new art is disregarded. In both, the transparency of the picture plane and the appearance of solid objects and their illusionary textures simulated in the smoothly painted image gave way to a palpable relief of pigment in more pronounced brushwork; in Cubism, segments of real objects were even pasted onto the tangible surface of the canvas. If, then, in returning to figurative painting in a quasi-traditional style after a few years, the Cubist artists restored to the human form a bulk and massiveness, by 1920 representation itself, whether of momentary appearance or of the primary qualities of objects,[47] had given way among certain followers of the Cubists to a concept of "abstract" or "pure" painting, like Piet Mondrian's and Malevich's: a free and imaginative construction of a few arbitrarily chosen elementary forms.

Not long before the emergence of Cubism, painters had been concerned with the instantaneous in the appearance of a rapidly moving object beheld from a fixed viewpoint and also in the look of a stationary one that, without displacement, undergoes visible changes in time. Manet's view of a horse race seen almost head-on in *The Races at Longchamp* is an example of the first; and of the second, time-implying type, there are the Cathedral, Haystack, and Poplar Tree series by

Fig. 12

Monet, each subject done on several canvases painted at different hours of the day from shifting viewpoints and displaying, from picture to picture of the same, static object, surprising, subtle variations of the observed light and color; these variations were due, according to science, to the earth's changing position relative to the sun and to the changing effect from sunrise to sundown. Our memory of such Impressionist scenes evokes *duration:* a season, a day, an hour, a condition of the weather, and the feelings, activities, and bodily movements of the represented occasions. In Monet's mural of a pond with water lilies, on the curved wall of a large oval room in the Orangerie, the spectator moving along that wall can follow, within the one vast painting, the changes of illumination and color from morning to evening light. By 1900 the newly invented cinematic film captivated an audience at rest by producing impressions of continuous movement on the same flat screen and dramatized that effect through the imaging of motion, uniform and accelerated, forward, inward, and transverse within the fixed field, with increasing or diminishing size of the object in perspective depth, as photographed from the changing positions of a moving camera.

It was actually not Braque and Picasso, the originators of Cubism, but certain of their followers, particularly Marcel Duchamp, and above all the Italian Futurists, who claimed for their art the introduction of time as a ("fourth") dimension. Their image of motion was of vehicles in mechanical and orderly motion, where their Impressionist predecessors had aimed to realize motion in light and atmosphere, though already they, too, were inspired by the spectacle of the modern city as a place of active human movement. In the Futurists' works we recognize certain features and relations borrowed from the Cubists: the fracturing, crossing, and interpenetration of geometrical forms by which they intensified the appearance of rapid movement and explosive force. But nothing in their imagery corresponds to the order and sequence of events in time forming a continuum in the mathematical sense. Although they attempted an extreme in rendering successive positions
Fig. 13 of a moving object, as in Giacomo Balla's *Dynamism of a Dog on a Leash* (1912), a picture of a running dog with multiplied legs and overlapping

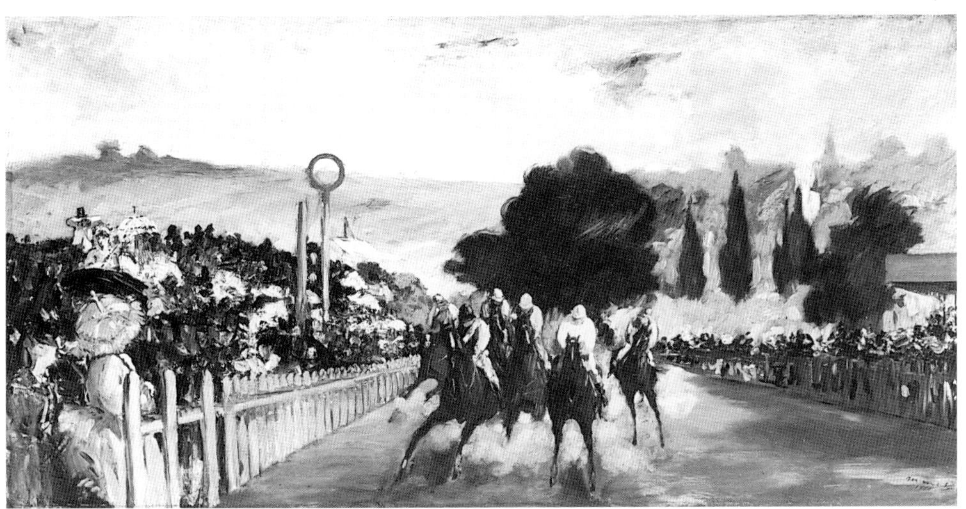

Figure 12. Edouard Manet, *The Races at Longchamp*, Paris, 1867, oil on canvas, 17¼ x 33¼" (43.8 x 84.5 cm), The Art Institute of Chicago, Potter Palmer Collection, 22.424.

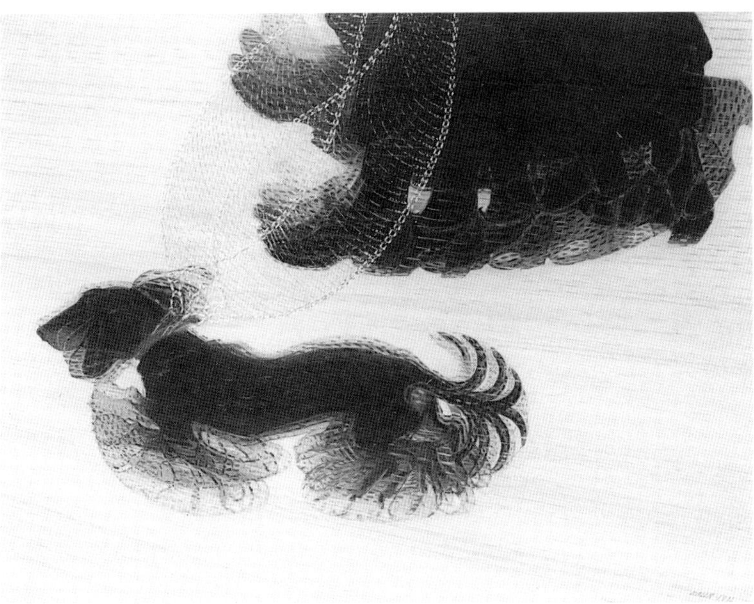

Figure 13. Giacomo Balla, *Dynamism of a Dog on a Leash*, 1912, oil on canvas, 35⅜ x 43¼" (89.8 x 109.8 cm), Albright-Knox Art Gallery, Buffalo, New York. Bequest of A. Conger Goodyear to George F. Goodyear, life interest, and Albright-Knox Art Gallery, Buffalo, New York, 1964.

positions of its body, nothing in their images corresponds to space-time in the senses of Minkowski and Einstein.

Simultaneity, with regard to painting, means the presentation of events in time while preserving unity peculiar to painting as a spatial art. For two hundred years before Cubism, artists and theoreticians had distinguished painting and literary art by their different relations to time and space, with objects and actions in a painting appearing as simultaneous, as if in the image of a single moment, whereas the literary text presented successive events in temporal sequence. As previously noted, this difference is the main theme of Lessing's *Laokoön*, which compares the classic sculpture of that name with Virgil's description of the subject. In deriving that normative principle from the nature of space and time, those artists and theoreticians were rejecting distasteful contemporary styles in which a writer indulged in lengthy descriptions of static persons, objects, and landscapes—things better portrayed in painting, which preserves the simultaneous, visible copresence of the various parts of the represented figures or objects. Moreover, they considered the painter to be at fault if he attempted to picture several successive moments or scenes of action within one image, like a naively primitive or popular story told in successive pictures within the same frame. In 1912, when that difference between the treatment of time and space in the arts was no longer a serious issue in criticism, and narrative painting was little practiced or even obsolete, the new Cubist works looked strange to those accustomed to more or less veristic painting; they were puzzled or outraged by the artists' liberty with the human and still-life forms. Simultaneity in painting of the past had meant the visible unity of the parts of the object as given together in the same glance; with the loss of the visible unity of the parts the *simultaneity* was shifting to the *plastic unity* of the elements that belonged to different viewpoints in time—so *time* became simultaneous (compare Einstein and Minkowski on the static aspect of space-time). Therefore, the concept of the simultaneous acquired a new sense by giving up the formulaic or axiomatic requirement of truth to appearance (in nature): If the viewer could not grasp the pictured object as an immediately given whole, he might rightly understand it as a coherent, though arbitrary, constructed set of operations upon an object form that the artist broke up into many small, faceted parts, especially lines and planes, arbitrarily continuous and discontinuous. But this conception has nothing to do, at least in inspiration, with the problem of simultaneity analyzed with acuteness by Einstein in 1905; nor does it express an experience of time as an ordered succession of points, matched with a series of positions in space from which the artist viewed separate parts of the model object. This practice bypassed Lessing's distinction, and satisfied the modern painter, who wished above all to achieve an appearance shaped by the desire to realize a conception of his art as the free exercise of his powers of invention of forms and expression of feelings. The term *simultaneity* described, then, the experience of the responsive observer, not the procedure of the artist before his object, in appreciating the harmony and plastic unity of the painting, which was founded on the cohesion of the constructive elements, the relations of forms, the carefully ordered lines, planes, and flecks of light and dark tones as units effecting a surprising transformation of the fractioned and paradoxically recomposed objects—paradoxically rearticulated with notations of the natural continuities, discontinuities, and spatial logic of actual objects in a three-dimensional space.

In connecting an art so complex and concrete with so broad and vague a concept as time, one easily loses sight of the distinctive qualities in the art as well as the importance of time as a root concept in philosophy of the nineteenth and twentieth centuries, especially after Hegel, Darwin, Marx, and Bergson—with the historical sense of nature as changing, as becoming. Time assumed prestige as the dimension of growth, change, fulfillment, and hope, as opposed to the older view of time as an eroding, destructive force, pertaining to the ruination of things and death. Modernity saw a new awareness of the time of the art, of the timeliness of one's present historical moment or century (consider, notably, Daumier and Rimbaud), in connection with a social-historical conception of time as representing significant change in culture, institutions, thought, marking the distinctiveness of a new historical epoch and attributing especially to the initiative of bold, innovating minds the motions of a historical process. How an idea of time as a continuum was indeed evoked after Impressionism we can judge from the works of advanced artists who found the Cubist style of Picasso and Braque deplorably static, while borrowing from it certain elements of their new forms: As a means of creating an appearance of motion, Duchamp's *Nude Descending a Staircase* and Balla's *Dynamism of a Dog on a Leash* both depict consecutive postures of an articulated moving body by superimposing, with effects of transparency and shuffled planes, the overlapping or intersecting forms of the body. In this way both works recall the successive, rapid camera shots of a figure in motion in a single photographic frame, evoking the duration of the instant of ongoing time, as seen in stroboscopic photography. The running horse, one said, has twenty legs. As such, the multiplied limbs in Balla's picture are a device anticipated a thousand years earlier in Viking tomb reliefs in Sweden, where a moving horse is shown with eight legs in a pattern of X's. But among modern painters the idea was short-lived and had little impact on later art. Far from expressing a new concept of space-time, such Futurist imagery has been likened by a mathematician to Newton's fluxions.[48]

The concept of absoluteness in Newton is of time and space as two separate "absolutes"; for Minkowski and Einstein it is of space-time as space and time connected, complementary, each being relative to the other. The Cubists' conception of time depends on the position of the viewer; it is still the qualitative effect, the *durée*, of contemplation by a moving spectator and painter. The notion of time as experienced in the picture also recalls theological ideas (for example, those of Giordano Bruno) of God's eternal and timeless contemplation of events.[49] We can hardly believe that the Cubists, Giedion, or Panofsky would accept that conception as scientifically valid, or as the same as Newton's *absoluteness* of time. Rather, they mean duration as an experience of movement or change in time and are careless in ignoring the distinctions between their views and the psychological and physical senses of duration, as well as the vitally relative nature of "felt time" and its variability.

Awareness of the history of Cubism and of its outcome in later works of the originators has not discouraged the pseudophysical interpretation of the new art, the analogizing of this art to science. A basic change in the scientists' conception of space and time seemed to illuminate for artists, critics, and historians the no less radical break with the past in painting. This break could be seen as a plausible and necessary counterpart, although artists continue to work in the traditional styles of representation to this day. Picasso returned to it after 1915 in new styles of his own while retaining some striking features of his Cubist phase. Coincidence of date has seemed a strong ground for ascribing the two revolutions, in physics and in painting, to a common outlook.

The artists and critics who found the analogy important were applying a cultural principle shared by certain philosophers and historians and by some scientists as well: the notion that a culture is an organic whole in which the state of one part varies significantly with the state of others at the same time and is intelligible through the latter as a functioning, mutually responsive part of the same social-cultural whole. According to one reading, all are rooted in a worldview or metaphysics manifest in the art, science, and social institutions of a time. But how artists and scientists may have arrived at the same conception of the world—whether through an influence of science on art or the reverse, or through a common set of philosophical assumptions, or through a shared experience of the life conditions of the time and of ideologies arising in response to them—remains virtually unexplored. For many writers, coincidence in time and place, even of a single feature in different fields, however vague the resemblance, is enough to warrant the idea that a deep connection exists between them. The Nobel Prize–winning chemist Ilya Prigogine declared a belief in the "essential unity of culture." He observed that it is possible to see similar thinking in the early twentieth century in Einstein's revision of the physics of space and time, Arnold Schoenberg's revision of music, and Cézanne's reconception of painting.

When a previous mode of thought is being reshaped, a dominant activity—a particular field of thought such as religion, economics, politics, art, philosophy, science, or technology—somehow impresses its new concepts on the other fields. Such simple intuitions of the totality and its parts often underlie and direct the search for connections and analogies of different fields. The unity of thought in a historical epoch has been formulated most sweepingly by Martin Heidegger in his essay "Die Zeit des Weltbildes" (The Age of the World Picture): "Metaphysics grounds an age, . . . it gives to that age the basis upon which it is essentially formed *(der Grund seines Wesensgestalt).* This basis holds complete dominion over all the phenomena that distinguish the age."[50]

Two master concepts shared by scientists and artists have disposed them to entertain the notion of correspondences between the work of the respective fields: (a) an organismic view of culture and history and (b) a concept of the science of different periods (and individuals) as styles of thought, and the idea that (a) and (b) are related. The concept of a *Weltbild* (a world picture) is common to science as well as to art history: witness Einstein, Max Planck, Werner Heisenberg, Erwin Schrödinger—and in philosophy, Heidegger.

Whatever doubts one may have of that master analogy of Cubism and the theory of relativity as a key to the art, one will recognize in it a way of thinking about art, philosophy, and science that has been common in the West during the last two hundred years. The notion of the unity of these fields in a particular culture or epoch was founded on an idea of the organic connectedness of different parts of a culture as a whole, including social life and institutions as supposedly shaped by a prevailing world outlook of a given epoch. Thus the term *Renaissance* was a unifying concept, embracing different fields, as in Jacob Burckhardt's classic work *The Civilization of the Renaissance in Italy* (1860). There two themes, the discovery of nature and the discovery of man as an individual, are keys to common features in the art, science, and social life (both secular and religious) of the age, and together are preconditions of the culture and thought of the modern age. The revival of Greek and Roman literary humanism in the fifteenth century was paralleled by a corresponding study of the classical models in the visual arts, and also of ancient philosophy, science, and even of political institutions of that age: See

Burckhardt's famous opening chapter on "The State as a Work of Art." The introduction of geometric perspective in painting, canons of mathematical ratios alike in architecture and the human body, geographical exploration, and Copernican astronomy, were all seen as different manifestations of the same worldview and of a new character type, in contrast to the manifestations of the very different worldview of the Middle Ages. The differences from the preceding medieval centuries in so many fields brought out that distinctiveness of the Renaissance as a whole.

Einstein, too (if we can trust the report), once admitted the organismic idea of a unity of art and science. At a meeting of the League of Nations Committee for Intellectual Cooperation in 1928, he was asked whether it was by "mere chance" that the theory of relativity, Freud's psychoanalysis, the League of Nations, and the World Court—all examples of an effort of unification—arose together in the same age as "an expression of the same revolutionary phase through which the contemporary world is passing." Einstein, after some reflection ("This synthetic vision is new to me, let me think it over"), is said to have replied, ". . . I endorse your Holism."[51]

In Einstein's earlier statement about the kinship of science and art, he had sidestepped the questioner's point and spoke of the artist and scientist in a timeless sense as alike in contemplating "the world" with the same disinterestedness—a view already evident in a talk that he gave at the celebration of Max Planck's sixtieth birthday, in 1918.[52] Is it the same "world" that both groups contemplate? Do Shakespeare, Rembrandt, and Bach bring to mind, for deeper and broader insight, the same objects, relationships, and ideas as their contemporaries Kepler, Galileo, and Newton? By what detailed observations and reasoning can the styles of those artists' works be likened to and illuminated by the theories of the scientists as expressions of a common worldview? Perhaps in replying to the question in 1928 Einstein meant nothing more than that the coincidence of those efforts of unification in different contemporary fields during the same period was in principle not a chance effect, since their causes lay in antecedent situations of crisis, intellectual and practical, in each of these contemporary fields, and in the shared commitment to resolve disagreements by rational means. The conditions that suggested analogous programs in the separate domains need not have entailed a similarity of basic concepts in those distinct tasks of unification nor have influenced each other, although the arts may for a time have shared with the sciences the interest in a progressively more comprehensive study of their problems. Together the different functions, problems, and proposed solutions shaped certain loosely described features of what was termed the "outlook" of the age—or superficial, sterile analogies that explain nothing, insofar as this "outlook" is a rather vague formulation of selected features pertinent to a particular interest and hardly as general and pervasive as it might appear. The important analogy is perhaps of the individual freedom of the artist and scientist, each occupied with problems he has set himself and respected for his originality.[53]

Perhaps Einstein's belief in strict determinism and his lifelong search for an underlying unity of physical laws, their interdependence and invariant relations, disposed him to that particular "holistic" conclusion. To speak of holism in that epochal frame was to imply an all-encompassing organismic concept of society, culture, and history, such as Spengler had made familiar a few years before. But Einstein had commented with amused skepticism on Spengler in 1920:

> Spengler has not spared me either. Sometimes one agrees to his suggestions in the evening, and then smiles about them next morning. One can see that the whole of his monomania had its origin in schoolteacher mathematics—Euclid versus Descartes is brought into everything, although, one must admit, ingeniously. These things are amusing; if someone should say the exact opposite tomorrow with sufficient spirit, it is amusing once more, but the devil only knows what the *truth* is.[54]

The organismic theory requires a theory, and not just an *ad hoc* one, of the nature of thought that permits deduction of its consequences in all fields and that, moreover, enables one to predict correspondences in newly discovered cultures. There is a difficulty in grounding this "thought," its transmission in different fields, its independence of the conditions peculiar to each field (see the Born-Einstein correspondence on independence of parts). Einstein's original 1921 statement opens the way: Art and science contemplate the same objective world, including the human, and differ in their grounds of validation—logical versus intuitive. Yet in the end, strictly within science, Einstein himself rejects quantum theory on affective, intuitive grounds: it doesn't feel right to him.

Alfred North Whitehead applied such an organismic concept in his eloquent book *Science and the Modern World* (1925), in ascribing to the English Romantic poets an outlook on nature anticipating evolutionary biology and atomic physics, as well as crediting painting and sculpture of the Middle Ages and the Renaissance with having advanced the perception of nature. He ventured to liken the poets' new perceptions of nature to the trend of scientific thought arising from the discovery of the electromagnetic field—and leading to a break with the assumptions of older mechanistic science. He compared that trend to the vision of nature as an organic totality and a *plenum*, proclaimed by William Wordsworth and Percy Bysshe Shelley.[55]

A similar analogy of art and science had been entertained by the Viennese historian of art Alois Riegl, a scholar of Whitehead's generation. In a subtle and far-reaching work, *Die Spätrömische Kunstindustrie*, he undertook to explain an epochal change in the visual art of late antiquity from closed forms on a neutral background plane to what he called the emancipation of the void: a treatment of the background as a field with distinct components in depth and with a rhythmic order in counterpart to the more pronounced figural pattern. It was, he supposed, the starting point from which the deep perspective and atmospheric perspective of the Renaissance eventually developed. Riegl's study, first published in 1901, has long been so little read in the English-speaking world that I venture to quote from it at some length as an example of an art historian's large-scale analogy of art and physical science:

> Since ancient man saw in the world merely closed, isolated forms, he could think of their connections only as mechanical, as pressure or push. Therein both the idealistic and materialistic (i.e. atomistic) systems of antiquity were in full agreement, and from this it followed that the connection (always leading from an individual object to its neighbor) could only be purely serial or a chain corresponding exactly to the rhythmic composition of single solid forms in contemporary visual art. [So art was charged with selecting a few individual shapes from the infinite confusion of phenomena and connecting them in a new, clearly defined unity by arrangement in a sequence on a flat surface. In the same way, ancient science had to disentangle the knot of phenomena and to arrange them in a coherent sequence of individual shapes according to the law of causality.][56]

In the late phase of antiquity, however, "one no longer felt satisfied by that kind of purely mechanical bond between single forms, and replaced it by another kind of bond—the magical—which the entire late pagan–early Christian world found its expression in Neoplatonism and syncretistic cults as well as in the concepts of the early Christian church"; and, "this change in the late-antique world view was a necessary transitional phase of the human mind in reaching from a concept (in the narrower sense) of a purely mechanical aligned *(reihenweisen)* connection of things projected on the plane surface to that of an allover *(breiteten)* chemical connection traversing space in all directions."[57]

In this transition the protoscience of alchemy had vital consequences for the very character of artistic form:

> Alchemy, which was as much magic as chemistry, forms a direct link between the late Roman concept of an occult connection between all things and modern chemical theory. But also, the modern conception of pervasive forces, for example, electricity, which is independent of the individuality of

> things, and the doctrine of cells and tissues, rests on the post-antique dissolution of the single form in the composition of masses and on the notion of the possibility of the influencing of a thing by thousands and thousands of other things, in part very distant from each other, in the same second.[58]

Thus, at the end of his great study, Riegl reflects:

> Of course, the late antique turn to magic meant a detour; but the necessity of this detour becomes perfectly clear to us as soon as one looks at it as it was in its own time; it appears then not as a matter of inventing a definite scientific theory, but as the surmounting of a common antique millennial conception of the composition of the world out of mechanically closed, isolated unit forms. The indispensable precondition for the turn was not just the shattering of the belief in the purely mechanical connection, but also the rise of a new positive belief in an extramechanical and thus magical connection of things, proceeding from the single forms. Only after this new belief had borne its indestructible fruit could the mechanical connection (which among Western Europeans had never been wholly forgotten) again receive its due consideration (alike in visual art and in the world view). Then was excluded once and for all the danger of falling back into the conception of an exclusively mechanical connection of a world conceived as composed of unalterable single forms. The idea of the existence of a connection other than mechanical of all things in creation had in the meantime become firmly rooted in the mind of the West, as had, to be the basic elements in art, the perception of mass composition (in place of the individuality of material shapes) and deep space (in place of a plane on which is disposed a sequence of individual shapes). Both of these, however, are indebted to the development of European humanity in the late Roman period.[59]

Riegl treated the voids in the background spaces as positive components of the compositional whole in interaction with the more pronounced forms and, as such, as establishing a precondition of subsequent art, through the Renaissance and on to the modern period. He regarded them as the outcome of a new worldview that, in replacing classic naturalism and scientific atomism by occult magic and action at a distance, thereby laid the foundation for future modern science with its investigation of gravitational and electromagnetic fields. This large-scale view of the history of ideas, embracing art, religion, occultism, and science, reappeared, interestingly enough, not long after Riegl but probably independently of him, in the history of science work of the physicist Pierre Duhem (especially his *Le Système du monde*, 1954–59). Expounding on the thirteenth-century debates concerning astrology and the forces that move both the heavenly bodies and those on earth, their immaterial source, and action at a distance, Duhem cites the decree of Archbishop Étienne Tempier of Paris, in 1277, against various propositions of the philosophers and physicists, particularly those that, in asserting direct influence of celestial bodies on earthly things, gave support to astrology; also condemned were the ideas of Aristotle and Averroës on the motion of the stars. Duhem wrote that this ecclesiastical condemnation "implicitly called for a new physics that, in reason, Christians could accept" and that consequently the effort to construct such a physics encouraged studies at the University of Paris in the fourteenth century, which can be considered one of the foundations of modern science.[60]

The analogy of stages of art and science was already an idea of Johannes Kepler's, who loved analogies in nature and mathematics as "our most reliable masters." He valued that of art and science enough to picture it on the engraved frontispiece that he designed for his publication of Tycho Brahe's catalogue of stars, the *Rudolphine Tables* (1627).[61] In his preface to the star catalogue Kepler traces the history of astronomy from the ancients to his own time as a growth from a stage of childhood, through adolescence and young manhood, to maturity ("step by step it climbs higher") and for the engraving he conceived a
Fig. 14 ten-sided temple with a dome supported by ten paired columns of vary-

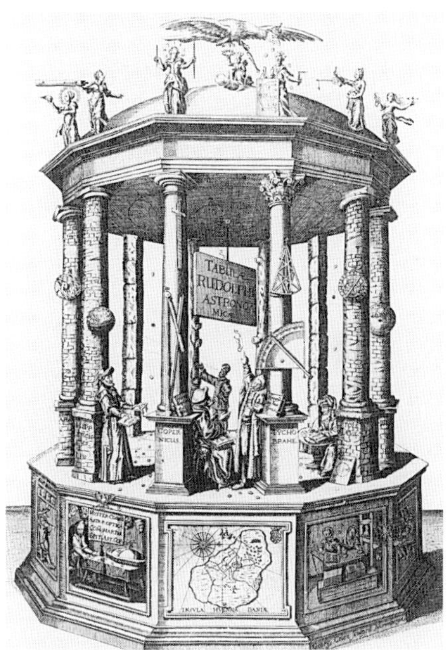

Figure 14. J. Kepler, *Rudolphine Tables*, frontispiece from *Tabulae Rudolphinae Ioannes Keplerus*, Ulm, 1627.

ing materials and form. The oldest pair—the most distant in the perspective view—are rough-hewn tree trunks between which a sage in oriental dress gazes at a star, determining its position by angular measurement with his forefinger and thumb. Next in the series and nearer to us are two stone pillars of large prismatic blocks of unmortared stone, uneven in surface and without capitals or bases; then come two pairs of brick columns, with simple stone capitals and bases on high pedestals, on which are inscribed the names of Meton and Aratus, Hipparchus and Ptolemy. These last two are portrayed with their writings in hand; their instruments and models, more exact than the old, are suspended from the columns. In the center foreground are the most advanced columnar forms, of smooth stone (perhaps marble); the left one, carrying a carved capital of the so-called Tuscan or Italic order, rests on a podium inscribed with the name of Copernicus, who sits beside it. In converse with him stands Tycho Brahe himself, pointing to the ceiling of the domed temple, on which are traced the orbits of his own planetary system. Brahe's column is crowned by a richly carved Corinthian capital, while the more refined instruments of their modern astronomy hang from both his and Copernicus' columns.

In Kepler's preface—as in the introductory poem by the rector of the high school of Ulm, who composed it under Kepler's guidance—the crudity of early astronomy is likened to the earliest art of building, and the progress of the science is matched to the development of architecture. Undoubtedly reporting Kepler's view, the poet asks, "What else are these columns but observations reworked by a sagacious mind when experience begot the art?" In the margin these Latin verses are condensed in a note: "The columns signify observations." The domed building, surrounded by allegorical figures symbolizing the various instruments applied in progressive scientific observation, signifies Kepler's immortal crowning achievement; and in a panel on the substructure of the temple appears a model of the dome set on the table at which Kepler sits at work, with the titles of his books inscribed on a sheet of paper suspended beside him. Kepler's frontispiece is not a simple simile or metaphor. The nature and function of his analogy are culture-historical, with special reference to the technology of observation, and have connotations of progress through increasing technical precision of observation and measurement, and their refinement through instruments and mathematical operations. Thus, it presents the viewer with a concept of progress as a more general feature of human history. Perhaps also embedded in his analogy of architecture and scientific thought (which served Hugh of St. Victor and Descartes in other contexts) are allusions to the dome as an image of the "heavens," to columns as exemplars of stability, and to the round temple as a constructed model of concentrated, contemplative knowledge. In any case, the science that discovers the true mathematical relations that underlie or constitute the beautiful order and harmony of the cosmos is here allied with the art, namely, architecture, in which beauty is realized through regularity and simple ideal proportions. In this view of the parallel progress of art and science we recognize a conception of history that draws upon the ancient accounts of the growth of civilization by

Lucretius and, especially for architectural theory, Vitruvius, as well as the Renaissance idea that the revival of antiquity was comprehensive, embracing many different fields. On the title page of his book Kepler has characterized the Rudolphine Tables (named for the Emperor Rudolf II, resident of Prague) as a "Restoration of astronomical science, after its long state of collapse, by that phoenix of astronomers, Tycho Brahe."

In the search for connections with particular events and circumstances in the field of the work of art, the organismic idea serves as a low-grade *heuristic* generalization. The organismic is different from other heuristic ideas in that it directs attention to general features of the society or culture as a whole, and above all to ways of thought, to outlook, and so on. It seeks, especially for art, a broad intellectual content, as if philosophic thought or a worldview is a basic factor in new artistic form and content, where otherwise one finds more direct connections in the subject matter and history of works, in their clearer connections with religion, patronage, styles of living, in literature, religion, and forms. Unfortunately, unlike the use of analogy within physics and mathematics, it rarely leads to close study of the two sides of the analogy or of the historical development of the supposedly analogous fields.

Besides the developmental organismic historical view, two concepts from the field of art have since then become more common in statements of scientists about their work as a creative activity. One is the notion of style as applied to differing methods and theories as distinctive forms and qualities of thought, whether by single, highly original innovators or by small groups of like-minded scientists, a vanguard who pursue new ideas and methods in their field. The second is the notion that the scientist's aims, like the artist's, are aesthetic, not utilitarian;[62] the interest and value of their work lies in the beauty of a result that unites hitherto unconnected phenomena or discloses new relations in nature. Such beauty, it is felt, can even be taken as a promising sign of the truth of a scientific theory or explanation.[63] If, as Francis Bacon said, "there is no excellent beauty that hath not some strangeness in the proportion" (Essay XLVII), one may also suspect that the surprising result or speculation in science is more likely to be right.

In the twentieth century a historian of art has imagined that Kepler was led to the discovery of the elliptical form of the planetary orbits by his aesthetic. As a man of the modern age, Kepler supposedly shared the taste for the ellipse in the contemporary style called Mannerist by modern students of art.[64] For the ellipse is a smoothly rounded form that, together with the oval, was often chosen then (and in the next century) for buildings, and also shaped pictorial fields, for its suave elongation and contrast of unequal axes—a departure from the perfect regularity of the circle, which had dominated science and art since the Greeks and Romans, though medieval builders in the Gothic style preferred the two-centered, pointed arch.[65] That Galileo, after Kepler's publications, could still write of the planetary orbits as circular has been explained accordingly as due to an opposed aesthetic taste, the Italian sharing with a new generation of "anti-Mannerist" artists a revived preference for the idealized forms of High Renaissance classicism exemplified by the great art of Raphael, Michelangelo, and Titian;[66] thus, in poetry Galileo placed the "classic" Ludovico Ariosto above the Mannerist Torquato Tasso.

Now of these aesthetic-stylistic explanations, the first ignores in Kepler's discovery the impelling weight of Tycho Brahe's more exact observations; it ignores, too, Kepler's struggle at first to reconcile the latter's tables with the traditional circle. Besides, was not Kepler devoted to the most regular geometric forms? In an earlier book, the *Mysterium cosmographicum* (1596), he supposed incorrectly that the radii of the spheres inscribed and circumscribed to fit the five regular solids were proportional to the distances between the five known planets and the sun. One may also note as important for his eventual formulation of the elliptical paths the availability of Apollonius of Perga's treatise on conic sections.[67] In the account of Kepler's journey of discovery, the aesthetic of Mannerism appears as a conjectured "fifth wheel." In their eccentricity the ellipses of the orbits deviate so little from the circle that they barely satisfy the norm of Mannerist taste. From the standpoint of stylistic analogy, one could as well refer to Kepler's acquaintance with Gothic architecture. Living in Germany and Bohemia, he certainly knew splendid medieval buildings in which the two-centered, pointed arch was adaptable to varying heights from spans of the same breadth: It provided a flexibility of proportions that architects of the Renaissance had rejected despite its practical advantage. Independently of that taste, however, Kepler, with his strong interest in optics and perspective, was surely aware of the ellipse as a regular transform of the circle. In planning an observation tower with a circular opening, he noted that through it the sun would be imaged on the floor as an ellipse. (In Renaissance painting well before his time, the ellipse appears often in the rendering of circular motifs of ornament on pavements drawn in perspective.)

As for Galileo's ignoring Kepler's discovery of orbital ellipticality and holding to the circle even after Kepler's later publication—a reluctance that Einstein and others have ascribed to feelings of rivalry—one may recall Galileo's explicit criticism of those who gave the circle a privileged rank in kinematics, as if nature had favorite curves.[68] His own investigation of the parabolic trajectory in ballistics should make his position clear; in the context of art, his discussion of a parabolic profile as the optimal design of a cantilevered wooden beam is an example of his readiness to accept a less regular conic as a suitable form in building.[69] Galileo's supposed "classic" taste did not keep him from describing painting as an art of *mixing colors* in order to produce the likeness of nature; and in treating of comets, he denied their solid state and tried to explain them as a phenomenon of light and atmospheric effects, as if he were an Impressionist.[70] If there was an aesthetic factor in Kepler's discovery of the elliptical orbits—a solution entertained earlier by Copernicus as a conjecture[71]—it may be found not so much in a prior taste for the beauty of the visualized ellipse as in the conceptual simplicity of that form in kinematics and the surprising ratios of periodic times and distances in the planetary system when compared to the cumbersome machinery of epicycles and deferents that had been contrived for the circular orbits in order to save the appearances.

While the Cubist-relativity linkage is a pure fancy, a conjecture, largely verbal, Kepler's text has another function. His book is also poetic and lyrical, a celebration in which he secures his membership in a line of great scientists from ancient times (perhaps even Babylonian), Egyptian and Archaic Greek, up to his own time. His comparison with architecture illuminates the great importance of the progress of observation and precision through the invention of instruments, including the telescope. I have devoted these pages to Kepler not only because his parallelism of astronomical science and the history of architecture may serve as a convincing model of such an approach, but also because a comparison with the modern ideas of so many writers on Cubism who assert a connection with relativity theory, especially space-time, in modern physics, will only make clearer what is vacuous in that analogy.

With the emergence of a more strictly nonmimetic style of painting, what was called "abstract" or nonobjective art, one continued to look for legitimating parallels in science and philosophy. Alfred North Whitehead locates his analogy of science and art in a historical context of the development of ideas, science, and philosophy, which suggests the common developments. In *Science and the Modern World* Whitehead calls attention to early mediaeval underpinnings of science and art, since as early as the sixth century, with the foundationally Greek "scientific mentality . . . in ruins," Gregory the Great and the Benedictines fostered not simply agriculture as such but that "alliance of science with technology, by which learning is kept in contact with irreducible and stubborn facts"; and "influence of this contact between the monasteries and the facts of nature showed itself first in art," even during the so-called Dark Ages.[72] Painters of the Renaissance and Baroque knew the ideas of scientists about light, perspective, anatomy, and representations of nature; and seventeenth- and eighteenth-century poets read Isaac Newton.[73]

Such parallels were echoed in the writings of modern physicists as well, so that while painters, critics, and historians of art were finding in physics analogies to Cubist forms, some scientists were likening their own new ideas to recent or contemporary art. The same Albert Michelson (a man of marked aesthetic sensibility, according to his niece's biography), who was engaged in the 1870s in measuring the velocity of light with extraordinary precision and ingenuity, painted luminous landscapes in an Impressionist vein. In his "Light Waves and Their Interference" (probably 1892) and *Light Waves and Their Uses* (Lowell Lectures 1899, published 1903) Michelson expressed his delight in the beauty of the colors produced by a laboratory instrument, the interferometer, and ventured to predict a future art of painting in pure color, without representation in scenes of bright daylight (already in the early nineteenth century the kaleidoscope, invented by a physicist, David Brewster, fascinated viewers by the spectacle of colors in motion).

In *The Nature of the Physical World* (1928) Arthur Eddington, astronomer and physicist, pointed to Impressionist painting as analogous to the notion of entropy as characterizing a molecular system as a whole in the kinetic theory of gases and heat:

> The artist desires to convey significances which cannot be told by microscopic detail and accordingly he resorts to impressionist painting. Strangely enough the physicist has found the same necessity; but his impressionist scheme is just as much exact science and even more practical in its application than his microscopic scheme.[74]

In this ingenious comparison Eddington ignored an important difference, though it is not altogether incompatible with his analogy and even suggestive of it on another order of magnitude. While the pattern of such a painting is formed of small random, seemingly chaotic brushstrokes that, at a certain distance, fuse in a summating glance to beget an impression of light as an intangible, pervading feature of the scene, that particle system was for the artist a controlled, macroscopic means in the visible and tangible fabric of the work. It was subject to a considered selection and balanced placing of each separate unit, such as Maxwell had imagined in the action of his tiny, purposeful demon sorting and redistributing the fast and slow molecules of a gas in order to overcome the entropy of a system.[75] And while it has been supposed that the discovery of the electromagnetic field by Michael Faraday and

Maxwell affected the practice of painters who introduced atmosphere and light as pronounced features of their paintings, this ignores not only the prevalence of these features in art since the sixteenth century, independently of any idea of the constitution of the electromagnetic field, but also that in Impressionism, with its particle-stroke structure of the fabric of the painting, the effects of vibrancy are not in accord with the wave theory of light.

From another side, the French premier Georges Clemenceau, himself an ex-physician, saw in his friend Claude Monet's Impressionist painting a correspondence to the microscopic "Brownian movements," as if the artist wished to suggest the molecular structure of water, which is invisible to the naked eye.[76] By then, Jean-Baptiste Perrin had already treated the phenomenon in his book *Les Atomes* (1913), in which he described his experiments confirming Einstein's theoretical papers of 1905 and 1906 dealing with the Brownian movement of gas molecules. Actually, Impressionism emerged as a new style in the late 1860s and the 1870s, well after the period when the concept of entropy was introduced in physics. And for the parallel interest of Brownian movement for the literary mind, I note that in her absorbing novel *Middlemarch* (1871–72) George Eliot has her physician character buy a copy of a study by the botanist Robert Brown (1773-1858), from whom the term for the apparently random movement of particles in suspension derives: He had discovered Brownian movement in the active effect of water molecules on suspended grains of pollen, in 1827, and had published the notion in *The Philosophical Magazine* in 1828, 1829, and 1830.

With Eddington's statement as corroboration, a historian of art or ideas could say that Impressionist painting and the physicist's concept of entropy had arisen at the same time in the nineteenth century as expressions of a common worldview; and that from that worldview came other basic changes in science and art such as the concepts of the electromagnetic field and the predominance of light and atmosphere over outlines and solid forms in Impressionist painting. But as far as Eddington, Impressionism, and Brownian movement are concerned, we find merely a literary analogy, since the comparison is of phenomena of widely different scale—Impressionism macroscopic, the movements of molecules in a liquid microscopic and only inferred through observation of their impacts on pollen grains. Relating Impressionism to the kinetic theory of gases is an ingenious analogy that might lead one to explain the Impressionist technique and structure and patterning of small flecks of color as somehow influenced by statistical mechanics or as an expression of a worldview shared by the physicist and the painter. I must add, however, that for the latter the strokes are deliberate choices responding to actual perceptions of color in nature, and his technique an invention designed to produce effects of light, atmosphere, movement, and vibrancy, with a new patterning of the surface fabric or weave of brushstrokes. Besides, such composition of a totality in which many components are vague, unlike everything ordered according to the principles of the "classic" line and mass structures of Renaissance art, has been developed since the sixteenth century and represents a pole of style also found in other cultures (later Roman, Chinese, and Japanese art).[77]

Whitehead's, Eddington's, and also Clemenceau's comparisons of science and art are not committed to a general view applicable to the interpretation of artistic content and form (though hints of such may possibly be found). And while in Eddington's and Clemenceau's cases they are similarly suggestive of *perceptions* of nature by an artist as like those of a scientist, even so they are not presented in art-stylistic language, as with Giedion and Panofsky.

Niels Bohr is reported to have remarked on seeing a Cubist painting in which the artist had represented a figure from more than one viewpoint—an analogy to his own concept of complementarity in the physical domain—that with "face and limbs depicted simultaneously from several angles . . . an object could be several things, could change, could be seen as a face, a limb and a fruitbowl."[78] On a broader front, artists of the last hundred years, especially, have recognized a fundamental complementarity or duality in the nature of figurative painting. The picture was seen as a veridical representation of objects in an illusory three-dimensional space; but by a slight shift of attention it could be grasped as a pattern of lines, colors, and textures on the plane surface of the canvas, what artists and critics in the later nineteenth century called the painting's "decorative" aspect, which painters of the twentieth century wished to isolate and reinforce as the necessary goal of their art, without illusory depiction of recognizable persons, places, or things.[79] Now, commenting on the factors outside physics—such as philosophy, psychology, language, and aesthetics—that are "the background of complementarity" in modern physics, Arthur I. Miller, a physicist, points to

> Bohr's interest in art, especially cubism. We might expect, therefore, to see in his study a painting by one of the acknowledged masters of this genre—for example, a Braque, a Gris, a Duchamp, or maybe a Picasso. Instead Bohr exhibited Jean Metzinger's 1924 painting *L'Écuyère* [The Rider]. This choice indicates a quite special interest in cubism, and perhaps a clue to yet another path to complementarity—that is, assuming that Bohr had known about Metzinger prior to 1927. It may be the case that after 1927 Bohr found in Metzinger's writings one more example of complementarity. Let's make the first assumption and attempt to find what it was in Metzinger that interested Bohr. Most art historians consider Metzinger to have been a minor cubist painter, but everyone agrees that he was a major theorist of the cubist school. In (1912) Metzinger and Albert Gleizes published a systematic exposition of cubist methods in their widely read book *Du Cubisme.* A cubist painting, they wrote, represented a scene as if the observer were "moving around an object [in order to] seize it from several successive appearances. . . . " Cubists achieved this motif through the interpenetration of figure and space in order to free the artist from a single perspective in favor of multiple viewpoints. And this was what impressed Bohr about cubism. Mogens Anderson (1967), a Danish artist and friend of Bohr, recollected Bohr's pleasure

> in giving "form to thoughts to an audience at first unable to see anything in [Metzinger's] painting—They came with a preconceived idea of what art should be." Such had been the case in 1913, when atomic physicists had a preconceived image of the atom. By 1925 atomic physicists had come to realize the inadequacy of visual perception, as had the cubists. In 1927 Bohr offered a motif for the world of the atom with striking parallels to the motif of multiple perspectives offered by cubism for glimpsing beyond and behind visual perceptions: According to complementarity the atomic entity has two sides—wave and particle—and depending on how you look at it, that is, what experimental arrangement is used, that is what it is.[80]

More recently, the conception of basic theory in physics as manifesting a style of thought that expresses the outlook of an age was advanced by Werner Heisenberg in expounding for lay readers the new principles of his science, physics. In acknowledging the experimenter's role in eliciting and affecting the phenomenon to be observed and measured, his "indeterministic" explication of quantum theory corresponds, Heisenberg believed, to that spirit of the age. The new science, unlike the old, formulates the calculated probabilities of knowledge rather than timeless certitudes about a nature independent of man. Our world today is constituted and known through man's works. The technology founded on science in turn provides the instruments with which the scientist explores nature. Artists, too, no longer simply represent nature as it appears but construct a coherent universe of their own choice that, by its abstract forms, expresses an outlook and values, the activity and inner life of the human being. So Heisenberg has written of modern physics and his principle of uncertainty as a style of thought, comparable to the styles of contemporary art. While recognizing the historical relativity of styles and their limited duration, each depending on unique conditions of its time and place—including the state of science, its problems, and its newly available techniques and instruments of research—Heisenberg was able to say that indeterminacy is not a transitional stage in the growth of physics but a lasting result, which new experiments or theoretical reflections are unlikely to change.

Besides the classicism of his schooling and family milieu,[81] the heritage of German idealistic philosophy perhaps also disposed Heisenberg to accept that assumption of a general unity of mind in the culture of his time, within which his own scientific outlook fitted as part of an organic whole, even though he questioned facile analogizing in writings by certain of his colleagues in science. I shall quote his views, here and below, in order to show that the declarations of painters, critics, and historians of art seeking to integrate the new art with the science and philosophical thought of their time have impressed an outstanding, highly reflective physicist. Heisenberg approached the similarity as a problem, not as a deep organic correspondence brought to view by the magic wand of analogy. Noting in a lecture on "Abstraction in Modern Science" the parallel growth of scientific thought and basic abstract forms in art, he remarked of the two terms of the analogy, "In science they have to depict reality, in art, to proclaim the content of life *(Lebensinhalt)* during the epoch." He was unsure whether abstraction in art was due to a striving for universality—the surmounting of local peculiarities of national cultures—or to a disarray of mind upon the loss of stabilizing faiths and loyalties, especially the religious, a change "reflected in art in the dissolution of traditional forms of which only particular abstract elements remain behind."[82] While disclaiming ability to decide, he inclined to the second view, since the new art appeared to him formless and unfocused, an "unshaping."[83] He missed in it a strong necessary content that could inspire an intelligible unified style as in the great art of the past. The state of art in the 1950s seemed to him to resemble the condition of physics in the first quarter of the twentieth century, when unresolved contradictions in the inherited science and the lack of unifying principles gave to physics a chaotic, unsettled aspect, until quantum mechanics, in the second quarter of the century, resolved the difficulties.

In his frankly groping approach, Werner Heisenberg was influenced, I believe, by the language of painters and critics who spoke of abstraction in painting to designate general properties and relations of form, independent of particular, real objects yet applicable to them, like the abstractions of logic and mathematics. In a dialogue published in 1919, well before Heisenberg's essays, Piet Mondrian had likened his own abstract paintings to the character of the city environment: "[I]sn't the primarily geometric character of our urban environment already very abstract in opposition to rural nature?" And his artist partner comments, "[A]bstract representation gives a more universal impression. Particularities disappear, leaving only the universal to reckon with."[84] In the same passage of *The Cubist Painters* in which he entertained the notion of the fourth dimension, Apollinaire had written, "Geometry, the science of space, its dimensions and relations, has always determined the norms and rules of painting";[85] and a decade later Ozenfant would declare, in *La Peinture moderne* (1925), "Analysis shows that our knowledge of the world is a matter of the *geometric system* which is a pure creation of the mind: the pleasures *(les jouissances plastiques)* of art all spring from the system of geometry."[86] With Mondrian, of course, the shapes of the elements of streets and buildings, the windows, doors, roofs, and entire city blocks, as sets of repeated regular units in an urban view, though no less concrete than the parts of a human figure in traditional art, are less individualized. But the concept of abstractness has also been applied in art criticism and theory ever since the eighteenth century to describe the forms of even richly detailed naturalistic works, even of so finely carved a classic statue as the fragmentary *Apollo Belvedere*, admired by Renaissance and Baroque artists for the sculptor's mastery of human forms; Joshua Reynolds, in 1780, explained the powerful effect of this piece upon our feelings by "the perfection of this science of abstract form."[87]

Actually, the points, lines, and figures of the so-called abstract paintings, both the simplest and the most complex, are designed and perceived—one cannot say emphatically enough—as parts of tangible, unique wholes articulated by concrete, often richly textural marks of the brush, by substantial dots, patches, strokes, and lines, subtly apportioned masses of colored paint on the material surface of the canvas, these with distinctive aesthetic and physiognomic qualities. While the specific form of a mathematically formulated physical law is that of a general proposition applicable as an invariant relationship between the variable qualities shared by an unlimited set of natural objects, the forms and whole of an abstract painting belong to a unique object, the individual work of art. If some works constructed with regular elementary shapes suggest the geometer's illustrations that serve to elicit and support intuition of relationships then demonstrable in a logical argument, mathematical diagrams lack the telling individuality of a strong painter's constructed and pondered "abstraction."[88]

By his or her choice of simple elementary forms executed with precision, an artist may realize for the eye an ideal of clarity and rigor that is shared by a geometer; but in no sense does the whole that is addressed to aesthetic sensibility derive from a mathematical theorem, though the relations may be described in mathematical terms. The resemblance of abstract art forms to geometric illustrations in proofs of mathematical theorems has misled interpreters of abstract art. If every curve is a continuum of infinitesimal straight lines and if two closed curves intersect in an even number of points, the general proposition is not proved or made evident for the mathematician in a curved line of an abstract painting or two intersecting closed curves. What suggests the mathematics is the *abstraction from* particular objects with these forms. Perspective in painting is an instance of a projective geometrical theorem; but in painting it belongs to physiological optics, an empirical science. In other abstract paintings—the earlier works of Kandinsky and Jackson Pollock, for example—the forms are conceived consistently as varied, impulsive strokes, irregular flecks, tracks and masses of colored pigment, composed or ordered as a balanced ensemble, however random they may appear in their distribution.

Despite the absence of recognizable object-forms, it is a mistake to regard this art as a matter of pure forms without connotations of feeling and personal taste. The writings of the pioneers of abstract art—Kandinsky, Malevich, Mondrian—make it clear enough that they conceived their new works as vehicles of ideas, emotions, and a spiritual content or symbolism. The expression and the implicit outlook have been criticized as shallow or incomplete, but the works are hardly formless or without meaning. Yet in their embodiment of a feeling or idea the forms are not so distinct as signs that they can be matched with the entities and concepts of science signified by algebraic symbols, though certain features, such as regularity, equilibrium, symmetry, and variation, may be found in both realms, and indeed in the ordinary experience of objects, and may satisfy a disposition of taste that accords with emerging values in public and private life (such as "freedom" in the relations, contingency or "energy" of simple abstract form, like the focus of a force). Even the geometric forms may be a schematic simulation of the qualities of objects and phenomena, as in the Futurist painter Balla's several images titled Abstract Velocity (1913–14), which recall the visual aspect of swiftness by a succession of repeated overlapping or nested angular units, as in stroboscopic photography. In older art, Velázquez had caught in his painting *The Spinners* (1657) the appearance of a rapidly rotating spinning wheel: The spokes disappear, and we see only the flicker of light in concentric rings (the "abstract" form here renders an observed phenomenon; it is not an arbitrary geometric construction).

While some abstract paintings suggest, by the regularity and simplicity of their elements, a scientist's search for order and constancy (qualities also realized in figurative art with more complex organic forms), the sensuous surface pattern remains an individual concrete object of our focused aesthetic attention. Some artists may be stimulated in their work by the discoveries of contemporary science, particularly by the fascinating documents of scientific observation—for example, photographs of hitherto unrecorded patterns of phenomena in particle physics, astronomy, chemistry, and cellular microbiology—as painters of the nineteenth century had responded to newly perceived sites and appearances in the landscape and city world or had undertaken to explore in their art congenial scenes from the social life of the time. The impelling new interests satisfied by such sites and states of the environment were rendered in a new style—Impressionism—that brought out concordant, reinforcing qualities and relations in the substance of the painting. In the twentieth century the aesthetic delight in those novel sights from the laboratory was anticipated by the growth of modern painting.[89] The new art enlarged the capacity to conceive and respond to a greater variety of forms, including those of exotic cultures and of tribal art, which in turn have influenced contemporary Western art.

If "abstractness," then, is the common term in the analogy of modern science and art, one has failed to search out deeply enough the origins, qualities, and significance of that feature in art. Some scientists entertaining the comparison were perhaps more ready to accept the unexplored analogy because artists, critics, and historians had ventured to assert a basic correspondence, without considering the unbridged gap between feeling and thought in the assumed convergence of relativity theory and art. Had the artists who read popularized expositions of the theory undertaken to translate the new picture of the physical world into painterly forms? Had their own concern with the paradoxes or contradictions of space and surface in figurative representation led them to imagine a mode of painting in which the canons of traditional representation were given up? And had the universals of artistic form, now more evident through the expanded scope of aesthetic judgment made possible by the taste for primitive and exotic arts and by the new demands of freedom of expression, inspired a style of painting in which those canons no longer applied (without representation, or with overt independence of those canons)? And if any of these motives prevailed, why the return to representation by gifted artists, including the inventors of Cubism themselves?—a development quite unlike relativity theory, which, be it Special or General Relativity theory, still remains essential for physics and astronomy.

In the analogies of modern art and modern science offered in explanation of what appears most novel and puzzling in the art, a single feature—abstraction or abstractness, energy or movement, space-time—has been selected as a common connecting term without sufficient searching of the history, qualities, and significance of that feature in the fields presumed analogous. Two rules in comparative studies of languages are pertinent in judging the explanatory worth of such analogies and of causal conclusions or connections drawn from them. In the last century, with the growth of a critical approach to etymology as a historical field long subject to far-reaching, often intriguing guesses about ancestry and kinship founded on the similarity of words, and applied in explaining religious beliefs, myths, folklore, and moral ideas, as well as language, linguists came to require that comparisons "must have in view the established lines of genetic connection, and the comparer must be thoroughly and equally versed in the material of both sides of the comparison."[90] The two demands are more likely to be satisfied by scholars in whose use of analogy both objects of comparison belong to human fields than by writers on art who venture to match an artistic style with a physical theory or by scientists who liken their concepts to those of contemporary painters.[91] Even within the humanities, notably in the frequent comparisons of a style of art with a particular philosophy, comparisons designed to explain the style as a product of a contemporary "feeling," outlook, or mode of thought, the grounds of the analogy are rarely explored with as critical a concern for validity as is evidence for the historical place of a work within a line of development and its connections with others, preceding and contemporary, or for determination of its structure, original form, and meanings.[92]

In a culture of which both scientists and artists are members, and the scientists respond to art and the artists to science, with both affected in varying degrees by events in political and social life, it seems likely that these fields will affect each other. But from their proximity and interaction we cannot say in just what parts of a domain and in what features the influence may be traced. A simple example is language, which is shared by all members of a society and is used in all fields. Yet the syntax and most of the vocabulary and sound system are quite constant and retain their forms and elements during and after the most revolutionary changes in practical and intellectual life. It is precisely because a language must serve in so many different contexts of thought and communication that it must be a quite stable instrument. If it were more specialized, it would be more plastic and variable, at least in vocabulary, like the language of mathematics and physics, yet also more restricted than the language of poetry (except, perhaps, regarding the form of the sentence, rhythm, and figurative usage).

If one did not know the history of the term *Cubism*, which was adopted by the innovating painters, though it had first been applied to their art by a disapproving viewer, one might be tempted to connect it with the cube in Picasso's Spanish tradition. The architect Juan de Herrera (c. 1530–1597), who built the palace of the Escorial, in Madrid, wrote a treatise on the cube as a model form embodying logical and occult relationships: *Discorso sobro la figura cubica*, a work (discovered by Goya's friend Gaspar Melchor de Jovellanos) inspired by the speculations of the medieval Catalan poet and mystic Ramon Llull[93]—in whose *Ars magna* operations on geometric schemes and symbolic notations served in logical deduction of properties of nature. On another level, one could look for a more personal link of Cubism with the art of the acrobat (a figure who appears so often in the canvases of Picasso, a lover of the circus, in the years shortly before his Cubist phase). A sixteenth-century writer on acrobatics, Arcangelo Tuccaro, referred to a feat of the circus called the *saut Cubistique*, in which, we suppose, the tumbler's body passed through a set of points defining a cube *(Trois Dialogues de l'exercice de sauter et de voltiger*, 1599). This risky stunt is mentioned by Edmond de Goncourt in his tragic novel *Les Frères Zemganno* (1879), a story of two brother acrobats who, like the two Goncourt brothers, collaborate in devising and executing daring projects in their art.[94] The acrobat, like the modern painter, is the object and subject of his art; he creates a fascinating spectacle in a high space with secure control of bodily movement and balance beyond the commonplace stability of ordinary active and sedentary life. The analogy appeared often in poetic writings and was reinforced by the painters' and poets' marginal bohemian existence; Baudelaire's prose poem *Le vieux Saltimbanque* is an earlier example of the comparison of poet and acrobat. But however striking as analogs and metaphors, these associations of the word *Cubism* seem irrelevant to the actual style of the paintings and their place in the history of modern art.

In the sciences analogy is welcomed as significant if it leads one to deduction of a confirmable law that applies in the two fields compared;

in social studies and history, the organic analogy provides a descriptive model that employs terms applied to certain features of organisms and their life histories, but features of the biological organism are disregarded. There is a sense of analogy in art as a principle that in alliance with contrast is artistically suggestive and fruitful (one thinks of Georges Seurat as well as the theoretical formulation of Charles Blanc); but then both terms belong to art and pertain to the work of art, whether in regard to style or period or subject matter. The comparisons of Cubist painting with geometry were not intended strictly as metaphors or analogs but as descriptions of the distinctive space of that art, just as Renaissance geometrical perspective was cited as the ground of much of Renaissance painting in the writings of artists (Leon Battista Alberti, Piero della Francesca, Leonardo da Vinci). Nor does the stricter sense of analogy justify the belief that Renaissance painting is to Cubist painting as three-dimensional perspective is to a "fourth dimension" that eliminates perspective; whereas three-dimensional perspective is clearly a means of picturing "real" objects in "real" space, picturing the ascription of four-dimensional space in Cubism is highly questionable and was so to the originators, though it was held a true description by some of their imitators.

One source of the error lay in ascribing to Braque and Picasso the intention to replace the space of Renaissance perspective by another form of pictorial space. The first was understood as the three-dimensional space of visual perception formulated in physical and physiological optics and pictured on the plane surface of a canvas in accord with the principles of projective geometry, or by an empirical approximation in close scrutiny of the appearance of objects in the visual field. Before Cubism arose, space as a category had become important in studies of the history of art (those of Alois Riegl especially): the term *Raumdarstellung* ("space-representation") was a technical term in the theory of art, and the interiors of buildings were analyzed with respect to the character of their distinctive three-dimensional forms. Painters have been aware since ancient times of the composition of pictures as a problem in distribution of the represented objects on a framed surface, with the distinctiveness of the recognizable objects and their coherence as an ordered whole through various correspondences, balances, and contrasts. This problem was complicated in the course of time by the artists' desire to represent, near and far, as if in three dimensions, the setting of figures in a landscape or building.

In rejecting the mathematical perspective of Renaissance art, Braque and Picasso were not seeking to replace it by another perspective system that represented a different form of real or imaginary space. They aimed, rather, to create a whole out of elements of painterly operation or construction that had been acquired in the previous process of veristic representation and composition—tangible brushstrokes, textures of pigment and elementary shapes, points, lines, planes, volumes, edges, articulated contours—and in such a way that the objects, most often still-life objects, are discernible through free construction. These elements of construction are more pronounced than the objects as familiar stable wholes. In Cubist painting the constituent shapes that define objects retain parts and features of familiar objects and give them relief and volume and distinct places in an apparent though fictive three-dimensional space. They appear discontinuous, paradoxically open, fragmented, intersecting, yet deliberate, consistent, systematic, as an organized, coherent, balanced perceptual whole. In their overlapping and intersection the forms violate basic principles of three-dimensional space as a set of points or planes with (invariant) relations of successiveness in forming a line, a plane, a volume; what appears as one plane in front of another plane, which the first overlays, will in places appear behind that second plane, without any folding or curvature of either fictive surface. In this new system the Cubist has overcome what Braque called the *préalable* (the relations required *a priori*) in perspective representation. All is manifest in a deliberate choice of the artist in willed disregard of the perspective laws as a whole.

For the parallel of Cubist painting and scientific thought, the importance given to time and change in evolutionary biology and philosophy since the mid-nineteenth century, while pertinent to Impressionist and Futurist art, is of little account in the works of the originators of Cubism (though artists and historians shared the idea that each age has an art of its own and its own unity of thought). If time and movement were taken as seriously by a certain follower, Marcel Duchamp, it was, as he said, in deliberate opposition to the static character of Picasso's art. Yet one can find in the writings of a contemporary philosopher, Samuel Alexander, a statement that a critic or historian who believed in a close connection of Cubist painting and relativity could cite as an impressive indication, a document of a common outlook in science and art. In reply to a critic of his book *Space, Time and Deity* (1920), Alexander explained his conception of historical reality as a system of perspectives of the world in space-time, unlike a static view of separate parts pieced together, which he compared to a cube sliced into sections:

> The slices do not add themselves together. But go round the cube and take its perspectives. You never get a slice; you take in the whole contour of the cube as far as you can see it; and (this is the point) the perspectives overlap; one cries out for the next to complete it; they fit together by themselves; and this is what happens when we see not the single perspective but the thing of which we have the perspectives, which I have therefore described as the system of perspectives unified within a certain volume of Space-Time which is its "substance."[95]

One could connect this with Cubism, though it was written after the comparable phase of Cubism. I do not know whether Alexander owed his example of the cube and its multiple overlapping perspectives directly or indirectly to the book of Gleizes and Metzinger, which was translated into English in 1913.[96] We have already seen in Leibniz the idea of multiple perspectives as the source of fuller knowledge of objects, and it reappears in our century in Edmund Husserl's philosophy. But the suggestive analogy with painting here would be with an incorrectly described Cubist art; it loses its explanatory force when applied to the pictures themselves. Although followers continued in the earlier mode, in the rapid course of Picasso's and Braque's development their works become less and less an imagery with multiple perspectives of solid objects and more decidedly a free construction of lines and planes in a shallow space, often with applied segments of real, flat objects of cut paper pasted onto the painted canvas surface.

In 1927, Alexander expressed doubts about an abstract art of painting concerned only with relations of space and forms in space:

> Painting in the past has been representative, though it has not been great art when it has descended, as it often has, to illustration. Now it is familiar knowledge that contemporary painting is passing through an experimental stage of new ideals; and a claim has even been preferred for abstract painting, which is said to be concerned with relations of space, as music is concerned with relations of time. No room, if this were true, would be left for subject matter in any picture. I cannot raise this question at the end of a lecture, even if I were competent. It may be that there is painting which has for its object merely "significant form," reducible to nothing but spatial relations and colour. But significant form is significant of something. And even music, the most abstract of the arts to which these innovators attempt to assimilate painting, according to the classic statement of [Eduard] Hanslick, has for its subject ideas of movement; and if this be true, it is hard to see how painting can avoid the question—form of what, or significant of what?[97]

It did not occur to Alexander that for the "formalists"—and there were such even among figurative painters who were impelled by a certain passion for rigor—all aspects, the smallest and the large, might be significant for their functions in building up the coherence of the whole.

In considering the validity or heuristic value of analogy, in this large field of synthesizing cultural interpretation and history, we must ask for specification of the correspondences in detail, and not as totalities; one must undertake a piecemeal description of the analogous objects, and particularly their history, the dates and conditions of their emergence, their duration, their changes and fates in subsequent times. Each field has its own conditions, tasks, methods, objects, results, distinct from others, and each is open to suggestions and impacts of the others. No necessary correspondence and no sign of convergence in time (excepting a forced will to unification in authoritarian systems): Art and science sometimes but *not* always represent the same world.

In conclusion, the stimulus of science to art at certain moments does not determine results. Theory in science must finally be tested by close observation of phenomena and by its agreement with other scientific laws as well as for logical consistency. Albert Einstein was surely aware that artists have knowledge and often reason in applying it. The distinction from science lies in the *response* to the result. The scientist, too, has intuitions and makes imaginative leaps that spring from unconsciously induced perceptions and thoughts, but their validity depends on their cogency to reason—the reader's and colleague's recognition of their consistency with both logic and observation. The "cogency" of the artist's work depends on a *feeling* of order, harmony, and expressiveness that is not of a logical or empirical order yet is analogous in some respects to logic and scientific knowledge—a felt "rightness" and "consistency." Since behavior occurs in individuals whose perspectives and thought are shaped by different experiences and circumstances, one must allow for a spectrum of different reactions to events that lead to changes in both art and the institutional frameworks of economy, politics, and social life. Much of the culture remains the same during and after wars and revolutions. With regard to artists and scientists, their response to such crises or climactic events may be quite varied, especially in large, complex populations and above all in fields that have acquired a considerable degree of interdependence as to the special content and high value of their achievement and the established tradition of their achievement in the past. In Einstein's admiration of Rembrandt, for example, there is a simple pathos in his aesthetic, as distinct from what Poincaré saw as an intellectual beauty (even lucid order) in Rembrandt or in Gothic architecture.

Is there not perhaps in the analogy of Cubism with science an intuition of an underlying structure of experience common to the physicist and the artist, both of whom seek to organize the spatial and the temporal with respect to an observing subject? (No doubt the belief of scientists that science is an art and an object of aesthetic interest encourages acceptance of a problematic analogy, supported by the role of intuition in the imaginative work of creating theories and proofs.) We acknowledge that since the seventeenth century traditional narrative representation had wrestled with the problem of representing and coordinating in a single plane the relations of space and time, as indeed was already done in the ancient astronomers' graphs of the motions of the planets, if not in the same way as by the painters' system. No more than that, however, are the subtler and more rigorous analyses of simultaneity by Einstein and of the measurement of space-time by Minkowski reflected or paralleled in Cubist constructions on the canvas.

It is not surprising that a style of painting could be likened to a contemporary science. Western visual art since the Middle Ages, increasingly attentive to observant rendering of appearances and details of natural forms, and in applying, since the fourteenth century, the principles of geometric perspective and the representation of subtle phenomena of color and light, had itself stimulated closer scrutiny of objects. The arts served the sciences, too, as an instrumental for recording their data. Drawing and painting were conceived by artists as avenues to knowledge subject to norms of precision and generality; a means of exploring and describing nature (see Joshua Reynolds on art as scientific; and see John Constable on painting as "natural philosophy"), which might achieve a beautiful unity through simple ordered relations in a closed, regular frame. Leonardo is the prime example of the imaginative artist as an investigator whose mimetic skills as a draftsman were also instrumental in his scientific studies.[98] Besides, since the Renaissance, aesthetic and practical treatises on painting have acquired a language of mathematical relationships in treating proportions and geometric forms as model schemata (such as Aristotle considered *eusynoptic*) of composition in effecting a coherent expressive whole through correspondences of rhythms and measures in unlike parts.[99]

When, in the twentieth century, painters replaced representation by a freer art of invented "abstract" forms, there were still artists and critics who believed that this new art embodied in its elements and relationships the most general structures (even "laws") of nature in ideal mathematical forms. The visual arts especially are open to analogizing with physics because of common terms in the language of the two fields. Both are representations, "world pictures," and even abstract painters speak of their nonmimetic art as disclosing basic structures of reality in visualizable geometric forms. The vocabulary of the reflective artist includes *order*, *unity*, *plane*, *point*, *line*, *axis*, *proportion* and other terms from the mathematical sciences. Theory, in both fields, employs, among other common technical terms, *form*, *structure*, *space*, *relation*, *simultaneity*, *light*, *surface*, *volume*, *mass*, *motion*, *equilibrium*, *symmetry*, and *asymmetry*, and in analysis of a painting's structure, in the practical teaching and criticism of art, one speaks of geometric schemata, of perspective as a projective system, of repetition, transformation, reflection, reversal, inversion, equality, and difference. In no other art were the ideas of truth to nature through close observation, and of principles, of order and harmony through simple numerical relations, so often associated as in the visual arts.[100]

Suggestive, too, for analogies are the classifying terms, the large-scale categories and systematic ordering features in histories of art. Styles are distinguished by names that match the works of art with broader historical cultural phases as unities in time and place, and with cultures and political regimes, during which there appear innovations in neighboring fields, like phases of religion and the state, significant for the content and forms of the visual arts. In these styles are imaged the religious beliefs and rites, the myths, social hierarchies, and dynastic events. Even architecture offers models of constructive imagination and ideal spaces of cult and civil life, in forms that recall the habitual modes of composition in painting and sculpture. Systematic comparison of period styles with reference to gradients of evolving features

of the time and the artist." The axioms were for him idealizations shaped, like those of art, by the spirit of the time. "The Zeitgeist," Heisenberg wrote,

> is probably a fact as objective as any fact in natural science, and this spirit brings out certain features of the world which are even independent of time, are in this sense eternal. The artist tries by his work to make these features understandable, and in this attempt he is led to the forms of the style in which he works.
>
> Therefore, the two processes, that of science and that of art, are not very different. Both science and art form in the course of the centuries a human language by which we can speak about the more remote parts of reality, and the coherent sets of concepts as well as the different styles of art are different words or groups of words in this language.

Heisenberg believes that a style of art is not "an arbitrary product of the human mind"; rather, it "arises out of the interplay between the world and ourselves, or more specifically between the spirit of the time and the artist":

> A style of art can also be defined by a set of formal rules which are applied to the material of this special art. . . . [T]heir fundamental elements are very closely related to the essential elements of mathematics. Equality and inequality, repetition and symmetry, certain group strictures play the fundamental role both in art and in mathematics. . . . [H]ow far the formal rules of the style represent that reality of life which is meant by the art cannot be decided from the formal rules. Art is always an idealization . . . [104]

The problem arises from the vagueness of the "spirit of the time" concept and what it is meant to cover. Is it not assumed thoroughly to pervade the totality of human activities, though constructed from a few selected phenomena? It is different when applied to characterize a civilization, an epoch, a decade, or a particular moment in history. The spirit of the time may be either an attitude that is the result of many varying circumstances and experiences during a particular span of time, or it may be a generating attitude that shapes these circumstances and experiences. The concept finally seems different from style in art, which is physiognomic (individual) and not only aesthetic, so that in the individual artist's work the style appears personal; whereas when distinguished as such, as distinct from the way of thinking or the process of reaching such a result, the *Zeitgeist* does not appear physiognomic.[105] In any case, the concepts of space-time and the fourth dimension have a different meaning and greater importance in physics than in painting or architecture.

Why, one may wonder, should Werner Heisenberg bring up the concept of "style" apropos of quantum theory? He does so to justify the acceptance of a theory that is founded on a notion of the necessary limits placed on physics by the human factor, the interaction of man and nature in all knowledge, and hence the continuity of physics with the human sciences. He recognizes art as not only engaging knowledge of nature and man but also as manifesting in its basic principles of style certain features common to theory in science, i.e., a system of elements and rules of operation that together are coherent and generate coherent individual works. How accurate and fertile is this description of art and the similarity to science has yet to be shown in thorough critical study. Common to modern science and art is the idea of free constructive activity of the imagination submitted to the requirements of order, simplicity, and consistency.[106] In physics, however, there is also the requirement of agreement with observation, unlike abstract art, which, as with music and architecture, is independent of representational reality and therefore more suggestive of mathematicians' work.

We have seen in the efforts to connect relativity theory with Cubism and Futurism, and abstract art with quantum theory, how analogy rests on disregard of the differing meanings of the terms *space*, *time*, and *simultaneity*—unlike, say, the meaning of perspective as projective transformation in geometry and painting. But the common features of modern science and art are more likely to be found in aspects such as the individual character of scientific imagination and discovery, in the inventive processes, in the ongoing collective activity, in the critical openness to the new, in the models science offers of sustained searching, questioning, and freedom of thought—those attitudes that Albert Einstein characterized so finely in the statement that I quoted at the beginning of this essay.

Appendix: Einstein's Letter on Cubism

I have referred in the first part of this essay to a letter of Einstein on modern painting in which, besides rejecting the analogy and the supposed connection of relativity theory and Cubism, he presents his own aesthetic thinking. In these last pages I wish to consider his letter and the views expressed in it.

Replying in 1946 to the inquiry of Paul Laporte, an historian of art who had submitted to him an unpublished article comparing Cubist painting and the concepts of space and time in the theory of relativity, Einstein spelled out his ideas on the grounds of aesthetic value and judgment in art and science. Professor Laporte undertook to defend his view and cited Gidieon and other scholars who had proposed the analogy of Cubism and relativity, having himself published two earlier articles on the subject. Although Laporte published an English translation of Einstein's reply in 1966, it has received little attention; I reprint it here, with a few changes of my own that I have ventured in the wording, as a unique and instructive document of his views on aesthetics and art, in which Einstein denied the supposed correspondence of Special Relativity and Picasso's Cubist style. In this document, which ends with the emphatic statement "This new artistic 'language' has nothing in common with the theory of relativity," Einstein has also stated more precisely his ideas on the nature of art and the grounds of aesthetic judgment.

> I find your comparison rather unsatisfactory. If I disregard the practical value of a science, I do see something similar in scientific and artistic activity. Both strive to constitute from parts, a whole which is in itself unclear, but in such a way that the order underlying that recomposition produces distinctness and clarity. The distinctness and clarity thus achieved gives us a deep satisfaction. This is realized in art as well as in science. In science the ordering principle that produces unity is the logical connection, while in art the ordering principle remains anchored in the unconscious. In the latter it is always a matter of traditional modes of connection, which are felt by those who live in that tradition to be just as compelling as the logical connection is felt by the scientifically oriented.
>
> The essence of traditional modes of connection in art is shown clearly in the simple forms of art, e.g., in musical melody and in ornament which rests on an intuitively grasped regularity. In both cases the means of effecting lucidity are perceived as necessary, in a way similar to logical inference in mathematics. With more complex forms of art those basic means of producing lucidity or "unity" are less easily grasped.
>
> A work of art can therefore be experienced and evaluated as such only by those in whom the relevant traditional modes of connection are alive. For them there is no other sanction than their living existence. If they are given, the work is good or bad in relation to them, according to the perfection with which, based on the traditional methods of composition, the impression of lucidity is achieved.
>
> If the foregoing is correct, it is absurd to try to evaluate traditional modes of composition (the languages of the periods of art, so to speak) relative to one another.

> Now, as to the comparison in your paper, the essence of relativity theory has been incorrectly understood in it, granted that the error is suggested by the attempts at popularization. For the description of a state of affairs *(Sachverhaltes)* one uses almost always a *single* coordinate system. The theory says only that the general laws are such that their form does not depend on the choice of the system of coordinates. This logical requirement, however, has nothing to do with how the single specific case *(Sachverhalt)* is represented. A multiplicity of coordinate systems is not needed for its representation. It is fully sufficient to describe the whole mathematically with reference to *one* system of coordinates.
>
> This is quite different in the case of Picasso's pictures *(Bildern)*, as I do not have to elaborate any further. Whether in this case the representation is felt as an artistic unity depends, of course, on the artistic antecedents of the viewer *(künstlerische Vorgeschichte des Beschauers)*. This new artistic "language" has nothing in common with the theory of relativity.

Einstein's formulation embraces, at least in part, beauty in science as well as in art. In both fields, parts of the visual world that appear unordered, even chaotic, are brought into "lucid unity," in science through logical connections formulated in mathematical language and in art through discovery of symmetries, correspondences, regularities, repetitions, proportions in a new context. In art such relations follow the established styles of a time: Only modes of connection in the viewer's tradition will be legible to him. In Picasso's Cubist paintings Einstein himself did not recognize the relations of forms to which he was accustomed, so he could not readily respond to their language.

Einstein's comment on Picasso's Cubism is interesting for his later scientific judgments as well as his doubts before the new art of his time. Committed to a strict necessity in the physical and even the human world, he was repelled by the indeterministic and seemingly acausal views of younger scientists.

This is an unclear statement of the effort to reconcile or assimilate science and art to each other. Both create an order, or disclose it, in what is apparently a disorder or is indistinct. The beauty of nature is given in perception; what interests Einstein is the "activity" of scientist and artist as an effort to achieve "distinctness and clarity," a "lucid unity." In his belief that the ground of value in painting lies in purely formal relations, a belief reinforced perhaps by his experiences of music and traditional architecture, Einstein was in accord with the aesthetic theory of the advancing artists who originated Cubist and abstract painting. But these painters were sustained in their faith in the validity of that aesthetic for their practice by their experience of primitive art and of a great variety of styles outside the Western tradition. The form-constructive and expressive power of those earlier and exotic arts had enlarged the scope of the aesthetic; the release of Western art from the requirements of idealized naturalistic representation had opened the eyes of artists to the "lucid unity" of works in those previously rejected or disregarded styles, inspiring a new freedom and innovation in modern art. In appreciating "lucid unity" as a universal of aesthetic value, Einstein retained, however, the requirement of a particular traditional system as a norm of lucidity and unity. His view may be compared to that of a linguist who recognizes in syntax structural principles of all language but still regards the syntactical rules and categories of a particular language or family of languages as normatively valid. In admitting that he does not understand Picasso's "language," Einstein seems to ignore the "lucid unity" and expressive force that many artists and a large public have sensed in it. His reaction to the new art leads us to ask whether that universality of forms is enough to characterize the new art, especially as distinct from normatively classical notions of form, balance, and "truth" to nature.

Between the letter's second and third paragraphs there is a non sequitur, or at least a considerable leap. Then in the third paragraph Einstein writes that if the impression of lucid unity is achieved, the work is good or bad only if sanctioned by the relevant traditional modes of connection, according to the perfection with which a conventional impression of lucid unity is achieved; but this ignores the fact that just that will no longer be practiced in whatever is the new style of a time. And why should the artistic antecedents of the viewer be so crucial, anyway, when it is very well known that Picasso was influenced by tribal art and by artists of many different styles and themes, as well as the classic art of Greece and the Renaissance and of artists of the seventeenth century. As for the "traditional modes of connection," one must distinguish two approaches to the required adherence to them: (1) one that includes the peculiarities of style (and representation) of a past art; and (2) one that ignores these peculiarities while recognizing universal form-relations that effect order in the old works, as Baudelaire held in his review of the Salon of 1846 and in writing on Édouard Manet and Constantin Guys, and on costume in general. A parallel in science would be the respect for older scientific work that still holds up by its logic, while freeing oneself from what is regarded as irrelevant or mistaken in the assumptions that are *a priori* in the old work and are later regarded as false through new empirical discoveries or contradiction by more comprehensive and consistent theories.

Let us not overlook the simple fact that the great physicist knew no more, comparatively, of Cubist, let alone abstract, painting than another modern painter who had absorbed Cubism in Paris but had already returned to a realistic mode: the Mexican muralist Diego Rivera. It happens that in 1934 Einstein had written a note, effectively a fan letter, to Rivera, in which he declared that he couldn't name another contemporary artist whose work was similarly capable of so basically impressing him. When Rivera wrote back in thanks, he praised Einstein only in the noticeably broad terms of "enlarging the perspectives of human thought toward space and light" and likewise as a figure of general enlightenment with a social conscience (however ironic the terms of the compliment might become a decade later), "against the actual overrunning of the earth by dark *(obscures)* forces which threaten to return the world toward the deepest depths of barbarism."

Defending the notion of "a common style for art and science alike at a given time," Laporte denies that "new scientific developments of a period are a cause of those in art" and maintains that "artists and scientists started from common roots and were compelled to move in the same direction by an inner logic in the situation." To our disappointment, he does not undertake to say what were these common roots or to clarify what he means by "an inner logic" of their "situation." There is the dogma that while the artist's personality, morals, and behavior may be socially determined, they are altogether separate from the choices, concepts, and subject matter in his work, which belong to his free imagination and not to the realities of his life (see Proust's *Contre Sainte-Beuve*). This view of the separateness of "life and art" runs counter to so much that is evident from studies of artists' and writers' responses to events and milieux that I regard it as an ideology; it serves a need, but itself has a social root. A more significant and important analogy is perhaps of the individual freedom of the artist and the scientist, each occupied with problems he or she has set himself or herself and each honored for originality and success. The greatly varied styles in the new contemporary arts would, in any event, associate with quite different aesthetic theories and norms of value.

It was possible and even easy to find analogies between the languages of art theory and science because of common features of the two domains. Both are representations of the observable, and in both representations are general abstract devices for grouping or relating the observables. In the nonmimetic arts of architecture and music, as in modern abstract painting and sculpture, the elements are connected and organized through correspondences and contrasts, as in the mimetic arts. But if one selects an object of scientific study that seems to lend itself to comparison with a quite similar object of the painter, let us say, light, and if one follows the changing ideas about that object in the two fields over a period of several centuries, the analogies will be difficult to sustain. Certainly the work of art belongs to its time, not only in the sense that it presupposes the art of the immediately preceding time and its tradition, but in that it shows in many features connections with events, conditions, interests, and ideas of its time and abiding traditions; but such connections are not deducible simply from analogies or similarities: They must be confirmed in some measure by demonstrable connections between the works of art and the other field or fields in question.

In the seventeenth century, one can match the opposed theories of Newton and Huygens on the corpuscular and wave properties of light with the coexistence of two modes of painting: the classic style of Nicolas Poussin, which gives to objects a solid, definitely defined form, sculptural and massive, and the style of Rembrandt, with its vaguely edged fields of light and shadow irreducible to the modeling of object forms. (I am aware, of course, that these descriptions and comparisons are loose and arbitrary; I adopt them from current literature on art in order to carry through the comparison in the following centuries.) In the eighteenth century, the painterly, flecked style prevails, though the Newtonian corpuscular conception is the dominant one in science. Yet one must also recognize the revived classicism in the second half of the eighteenth century in England, France, and Germany, that continues on even as Augustin-Jean Fresnel and Thomas Young, early in the next century, contemporary with the paintings of Jacques-Louis David, Henry Fuseli, and William Blake and the sculptures of Antonio Canova, revive the wave theory of light and establish it for the nineteenth century as a whole. It is not until the last third of the nineteenth century that Impressionist painters seem to respond to the qualities of light in a style that is characterized by what painters and critics called vibration. More recently, in the twentieth century, with the discovery of the particle properties of light, its mass as well as waves, one can find analogies to this dual character in the coexistence of styles of regular closed forms and styles of undulatory movement; in America there is the contrast of Mark Rothko and Jackson Pollock—and even both aspects on the same canvas, as in late works of Adolph Gottlieb.

I have no reason to believe that these artists were inspired by scientific ideas. In the 1940s, in the studio of a well-known painter friend, I saw pinned up clippings of microphotographs of cloud chambers and tracks of atomic particles, which the artist found exciting and borrowed as motifs for his abstract canvases. But although this painter enjoyed the imagery of the new physics, and liked to give his paintings titles with terms from the language of nuclear physics, his startling canvases could hardly be said to convey the essential concepts of physical theory. It was their phenomenal aspect that attracted him, as in an earlier time he might have represented newly seen landscapes in changing light. A colleague in physics might just as well characterize particle tracks by naming them after painters, Picasso and others, whose linear patterns resembled these tracks.

(1979, with later additions)

[1] The response as published: Albert Einstein, "Das Gemeinsame am künstlerischen und wissenschaftlichen Erleben," *Menschen; Zeitschrift neuer Kunst*, 4th year (vol. 2, no. 100, February 1921):19.

[2] Paul M. Laporte, "Cubism and Relativity; with a Letter of Albert Einstein," *Art Journal* 25, no. 3 (spring 1966): 246–48; discussed in Appendix, below.

[3] Siegfried Giedion, *Space, Time and Architecture; The Growth of a New Tradition*, 5th ed. (Cambridge, Mass.: Harvard University Press, 1967), 14.

[4] Ibid., 436. The emphasis on simultaneity perhaps suggests Futurism even more than Cubism. (Actually, it is reported that Einstein considered Giedion's book "*scheisslich*" [= "crappy"] .)

[5] For a detailed exposition of which, see A. D'Abro, *The Evolution of Scientific Thought from Newton to Einstein*, rev. ed. (New York: Dover, 1950), esp. appendix "The Space and Time Graphs," 467–81.

[6] Albert Einstein, "Die Grundlage der allgemeinen Relativitätstheorie," *Annalen der Physik*, n. s. 49 (1916), repr. in his *Collected Papers*, ed. John Stachel et al. (Princeton: Princeton University Press, 1987–), 6 (*The Berlin Years; Writings, 1914–1917*): 284-338, here §§ 3–4, pp. 288–95.

[7] Erwin Panofsky, *Early Netherlandish Painting; Its Origins and Character* (Cambridge, Mass.: Harvard University Press, 1953), 5, continuing on 362, n. to p. 5; see also Panofsky's *Renaissance and Renascences in Western Art* (1960; New York: Harper, 1969),

122; and for another version of the same idea, his "Die Perspektive als 'symbolische Form,'" *Vorträge der Bibliothek Warburg*, 1924-25 (1927), this last discussed below.

[8] Albert Gleizes and Jean Metzinger, *Du Cubisme* (Paris: Figuière, 1912); in the anon. English trans., *Cubism* (London: Fisher Unwin, 1913), 55: "moving around an object to seize several successive appearances, which, fused in a single image, reconstitute it in time"; there were also German and Russian translations. (Compare Gleizes's later account in a 1932 lecture on art and science.)

[9] Henri Poincaré, *Science and Hypothesis* (1st English ed., 1905; repr. New York: Dover, 1952), chap. v, 72–88, treats non-Euclidean geometry and a "law of relativity." But see Poincaré, *Science and Method*, trans. Francis Maitland (New York: Dover, n. d.), sec. II, chap. i, "The Relativity of Space," 93–116; sec. III, chap. ii, "Mechanics and optics," esp. pt. ii, "The Principle of Relativity," 217–21. This latter part may reprint an article published before Einstein's; but Poincaré notes (228 n) that as the book goes to press he learns that A. H. Bucherer in 1908 has repeated an experiment of W. Kaufmann that had seemed to contradict Lorentz's view, and got a result that confirmed Lorentz and Einstein; Bucherer's 1908 experiment was published in the *Physikalische Zeitschrift* 9 (1909), 755–62, subtitled "Die experimentelle Bestätigung der Lorentz-Einsteinschen Theorie" (this according to Max Jammer, *Concepts of Mass in Classical and Modern Physics* [Cambridge, Mass.: Harvard University Press, 1961], 166 n. 18). Since Poincaré refers in his 1908 book to Kaufmann's article "Über die Konstitution des Elektrons," in the *Annalen der Physik*, ser. 4, vol. 19 (1906), 487–553, he must have known already of Einstein's work; there Kaufmann summarizes his own findings, "These results speak decisively (*entschieden*) against the correctness of Lorentz's and hence also of Einstein's theory" (534), after announcing that "the results of [his] measurement are not compatible with the basic assumption of Lorentz-Einstein" (495), with citations to Einstein's article of 1905 (492, 494). Kaufmann accepts the idea that "physical phenomena depend on movement relative to an altogether definite coordinate system, which we designate as the *ether in absolute rest*," and "if one hasn't yet succeeded in demonstrating such an influence of movement through the ether by electrodynamic or optical experiments, one must not yet conclude that such a proof (*Nachweis*) is impossible" (535; italics in original). Had Poincaré summarized Einstein's work, as he did Lorentz's, Einstein's ideas would have become familiar to French readers several years before the first references to his article on Special Relativity in French publications in 1911 and 1912—by Paul Langevin, on whose 1908 academic course Picasso's philosophic friend Eugeni d'Ors had sat in, interested in analogies of art and science.

[10] In *"Subtle is the Lord"; The Science and Life of Albert Einstein* (Oxford: Clarendon Press, 1982) Abraham Pais quotes (126–27) a summary of "an utterly remarkable article by Poincaré entitled 'La Mesure du temps'" [trans. Halsted in *The Value of Science* (1913)] from the *Revue de Métaphysique et de Morale* 6/1 (1898): "*we have no direct intu-*

ition about the equality of two time intervals. People who believe they have this intuition are the dupes of an illusion" (Poincaré's italics). And in a chapter on classical mechanics in *Science and Hypothesis*, Poincaré writes, "There is no absolute time; to say that two durations are equal is an assertion which has no meaning and which can acquire one only by convention. . . . [ellipsis in source] Not only have we no direct intuition of the equality of two durations, but we have not even direct intuition of the simultaneity of two events occurring in different places" and refers to his article of 1898, "La Mesure du temps." Of this, Poincaré's 1902 book, Maurice Solovine, Einstein's fellow student at the E. T. H. (Federal Institute of Technology) in Zurich, remembered that it "profoundly impressed us and kept us breathless for weeks on end" (qu. in Pais, op. cit., 133–34).

[11] James Clerk Maxwell, *Matter and Motion* (1877; American ed., 1878) (New York: Dover, 1991): "The phrase 'absolute velocity' has as little meaning as absolute position. It is better, therefore, . . . to regard [a certain] . . . diagram of velocity . . . as expressing the relations of all the velocities without defining the absolute value of any of them" (46). "'At rest' means in ordinary language 'having no velocity with respect to that on which the body stands,' as, for instance, the surface of the earth or the deck of a ship. It can not be made to mean more than this" (ibid.); "It is therefore unscientific to distinguish between rest and motion as between two states of a body in itself, since it is impossible to speak of a body being at rest or in motion except with reference, expressed or implied, to some other body" (47). Compare William Kingdon Clifford (1845–1879), *The Common Sense of the Exact Sciences* (New York: Knopf, 1946), a posthumous work first published in 1885 (edited and completed by Professor R. C. Rowe and Karl Pearson from Clifford's notes and papers), the 1946 edition with a preface by Bertrand Russell. Ernst Mach: *The Science of Mechanics* (1883), 5th English ed. (La Salle, Ill.: Open Court, 1942), 272–76, on time as an abstraction arrived at by the changes in things (likewise space: 337); also *History and Root of the Principle of the Conservation of Energy* (1872), trans. E. B. Jourdain (Chicago: Open Court, 1911); *Popular Scientific Lectures*, trans. Thomas J. McCormack (Chicago: Open Court, 1895); and *Erkenntnis und Irrtum; Skizzen zur Psychologie der Forshung* (1905), 2nd ed. (Leipzig: Barth, 1906), 446 n. 1, with ref. to an earlier statement of his, concerning the inseparability (*Unbetrennbarkeit*) of space and time, in *Zeitschrift für Philosophie*, 1866, and others.

[12] Modern astronomers had recognized the difficulties in determining the distance of a star, or the simultaneity of events in the heavens; e.g., "Measurement" by R. S. Ball, Royal Astronomer for Ireland, in the *Encyclopedia Britannica*, 9th ed. (1875–89); also "Astronomy" (historical article) and "Parallax."

[13] George Gissing, *The Odd Woman* (London: Bullen, 1905), 231. Gissing was perhaps inspired directly by Karl Pearson's *The Grammar of Science* (1892; 3rd ed., New York: Macmillan, 1911); see esp. chap. vi, sec. 5, 191–94, and sec. 12, 208; also, 212 n. i, 217.

I learn from Adeline Tintner that in December 1892, while writing his novel, Gissing refers in his diary to his then reading of Pearson's book.

[14] See Albert Einstein and Leopold Infeld, *The Evolution of Physics; the Growth of Ideas from Early Concepts to Relativity and Quanta* (New York: Simon and Schuster, 1938); also, Pais, "*Subtle is the Lord.*"

[15] Consider Honoré Daumier's prints of figures caught in showers, or Camille Pissarro's boulevard scenes conveying an instant in a scene of crowded movement.

[16] Giedion, *Space*, 443–44, 445.

[17] See H. A. Groenewegen-Frankfort, *Arrest and Movement; An Essay on Space and Time in the Representational Art of the Ancient Near East* (London; Faber, 1951). Compare the rhythms of the legs of the horsemen in series on the Parthenon frieze; also, Scandinavian reliefs of the eighth and ninth centuries.

[18] Compare the critics Roger Fry and Maurice Raynal. See Maurice Denis, "De la Gaucherie des primitifs" (1904), in his *Théories 1890–1910; Du symbolisme et de Gauguin vers un nouvel ordre classique* (Paris: Rouart and Watelin, 1920), 172–78, as well as Fry on conceived versus perceived forms.

[19] Not that there are no differences between archaic and Cubist fractioned representations: In many Cubist works the outline of an object is discontinuous, and parts of that outline reappear in neighboring objects; the figure or object seems to be merged with "constructive" lines or flatly layered planes of the background surface that represent no apparent or constructable object.

[20] Compare one of the miniatures of the *Vienna Genesis* showing what looks like a family on the march crossing a bridge [apparently the image of *Jacob Going Home*—Ed.].

[21] Erwin Panofsky, "Perspektive," trans. as *Perspective as Symbolic Form*, trans. Christopher S. Wood (New York: Zone, 1991), 153–54 n. 73.

[22] Time itself is symbolized in the Middle Ages by a figure with three faces on one head, one frontal and two in profile; all the more curious, then, is the combination of front and profile views in the representations of the Holy Trinity, indicated by a frontal head merged at the sides with two profiles, for the different views can hardly imply a succession in time, symbolizing as they do the three mysteriously *coeternal* "persons" of the singular Trinity.

[23] See Wilhelm Busch, *Comedy of Frustration: An English Anthology*, ed. and trans. Walter Arndt (Berkeley: University of California Press, 1982), 156.

[24] Robert Delaunay, "Historical Notes on Painting: Color and the Simultaneous" (probably 1913), in *The New Art of Color: The Writings of Robert and Sonia Delaunay*, ed. Arthur A. Cohen, trans. David Shapiro and Arthur A. Cohen, *The Documents of 20th-Century Art* (New York: Viking, 1978), 52.

[25] In sculpture, consider too the statue of *Maréchal Ney*, in Paris, by François Rude (1853).

[26] Charles Cros, *Oeuvres complètes*, Pléiade ed. (Paris: Gallimard, 1970), 531–32. His poem *Le Fleuve*, describing the successive appearances of a winding river in its long course, was published with a series of illustrative etchings by Manet (1874). Compare with Cros, Arthur Eddington, *The Nature of the Physical World* (1928; London: Dent, 1935), 98, 274, on the constitution of a viewpoint; also Umberto Boccioni's Futurist manifesto as quoted by Giedion.

[27] Max Weber, "The Fourth Dimension from a Plastic Point of View," *Camera Work*, no. 31 (July 1910): 25. Weber entitled one of his paintings *Interior of the Fourth Dimension* (1913; coll. Natalie Davis Springarn); illus. in the exhibition catalogue *Max Weber: American Modern* (New York: Jewish Museum, 1982), cat. no. 31 on 54; the work shows repeated forms with Gothic elements—interior vaulting, concavities, pinnacles, buttresses, arches, intersecting lines—perhaps suggested by the work of Robert Delaunay; see also other works by Weber in the years 1908–14. Weber also published a book of his poetry as *Cubist Poems* (London: Mathews, 1914).

[28] Guillaume Apollinaire, *The Cubist Painters: Aesthetic Meditations* (1913), trans. Lionel Abel, *The Documents of Modern Art* (New York: Wittenborn, Schultz, 1949), 13–14. (There was a concept of infinity of space in projective Euclidean geometry already well before the modern period, though the depth axis in perspective vision is a finite distance in actual perception.)

[29] Apollinaire and Weber met in Paris in 1908, in the studio of Henri Rousseau, who painted the portraits of both men. Apollinaire was close to the circle of the Cubist painters Gleizes, Metzinger, Delaunay, Villon, and Duchamp, and doubtless open to their ideas.

[30] Felix Klein, *Elementary Mathematics from an Advanced Standpoint: Geometry* (1908), 3rd ed., trans. E. R. Hedrick and C. A. Noble (New York: Macmillan, 1939), 62–63. On the "fourth dimension" and the contemporary occultists, see, for instance, Jammer, *Concepts of Mass*, 215 ff.

[31] For Picasso's denial, see the interview by Marius de Zayas (1923), in Alfred H. Barr, *Picasso: Fifty Years of His Art* (New York: Museum of Modern Art, 1974), 271.

[32] Maurice Raynal, "Le Cubisme," *Gazette des Beaux-Arts*, 6th period, 13 (1935): 179–91, esp. 181. Raynal's mathematics teacher was also, coincidentally, named Riemann. I had supposed that Raynal confused the name of the great German mathematician Georg Riemann (1826–1866) with that of Othon Riemann, a professor of Latin at his school; but Yve-Alain Bois has written me of a David Riemann, who taught mathematics there at the turn of the century.

[33] Alexandre Mercereau, "Introduction to an Exhibition in Prague" (i.e., 45th Exhibition of the Mánes Society, Prague, February–March 1914), trans. Jonathan Griffin in Edward F. Fry, ed., *Cubism* (London: Thames and Hudson, 1966; repr. New York: Oxford University Press, 1978), 133–35, esp. 134.

[34] Vladimir Nabokov, "The Overcoat (1842)," in his *Lectures on Russian Literature*, ed. Fredson Bowers (New York; Harcourt, Brace, Jovanovich, 1981), 54–61, here 58. Nabokov was perhaps influenced by his Russian emigré milieu in Berlin. On the vogue of the fourth dimension in connection with philosophy in Russia, consider P. D. Uspenskii. There is also Kazimir Malevich (among other places), in a discussion of the Cubists with their apparent multiple viewpoints: "They reasoned that hitherto artists had been conveying the object from only three sides, using three dimensional measurement."; Kazimir Malevich, *On New Systems in Art* (1919), collected in his *Essays on Art; 1915–1928*, trans. Xenia Glowacki-Prus and Arnold McMillan, ed. Troels Andersen, 2 vols. (Copenhagen: Borgen, 1968), 1: 83–119, here 95.

[35] Georges Poulet, *Studies in Human Time* (1956), trans. Elliott Coleman (Westport, Conn.: Greenwood, 1979), 318–19; compare Proust's account (in *Swann's Way*, 1913) of the Columbray church. For a musicological example, see Ernst Křenek, *Über neue Musik* (1937), trans. Barthold Fles as *Music Here and Now* (New York; Norton, 1939), 205–6, suggesting an axiomatic view of relations of musical elements in analogy with David Hilbert's *Foundations of Geometry*.

[36] R. Buckminster Fuller, in American Academy and Institute of Arts and Letters *Proceedings*, 2nd ser., no. 29 (1978): 75.

[37] Paul Langevin, "L'Evolution de l'espace et du temps," *Revue de Métaphysique et de Morale* 19 (1911): 455–66; Emile Meyerson, *Identity and Reality*, trans. Kate Loewenberg (New York: Gordon and Breach, 1989), esp. 136–37, 257–58 n. 73. In Germany there had appeared in 1910 the book of the neo-Kantian philosopher Paul Natorp, *Die logischen Grundlagen der exakten Wissenschaften* (1910), 2nd ed. (Leipzig and Berlin: Teubner, 1921), with an attempt to save the Kantian priori nature of space and time from the consequences of the new work of both Einstein (392 ff) and Minkowski (395 ff); Natorp's work was reviewed by Philip E. B. Jourdain in *Mind*, n. s. 20 (1911): 552–60.

[38] *Letters of Juan Gris (1913–1927)* (London: privately printed, 1956), Letter to Maurice Raynal, January 3, 1922, 135.

[39] Eugeni d'Ors, *Pablo Picasso* (Paris: Chroniques du Jour; New York: Weyhe, 1930); there is a study by Enric Jardí, *Eugenio d'Ors; obra y vida* (Barcelona: Ayma, 1967). In art criticism, d'Ors decried the concept of a relativity of taste, believing in the eternal canons and universals of great art. For his book on Picasso, see also the expanded edition *Picasso; en tres revisiones* (Madrid: Aguilar, 1946), which adds to the original text some severely skeptical doubts written down in 1935 and 1945.

[40] Filippo Tommaso Marinetti, "Destruction of Syntax—Imagination without Syntax—Words-in-Freedom" (1913), in *Futurist Manifestos*, ed. Umbro Apollonio, trans. Robert Brain et al., *The Documents of 20th-Century Art* (New York: Viking, 1973), 95–106, here 97.

[41] These last three quotations from the Futurist manifestos (as trans. anonymously in

1912) in Joshua C. Taylor, *Futurism* (New York: Museum of Modern Art, 1961), 124, 125, 127, respectively.

[42] Hermann Minkowski, "Space and Time; An Address Delivered at the 80th Assembly of German Natural Scientists and Physicians at Cologne, 21 September 1908," in H. A. Lorentz, Albert Einstein, and Hermann Minkowski, *The Principle of Relativity; A Collection of Original Memoirs on the Special and General Theory of Relativity*, ed. A. Sommerfeld, trans. W. Perrett and G. B. Jefferey (London: Methuen, 1923; repr. New York: Dover, 1952), 73–96, here 75, 79–80. Minkowski considers the term "*relativity-postulate*," which "comes to mean that only the four-dimensional world in space and time is given by phenomena, but that the projection in Space and Time may still be undertaken with a certain degree of freedom," rejecting it in favor of a "*postulate of the absolute world* (or briefly, the world postulate)" (83).

[43] See P. D. Uspenskii, *Tertium organum; The Third Canon of Thought: A Key to The Enigmas of the World* (probably 1931), trans. (London: Routledge and Kegan Paul, 1981), with allusions to Einstein and Minkowski.

[44] Compare Roman Jakobson, "On a Generation that Squandered Its Poets," in his *Language in Literature*, ed. Krystyna Pomorska and Stephen Rudy (Cambridge, Mass.: Harvard University Press, 1987), 273–300, esp. 285, 287.

[45] [Compare Meyer Schapiro, *Paul Cézanne* (New York: Abrams, 1952), 112: "[T]he painters of the beginning of this century found picturesque the geometric intricately grouped, the disorder of regular elements, the decided thrust and counterthrust of close-packed lines and masses in the landscape. A scene like this one was fascinating to the artist as a problem of arrangement—how to extract an order from the maze of bulky forms. It is one aspect of the proto-Cubist in Cézanne."—Ed.]

[46] Albert Gleizes, *Du Cubisme et des moyens de le comprendre* (Paris, 1920), 18.

[47] The selection of (object) qualities that constitute "real" objects is arbitrary and practical, according to the pertinence of the qualities to particular aesthetic and practical interests or goals.

[48] Joachim Weyl, "Science and Abstract Art," *College Art Journal* 2 (January 1943): 42–46, esp. 45, on space in Cubist painting as specifically Cartesian, while Cézanne's is Galilean, with Futurist space likened to Newtonian fluxions.

[49] See Milič Čapek, "The Conflict Between the Absolutist and the Relational Theory of Time Before Newton," *Journal of the History of Ideas* 48 (1987): 595–608, though Čapek is wrong to attribute the Newtonian concept of the separate absoluteness of time and space to James Clerk Maxwell.

[50] Martin Heidegger, "The Age of the World Picture" (lecture of 1938, published in *Holzwege*, 1952), in his *The Question Concerning Technology and Other Essays*, ed. and trans. William Lovitt (New York: Harper and Row, 1977), 115–54, here 115 (German phrase, 115 n. 2).

51 The exchange is reported in the autobiography of Ernst Jackh, *Weltstaat, Erlebtes und Erstrebtes* (Stuttgart: Deutsch und Verlagsanstalt, 1960), 35–36; see also Ronald W. Clark, *Einstein; The Life and Times* (New York: World, 1971), 364. The occasion of this committee arose from the disastrous and unforseen effects of the World War I—a resort to irrational means—which are still with us after more than sixty years, while science (and even art) contributed to its effects. Another example of the currency of the idea of a connection between the new science and the League of Nations as examples of unification: In a speech in a fictional symposium on world unity, in a book by the Irish poet—and artist—George William Russell, who signed his books "A. E.," the speaker says, "To men of science the universe is demonstrably under the dominion of unalterable and inflexible law"; A. E., *The Interpreters* (New York: Macmillan, 1923), 66. The international practice of modern styles, in contrast to the many local or national schools in older art, is peculiar neither to art nor to science; indeed, one must recognize the superficiality by which "internationalism" as a concept applies to multinational corporations, communist and socialist governments, terrorism, export-import trade, Olympic games, movies, and so on.

52 Max Planck himself, in his 1920 Nobel Prize address on relativity and quantum theory as contemporary with but different from Einstein's search for a "unified field theory," rejected the indeterminacy principle in quantum theory: *The Origin and Development of the Quantum Theory*, trans. H. T. Clarke and L. Silberstein (Oxford: Clarendon Press, 1922); his reluctance to accept its consequences has been ascribed to his lifelong faith in the deterministic idea in his own physical approach.

53 Thus, the change in painting from representation to abstraction is better understood as an effort of autonomy, a desire for emancipation by artists from the functions that sustained representation in the eighteenth and nineteenth centuries, than as the outcome of a desire for universality or generality of forms.

54 Albert Einstein and Hedwig and Max Born, *The Born-Einstein Letters; Correspondence Between Albert Einstein and Max Born from 1916–1955*, ed. Max Born, trans. Irene Born (London: Macmillan, 1971), Letter to Max Born, January 27, 1920, pp. 22–23. It is interesting that Oswald Spengler, while discussing relativity in at least three places in *The Decline of the West* (1918; 1926–28), credits Lorentz, Minkowski, Niels Bohr, and others without mentioning Einstein.

55 Alfred North Whitehead, *Science and the Modern World*, Lowell Lectures 1925 (New York: Free Press, 1967), esp. chap. v, "The Romantic Reaction," 75–94. One also thinks of German Romantic poetry—Novalis (Friedrich von Hardenberg) and August and Friedrich von Schlegel, and Samuel Taylor Coleridge. Whitehead was also aware of the contribution of medieval crafts and art to progress in instrument making, without which the growth of science could not have advanced as it did in the following and modern centuries.

[56] Alois Riegl, *Spätrömische Kunstindustrie* (1901), 2nd ed. (Vienna: Österreichischen Staatsdrukerei, 1927; repr. Darmstadt: Wissenschaftliche Buchgesellschaft, 1964), 402. [Owing to a break in the manuscript, the continuation in square brackets is taken from Riegl, *Late Roman Art Industry*, trans. and ed. Rolf Winkes, Archaeologica, 36 (Rome: Bretschneider, 1985), 232.—Ed.]

[57] Ibid., 403.

[58] Ibid., 404 n. 1.

[59] Ibid., 404–05.

[60] Pierre Duhem, *Le Système du monde; histoire des doctrines cosmologiques de Platon à Copernicus*, 10 vols. (Paris: Hermann, 1954–59), 6: 66. Duhem discusses the same problem in Maimonides and his disciples (5: 178–82). Interesting complexities of the Paris disputes include comments (8: 500–501) of Nicholas Oresme and Jean de Gerson, in the fourteenth century: "Thank God they did not reject the whole of Astrology. For beneath its monstrous errors it enclosed the germ of great and fruitful (*féconde*) verities" (500). According to Jacques Hadamard, *An Essay on the Psychology of Invention in the Mathematical Field* (Princeton: Princeton University Press, 1949; repr. New York: Dover, 1954), 128, Duhem "was a remarkable artist as well as a prominent physicist."

[61] On Kepler's frontispiece, see the study by Horst Bredekamp, "Antikensehensucht und Maschinenglauben," in Herbert Beck and Peter C. Bol, eds., *Forschungen zur Villa Albani; Antike Kunst und die Epoche der Aufklärung* (Berlin: Mann, 1982), 509–59, with pls. 158–78, figs. 304–43; esp. 542–43 and pl. 172, fig. 333. Missing the point of the varied columns, Bredekamp says of the temple, "Ein offenbar ruinöser antiker Rundtempel . . . scheint in Auflösung begriffen, jedenfalls befinden sich die mittleren und besonders die hinteren Säulen in Erosion. Die beiden vorderen Säulen aber geben dem Bauwerk als Verkörperungen der Lehren von Kopernikus und Tycho Brahe, die die Ordnung des Himmels und der Erde vor dem Zusammenbruch bewahren, neue Stabilität." (An obviously ruined ancient round temple . . . appears to be disintegrating, but in any case the middle and especially the back columns are eroding. These two front columns present the building as the embodiment of the lessons of Copernicus and Tycho Brahe, which with a new stability guard the arrangement of the heavens and the earth from collapse.) He cites for this last point on the threatened ruination of the heavens Kepler's poem in the *Astronomia nova* (1609), which speaks of the danger that threatens the cracked walls of the heavens (if the system of Tycho Brahe and Copernicus is correct)—so Kepler gets to work in hope that he will succeed in supporting the heavenly roof with a new architrave (*Gebälk*); see German translation of Kepler's *Astronomia nova* by M. Caspar (Munich: Beck, 1937–), 3: 60. Eva Chojecka, "Johannes Kepler und die Kunst; zum Verhältnis von Kunst und Naturwissenschaften in der Spätrenaissance," *Zeitschrift für Kunstgeschichte* 30 (1967): 55–72, esp. 61, on the engraving (attributed by Chojecka to Johann Cöler), to Kepler's design; here the building is considered to be a "Temple of

Urania," i.e., of the muse of astronomy and, according to Kepler himself, the sign of victory, of triumph over the incapacity of forebears.

62 Hermann Weyl, *The Open World; Three Lectures on the Metaphysical Implications of Science* (New Haven: Yale University Press, 1932), 82, opposes to the reflective realm of the philosopher "the domain of creation (*Gestaltung*), of construction, to which the active artist, the scientist, the technician, the statesman devote themselves."

63 See Jacques Hadamard, *Essay*, 31, citing, for example, Jules-Henri Poincaré on "the intervention of sense of beauty playing its part as an indispensable *means*" of finding right choices in scientific investigation; also on Bernoulli and Vito Volterra (129–30). P. A. M. Dirac, "The Evolution of the Physicist's Picture of Nature," *Scientific American*, May 1963, 45–53, esp. 46–47, on Schrödinger's discovery of the wave equation in wave mechanics: "Schrödinger got this equation by pure thought, looking for some beautiful generalization of [Louis] De Broglie's ideas. . . . [I]t is more important to have beauty in one's equations than to have them fit experiment. . . . It seems that if one is working from the point of view of getting beauty in one's equations, and if one has really a sound insight, one is on a sure line of progress."

64 Erwin Panofsky, *Galileo as a Critic of the Arts* (The Hague: Nijhoff, 1954); also (with revisions stimulated by Alexandre Koyré, "Attitude esthétique et pensée scientifique," *Critique* IX, tome 12, no. 100–101 (1955), 835 ff): "Galileo as a Critic of the Arts; Aesthetic Attitude and Scientific Thought," *Isis* 47, pt. 1, no. 147 (March 1956): 3–15.

65 A systematic attempt to interpret the history of Western art since the Middle Ages through the types of relations of space and time is Dagobert Frey's *Gotik und Renaissance als Grundlagen der modernen Weltanschauung* (Augsburg: Filser, 1929).

66 Panofsky, *Galileo*, and "Galileo"; Otto Benesch, *The Art of the Renaissance in Northern Europe; Its Relation to the Contemporary Spiritual and Intellectual Movements*, rev. ed. (London: Phaidon, 1965), chap. viii, esp. 184 n. 42.

67 See George Sarton, *The Appreciation of Ancient and Medieval Science During the Renaissance* (Philadelphia: University of Pennsylvania Press, 1955), 143–44, for the influence of Apollonius's *Conica* (c. 200 B.C.).

68 Galileo Galilei, *Il Saggiatore*, sec. 38, in his *Opere*, ed. Ferdinando Flora (Milan and Naples: Ricciardi, 1953), 264: "[A]s for me, never having read the chronicles and the particular nobility of figures, I don't know which ones are more or less noble and more or less perfect; but I believe that all are in a way ancient and noble, or to put it better, that in themselves they are neither noble and perfect nor ignoble and imperfect: except in building a wall I believe that square blocks are more perfect than spheres, and for rolling or conducting wagons I judge the round more perfect than the triangular."

69 A. Wolf, *A History of Science, Technology and Philosophy in the 16th and 17th Centuries* (New York: Macmillan, 1935), 469 with fig. 235.

70 Galileo Galilei, *Dialogues Concerning the Two Chief World Systems, Ptolemaic and*

Copernican (1632), trans. Stillman Drake (Berkeley: University of California Press, 1962), 104–5 (close of "First Day"), citing Michelangelo, Raphael, and Titian.

[71] See Alexandre Koyré (besides his "Attitude esthétique"), *La Révolution astronomique; Copernic, Kepler; Borelli* (Paris: Hermann, 1961), 269 et passim.

[72] Whitehead, *Science*, 15.

[73] Although twentieth-century analogical interpretation is often ahistorical, coincidental, lacking in concreteness, one admires Whitehead's strong sense of history, of progress, growth, and individuality in the natural and social world, his effort to integrate the aesthetic and ethical sphere with the pursuit of science and philosophy. He was an inspiring teacher and intellectual personality, eloquent and acute, and in some ways more attractive than Bertrand Russell, with a generous and bountiful mind—appreciative and insightful.

[74] Eddington, *Nature*, 107–8. Apropos of Eddington's comparison of entropy and Impressionist painting, compare Pearson, *Grammar*, 364, on the electromagnetic constitution of the atom: "We have a new picture of the universe. Seen from a distance it looks like the old. The details cannot be seen; the masses are the same as a hundred years ago. But coming nearer we perceive how these mass effects are produced. We seem to see more of the detailed touches of the artist's brush."

[75] James Clerk Maxwell, *Theory of Heat* (London: Longmans, Green, 1871), 308–9.

[76] Georges Clemenceau, *Claude Monet; Les Nymphéas* (Paris: Plon, 1928), 95. (Compare Paul Klee's notion that the purpose of painting is to render the invisible visible.)

[77] [See "Impressionism and Science," in Schapiro's *Impressionism: Reflections and Perceptions* (New York: George Braziller, Inc., 1997), 206–29.—Ed.]

[78] Mogens Anderson, "An Impression," in *Niels Bohr; His Life and Work as Seen by His Friends and Colleagues*, ed. S. Rozental (New York: Interscience, 1967), 322, as quoted by Arthur I. Miller, "Visualization Lost and Regained," in Judith Wechsler, ed., *On Aesthetics in Science* (Cambridge, Mass.: M. I. T. Press, 1978), 72–102, here 76.

[79] Even before they turned to abstraction, it was a practice of painters to invert a canvas being painted in order to test its "rightness" as a balanced, coherent structure without influence of its recognizable objects and perspective, so that the structure of the composition might be judged "in itself."

[80] Arthur I. Miller, "On the Origins of the Copenhagen Interpretation," in *Niels Bohr: Physics and the World*, Proceedings of the Niels Bohr Centennial Symposium, Boston, November 12–14, 1985, ed. Herman Feshbach, Tetsuo Matsui, and Alexandra Oleson (Chur [Switzerland]: Harwood Academic Publishers, 1988), 27–43, esp. 28, 40–41 (brackets and parentheses in this source).

[81] Heisenberg's father was a professor of Greek, a noted investigator of Byzantine architecture, and the editor of the *Byzantinsche Zeitschrift*.

[82] Werner Heisenberg, "Die Abstraktion in der modernen Naturwissenschaft" (1960–61), in his *Gesammelte Schriften/Collected Works*, ed. H. Blum, H.-P. Durr, and H.

Rechenberg (Berlin and New York; Springer, 1984–), C2: 302–25, here 323–24.

[83] Yet consider Heisenberg, "Science and Religion" (1927), in his *Physics and Beyond: Encounters and Conversations*, trans. Arnold J. Pomerans (New York and Evanston: Harper, 1971), 82–92, on Paul Dirac and his "uncompromising" logicality and perfectionism: "Recently the two of us went to an exhibition which included a glorious gray-blue seascape by Manet. In the foreground was a boat, and beside it, in the water, a dark gray spot, whose meaning was not quite clear. Dirac said, 'This spot is not admissible.' A strange way of looking at art, but he was probably quite right. In a good work of art, just as in a good piece of scientific work, every detail must be laid down quite unequivocally; there can be no room for mere accident" (87).

[84] Piet Mondrian, "Natural Reality and Abstract Reality" (1919–20), in *The New Art—The New Life; The Collected Writings of Piet Mondrian*, ed. and trans. Harry Holtzman and Martin S. James (Boston: Hall, 1986), 82–123, here 98.

[85] Apollinaire, *Cubist Painters*, 13.

[86] Amédée Ozenfant and Charles-Édouard Jeanneret (called Le Corbusier), *Le Peinture moderne* (Paris: Crés, n.d.), ii (at least twice in the book the name of Einstein is invoked: 10, 151). Here Ozenfant, who was an active participant in the cult of geometry of the "L'Esprit Nouveau" circle, which had political affinity with the *Rappel à l'Ordre*, also says, "Geometry, through its development of machines, is everywhere. . . . [O]ur mind itself, satisfied to discover this geometry, its creation, everywhere, rebels against the inconsistent, often ungeometric aspects of painting, and particularly the incoherent blurs of impressionism. The present spectacle is essentially geometrical, our senses and our mind are impregnated with it. Man is a geometric animal, animated by a geometric mind. . . . " See also the section "Vers le crystal" (135 ff) and Ozenfant's *Foundations of Modern Art* (1928).

[87] Joshua Reynolds, *Discourses on Art* (New York: Collier, 1961), Discourse X (1780), 153-65, here 157; and in the same place: "[T]he beauty of form alone, without the assistance of any other quality, makes of itself a great work, and justly claims our esteem and admiration."

[88] The mathematician Hermann Weyl, in his *Philosophy of Mathematics and Natural Science*, trans. Olaf Helmer, rev. ed. (Princeton: Princeton University Press, 1949; repr. New York: Atheneum, 1963), quotes David Hilbert on the concreteness of mathematical symbols as "independent of time and place, of the particular conditions of their manufacture, and of trifling differences in their execution" (35), and on mathematical cognition as concerned with "extra-logical, concrete objects, which can be overlooked completely in all their parts, and whose exhibition, differentiation, and succession or coordination are given along with the objects as something neither capable nor in need of reduction to anything else" (64); Weyl comments (113) on the dependence of a sense of multiple viewpoints on symbolization.

[89] [Compare John Dewey, in *Art as Experience* (New York: Minton, Balch, 1934), projecting scientific and artistic development returning from parted ways to a common concern with "making natural rhythms manifest," so that even "subject matter that now exists only for laborious reflection, that appeals only to those who are trained to interpret that which to sense are only hieroglyphics, will become the substance of poetry" (150); also Dewey's quotation of Wordsworth's prophecy: "The remotest discoveries of the Chemist, the Botanist, or Mineralogist, will be as proper objects of the Poet's art as any. . . if . . . the relations under which they are contemplated by the followers of these respective sciences shall be manifestly and palpably material to us as enjoying and suffering beings" (319).—Ed.]

[90] William Dwight Whitney, *The Life and Growth of Language; An Outline of Linguistic Science* (1875; New York: Appleton, 1897), 314.

[91] And often scientists' own comparisons are essentially metaphorical (or poetic), e.g., the term *flavor* as applied to particles.

[92] In an unpublished paper, "On a Parallel in Islam and Hiberno-Saxon Art," presented at the annual meeting of the College Art Association, in Philadelphia, in 1964, I have considered the Matthew symbol of the Echternach Gospels and an Islamic figure as two works separated by time and place yet surprisingly similar in conception and form, though one is late-seventh-century Hiberno-Saxon and the other from eleventh-century Fatimid Cairo—as identical words may occur in different languages, far separated in time and space, yet with related meanings. In "The Miniatures of the Florence Diatesseron (Laurentian MS Or. 81); Their Place in Late Medieval Art and Supposed Connection with Early Christian and Insular Art," *Art Bulletin* 55 (1973): 495–531, I trace the resemblance of the Hiberno-Saxon ornamented page and a similar page of complex intricate ornament in a Persian Christian manuscript of the sixteenth century to a diffusion of such interlace ornament from Mediterranean art of the Greek and Roman world to both the Near East and to the Celtic and Germanic peoples of northwestern Europe in the sixth and seventh centuries (as in their languages). The spread of Christianity from the eastern Mediterranean introduced in the native languages of northwestern Europe terms clearly derived from the Greek and Latin Bible and the usage of the Church of the Early Christian period.

[93] Juan de Herrera, *Discurso . . . sobre la figura cubica*, ed. Edison Simons and Roberto Godoy (Madrid: Editiona Nacional, 1976). Herrera was a leading mathematician and metaphysician who also taught applied mathematics and physics, cosmography, fortification, hydraulics, clock making, etc.; see Marcelino Menéndez Pelayo, *Historia de las ideas estéticas en España*, 5 vols. (Buenos Aires: Espasa-Calpe, 1943), 2: 370–79.

[94] Edmond de Goncourt, *Les Frères Zemganno* (Paris: Nizet; Naples: Liguori, 1891), 149, 220. One also recalls not only Baudelaire's, Apollinaire's, and Cocteau's love of the circus, including a poem by Apollinaire about an acrobat, but perhaps also Picasso's

identification with the daring Wright brothers while collaborating so closely with Braque in the formation of Cubism.

[95] Samuel Alexander, "Some Explanations," *Mind* 30 (1921): 409–28, here 417, (written response to a critique by C. D. Broad, "The External World," 385–408 in the same volume). John Passmore, *A Hundred Years of Philosophy* (London: Duckworth, 1957), comments on Alexander's notion: "A doctrine similar in certain respects had been maintained by physicists like Minkowski and Einstein. But Alexander's theory of Space-Time was arrived at, he says, by independent metaphysical speculation; he is glad to have the support of physics but makes no direct use of physical theory. Nor does he wholly accept the new physical conceptions. Indeed, one can easily detect two different approaches to Space-Time in Alexander, one relativist, the other not" (273 n. 2, with refs.).

[96] Passmore's paraphrase, "In the same way, spatio-temporal perspectives 'demand' Space-Time for their completion, as slices of simultaneous events would not" (loc. cit., 277 n. 2), might seem a good equivalent of Gleizes et al. in Cubism.

[97] Samuel Alexander, "Art and Instinct," Herbert Spencer Lecture, at Oxford, May 23, 1927, in his *Philosophical and Literary Pieces*, ed. John Laird (London: Macmillan, 1939), 254–55.

[98] Compare Michelangelo on drawing as a universal instrument of knowledge and design, in Francisco de Hollanda, *Four Dialogues on Painting* (1548), trans. Anthony F. G. Bell (London: Oxford University Press, 1928; repr. Westport, Conn.: Hyperion, 1979), Dialogue III, ii, pp. 36–38).

[99] Anthony Ashley Cooper, 3rd Earl of Shaftesbury, *Characteristics of Men, Manners, Opinions, Times* (1711), 2 vols., ed. John M. Robertson (1900), ed. Stanley Green (repr. Gloucester, Mass.: Peter Smith, 1963), 1, sec. iii, p. 94, n. 3, emphasizes that which Aristotle calls the painter's "unity of design," such that "particulars . . . yield to the general design and all things be subservient to that which is principal, attributing in a long note the term and concept to the *Poetics* (expecially chaps. vii, xxiii).

[100] Excepting, that is, for the Pythagorean mathematics of musical harmony, as influential in the nonmimetic visual art of architecture

[101] Compare Gottfried Kinkel on domed and columnar buildings as corresponding to monarchy and democracy, an idea advanced independently, it seems, by Eugeni d'Ors in his *Picasso* (1930): "Die Sophienkirche von Konstantinople," in his *Mosaik zur Kunstgeschichte* (Berlin: Oppenheim, 1876), 275–301, esp. 299–300.

[102] Albert Einstein, "Principles of Research" (1918; lecture at the Berlin Physical Society), from Einstein's *Mein Weltbild* (1934), ed. Carl Seelig, in his *Ideas and Opinions*, ed. and trans. Sonja Bargmann (New York: Crown, 1954, repr. 1963), 224–27, here 225. This also concerns the life problems of viewers as members of an unstable, changing society, exposed to wars, economic and political crises, and the challenges of new ways, which may also stimulate reaction in artists and others.

[103] Richard von Mises, *Positivism: A Study in Human Understanding* (Cambridge, Mass.: Harvard University Press, 1951; repr. New York; Dover, 1968), 312, on style as an important classificatory "order concept" for the "empirical description of the phenomenon of art," even as "science in particular cannot do anything but classify by description." Style in science is a historical as well as an "artistic" category, changing with basic ideas, procedures, and knowledge; it includes the standards of correct science in each epoch, the tacit assumptions and ignored contradictions and the notions of plausibility and accepted philosophic interpretations (unless these may already be more than the style?). The concept of "paradigms" of scientific thought (see Thomas S. Kuhn, *The Structure of Scientific Revolutions*, 1962) as created by leading scientists—Kepler, Galileo, Descartes, Lagrange, Laplace, Maxwell, etc.—is like the concept of styles of art as initiated by Brunelleschi, Giotto, Donatello, Michelangelo, Raphael, Jan van Eyck, whose works were models for each artist's next generation.

[104] Werner Heisenberg, *Physics and Philosophy; The Revolution in Modern Science* (New York: Harper, 1958), 109, 108.

[105] Compare Ernst Mach on John and Jacob Bernoulli's two different styles in solving a problem.

[106] Einstein, *Ideas and Opinions*, offers several possible points of reference here from papers of the earlier 1930s (e.g., 266, 272, 282, 301); especially pertinent may be "On the Generalized Theory of Gravitation" (repr. from *Scientific American*, April 1950), 341–56, esp. 342–43, 352.

[107] Paul M. Laporte "Cubism and Science," *Journal of Aesthetics and Art Criticism* 7 (1949): 243–56, and "The Space-Time Concept in the Work of Picasso," *Magazine of Art* 41 (1948): 26–33; and more recently, an article on painting in relation to modern mathematics and physics from nineteenth-century non-Euclidean geometry and the revision of classical picture space to quantum mechanics and post-Cubist, even Abstract Expressionist, painting: "Turner to de Kooning: Non-Euclidean Geometry to Quantum Theory," *Bulletin of the New York Public Library* 79 (Autumn 1975): 4–39.

[108] Paul M. Laporte, "Cubism and Relativity"; Einstein's letter is dated May 4, 1946. I thank Helen Dukas for a photocopy of the original letter and permission to publish the translation. An extract from the letter has been quoted by Professor Gerald Holton in his preface to the volume of papers presented in the Jerusalem meeting of 1979 commemorating the centenary of Einstein's birth: *Albert Einstein: Historical and Cultural Perspectives; The Centennial Symposium in Jerusalem*, ed. Gerald Holton and Yehuda Elkana (Princeton: Princeton University Press, 1982).

[109] Compare Jean Leymaire, *Picasso; Artist of the Century*, trans. James Emmons (New York: Viking, 1972), vii: "'Picasso,' declared Albert Einstein, 'freely justifies the saying which has it that man and the world are daily created by man.'"

[110] On beauty as a criterion in mathematics and theoretical physics, see (among other

things) Hermann J. Weyl's statement reported in Freeman J. Dyson's obituary of Weyl in *Nature* (March 10, 1956), as quoted in James R. Newman, ed., *The World of Mathematics*, 4 vols. (New York: Simon and Schuster, 1965), 3, pt. xvii, "Mathematics as an Art," 1831 n.

[111] Fifty years earlier, John Ruskin had written that it was the duty of Englishmen to preserve the art of western Europe, "in which alone . . . pure and precious ancient art exists, for there is none in America, none in Asia, none in Africa"; John Ruskin, *The Political Economy of Art; Being the Substance (with Additions) of Two Lectures Delivered in Manchester, July 10th and 13th, 1857* (New York: Wiley, 1885), 68. The same Ruskin had included in his family of true art the works of the later Middle Ages, while earlier medieval art was for him barbaric or savage or merely embryonic—though he noted in it interesting signs pointing to later growth. He was repelled, too, by the new art of the French Impressionists, artists twenty years younger than himself.

[112] I quote from photocopies of the originals: Albert Einstein, Letter to Diego Rivera from Princeton, February 13, 1934 (in German); Diego Rivera, Letter to Einstein from Mexico, March 5, 1934 (in French).

[113] Compare Hadamard, *Essay*, 134: "Social influences govern mathematical development in the same unconscious and rather mysterious way as they do literary or artistic ones." In answer to questions of Hadamard, Einstein wrote in a letter, "It seems to me that what you call full consciousness is a limit case which can never be fully accomplished" (143).

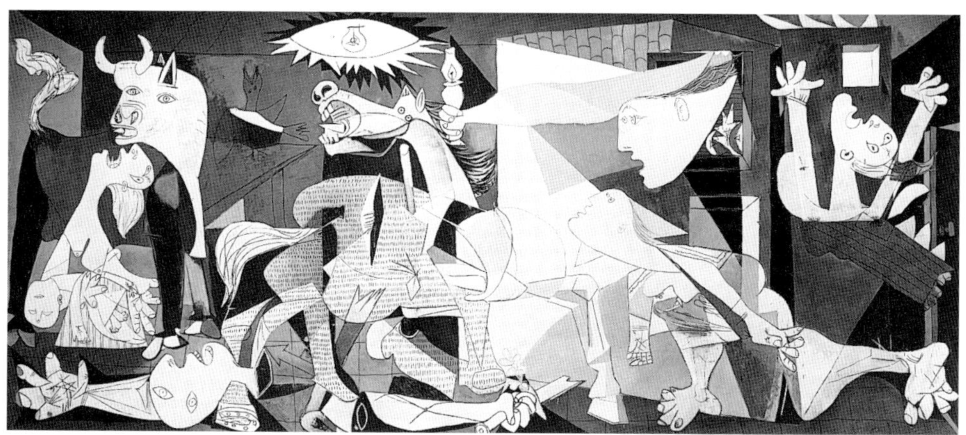

Figure 1. *Guernica*, May 1–June 4, 1937, oil on canvas, 11'5⅜" x 25'5½" (349 x 776 cm), Museo Nacional Centro de Arte Reina Sofía, Madrid.

GUERNICA: SOURCES, CHANGES

Most of you, I suppose, have heard or read Rudolf Arnheim on the subject of *Guernica*, reconstructing as a Gestalt psychologist the course of a great work of art through many sketches and through the successive states of the canvas as recorded in photographs.[1] Professor Arnheim presented these as single elements of the process in order to demonstrate how one followed from the preceding, and how a certain one was a leap beyond the others, all leading to the final work. I propose to deal with the same process from another point of view that, while being a historian's, also concerns the psychology of invention of forms. Fig. 1

I must say, first, that the way in which we look at the preliminary stages of a work toward a goal depends on how we characterize and judge the result. If you believe that the finished work is perfect, if you characterize the artist and the qualities of the work accordingly, you will undoubtedly discover along the way anticipations of the result, a movement toward the goal, a progress. On the other hand, if you raise critical questions as to the nature of the work, its character, if you see in its course not an anticipated unity but a struggle for unity, with elements of incompleteness and imperfection—and this you may find in the greatest works—then the process will assume another face. The same applies to characterization, which is not only of the complete result, but also of the meaning of its form—its particular expressiveness, its relation to the character of the image, which is the carrier of the meaning in both a poetic sense and the sense of everyday reality. We are imagining and contemplating through the work signified objects that we know and with reference to which we have ideas and interests. Besides this aspect of interpretation, there is the question of what is meant by the creative moment. It is possible, of course, to limit the concept of the creative moment to a single flash of understanding, the moment of discovery as an ideal, decisive instant within a long habitual process. It is much, then, like comparing the discovery made by a scientist, after much reflection and experimentation, with an artist's hitting upon an idea of form that will resolve a difficulty in composition. On the other hand, we may approach the concept of the creative moment as the more or less prolonged period of time during which something new is achieved; if we do that, we must recognize that the conditions at the start are important for what follows. Moreover, we suppose that changes in the surrounding conditions during the course of a work have a bearing on the subsequent stages, the failures, or the advances. Finally, all these become more intelligible according to our estimate of the value (the place and our sense of its character) of the final work. So we are involved in history, and not only the history of an individual; it is also of a community, since our grasp of the work, our idea of its very possibility of existence, would be different if the painting had been undertaken in the year 1938 or 1939 rather than 1937. I shall try to show how the creation of *Guernica* in the month of May 1937 is inseparable from certain conditions at that time in France, more particularly in Paris and in the circle of Pablo Picasso and his friends. In the work are many signs of these conditions; they affect not only the initial moves of the artist in undertaking it, but have also an important role in its final organization, its completion. I must add to these the importance of earlier experiences that have provided the painter—and this will hold true for anyone engaged in intellectual as well as artistic work—with the skills and models of action, the various means of coping with difficulties, that have given him a rich stock of ideas and forms that are at hand and that he can call upon. Of course only certain ones will be applied, and we shall understand why just these, in the light of the conditions of the moment, the personality, and the final outcome itself. The result guides us as a kind of boundary of the whole process that gives us some insight into what may be regarded as a latent tendency of the artist.

I wish to say at this point that in adopting such an approach I take the risk of imposing upon what is personal, complex, and known to us only indirectly (my own predispositions, interests, and way of thinking). Picasso himself has warned us against doing that. In a statement that has been published in the catalogue of the current exhibition in Paris, he says:

> Those who seek to explain a picture most often go astray. How can a spectator live a picture as I have lived it? How can one penetrate into my dreams, my instincts, my desires, my thoughts, which have taken so long to work themselves out and to come forth? And especially, how can one grasp what I have put into the work, perhaps in spite of my will?

Yet he would have been, I suppose, the first to recognize that he was often surprised by a result. Returning to works that he had done many years before, he viewed them in an altogether new light. If we intend not only to describe his work but to reconstitute the process, to imply, even if we do not assert it, certain tendencies or motives in the passage from one stage to another, we shall be moving in the dark ourselves—making doubtful guesses and conjectures. We can only hope that in the light of other facts that will emerge in the course of time, and in the light of our knowledge of the artist and other artists, even of the whole of modern art (that we do not start from but that we reach by a collective effort of studying, sifting, criticizing, matching one judgment with another), some of these features of the work will become clearer to us, and our reading of them more (or less) plausible. So I take this chance in dealing with the work. I must say, however, that although Picasso has challenged and discouraged others who tried to explain his work by denying it was possible to do so (he himself did not understand how the work came to be what it is), he took the trouble to assemble its stages as no artist in the past had ventured for a picture of his own. A few years before, he had permitted his friend Christian Zervos, the editor of *Les Cahiers d'Art*, to reproduce in their order of becoming the sketches for a finished painting and to comment on the intrinsic interest of such preparatory sketches for the understanding not only of the final canvas but of the artist's activity itself as a process stirring to one who responds to a work of art in its completed form. Other modern artists have expressed the same thought. Henri Matisse had a painting of his photographed in its successive stages and allowed those photographs to be exhibited, as if the documents of the gestation of a work were worth presenting beside the completed object. The poet Paul Valéry has written about sitting for a sculptured bust and watching the artist at work. He confessed he was more interested in her manipulations, her changes of mind, than he was in their outcome in the finished work. This concern with process has, of course, been a real ingredient of the modern artist's consciousness; he values to such an extent the process of making—and this has been recognized for two hundred years—that he will sometimes preserve in the finished work visible traces of underlying layers beside accidents of the brush and bare spots of the canvas, a succession of superimposed paintings in time, as if the whole were a palimpsest. *Guernica* is, therefore, a work that exists for us not only as a finished product but as a process in time, made visible through the photographs of its successive stages on the canvas, as well as through many preparatory sketches and studies and a remarkable series of "postscripts," drawings and small paintings of single parts. Seen together, they exhibit his creation as a struggle, a sum of destructions comparable to the suffering and violence in the subject of *Guernica*. Picasso couldn't do this with a Cubist work of 1912, which would have a more intellectual and technical interest—a kind of demimagic (or dramaturgic) process.

Let us turn to the actual situation in the making of the work (at least as it belongs to the historical record that we owe to the painter himself). Picasso in 1937 was the artist who more than any other of his time and perhaps in our whole tradition has sought out new problems; he has been happy with innovation and has been ready to change his way of working year after year and to follow out the consequences of a new idea far beyond what he could have imagined when he first conceived it. Nevertheless, when commissioned to paint a mural-sized work for the pavilion of the embattled Spanish Republic at the World's Fair, he reacted in a different way. As a type of project, Guernica, the theme he had chosen, was a novelty to him. Until then he had worked solely from his own initiative, so to speak, only rarely accepting a commission from outside, as in painting in 1917 a curtain for the ballet *Parade*, for which he also designed the costumes. But he had undertaken no large canvas with a theme of history or action or a subject proposed by someone else, and least of all for an official, public context. He might portray a friend, a member of his family, a poet, or a composer—individuals who belonged to his own world of art. But in undertaking to paint *Guernica*, he accepted a challenge without precedent in his past: a monumental painting with a political significance (and likely political impact). The Spanish Republic had honored him by appointing him director of the Prado, and he was bound to Spain not only by his birth but by ties with Spaniards in the past and at the moment of the Civil War. But for him to undertake a painting with a subject of this kind was a reversal of a long-held belief about the nature of his art. The year before he undertook this painting, Picasso, like many painters, poets, and novelists in France and elsewhere in Europe and America, had been solicited by the Communist Party and its sympathizers to place their art at the service of humanity by representing the realities of our time in a spirit of radical partisanship. His friend Zervos had criticized that appeal in writing about Picasso in 1936, just before the Spanish Civil War broke out. To paint such pictures, Zervos said, was to paint *faits divers*, commonplace events, the items that fill a few lines in a daily newspaper and have no importance beyond the moment. The artist can only paint, he said, from feeling, and only image what attracts him as a sovereign individual. The world of politics, of social interests and conflicts, all these are essentially foreign to the nature of art; for Zervos, it was as if the artist could have no feelings about a world beyond his immediate, personal relationships—his family, his loves, his friends, and his occupations, as if even these were not also subject, and often tragically, to the course of events.

This view was shared then by Picasso and other painters in France who were sympathetic to the Left and felt the great urgency of political partisanship at that time. Within a few months the Spanish Civil War broke out. During that period—from the summer of 1936 until May 1937 when he began to paint his picture—Picasso was in constant touch with Spaniards in Paris; and though accepting the directorship of the Prado as an honorary post, a sign of his support of the Republican government of Spain, he had produced no painting that alluded to those events or to that partisanship. His paintings were mainly of nudes and still lifes, works relating to the studio milieu, and with forms adapted from his preceding Cubist and figurative art. There was an exception: He had undertaken, in connection with the Spanish cause, the two etchings entitled *The Dreams and Lies of Franco*, on which I will comment later. But they were not finished and distributed until June 1937, when he had completed *Guernica*; and they were certainly affected in part by his experience in making that large and exceptional canvas. His identification with the political cause that was so important to him—even a matter of great anguish—did not excite in him the will to represent such subjects nor related symbols, a significant fact to which I shall return.

When he undertook to paint for the Spanish Pavilion of the World's Fair in Paris and chose the theme of Guernica, an old Basque town that had just been destroyed by German bombers—a choice fateful for the character of the painting—what was his first thought in conceiving the work? One may reconstruct it from the earliest sketches. Let us look at
Fig. 2 several of those drawings. In the first one (which he marked number 1 and dated the first of May, 1937), he drew rapidly and impulsively a

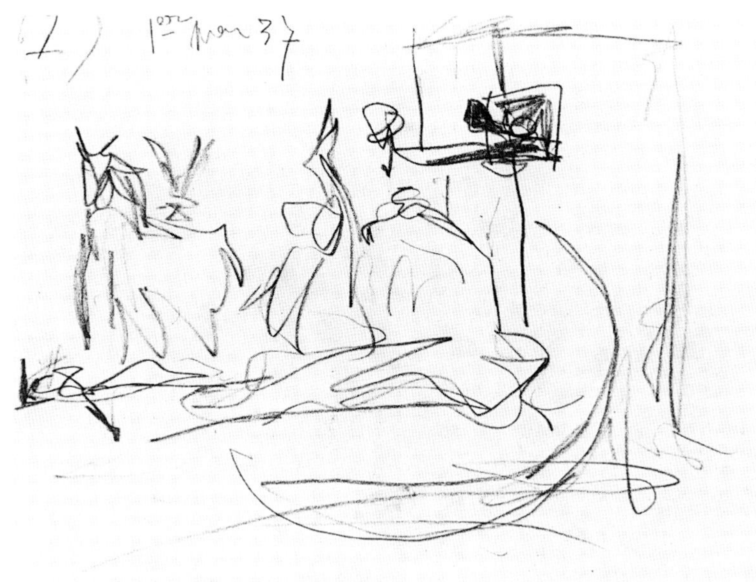

Figure 2. Sketch 1. *Composition Study for Guernica*, May 1, 1937, pencil on blue paper, 8¼ x 10⅝" (21 x 27 cm), Museo del Prado, Madrid.

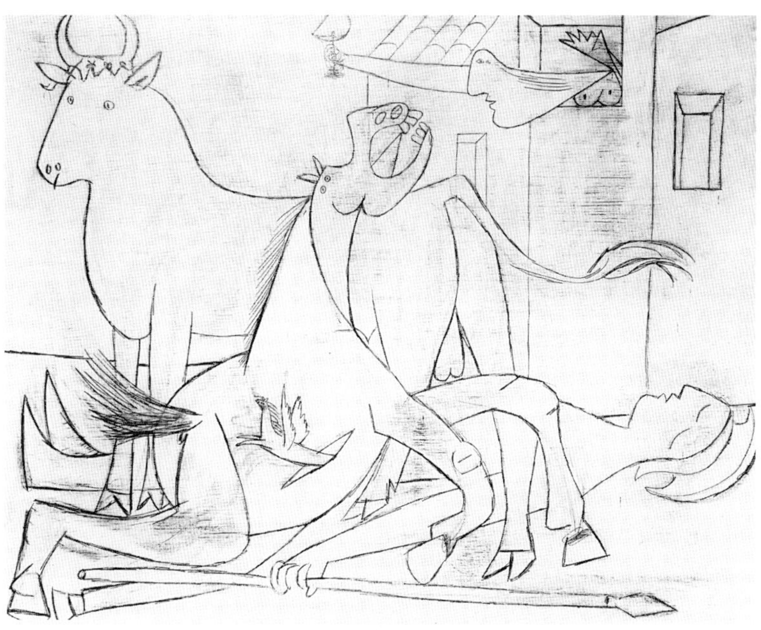

Figure 3. Sketch 6. *Composition Study for Guernica*, May 1, 1937, pencil on wood panel, 21⅛ x 25½" (53.7 x 64.8 cm), Museo del Prado, Madrid.

horse with a bird flying over its back; under the horse is a recumbent figure; a woman, holding a lamp, extends her arm from a window; and at the lower right, a big curve reminds us of the source of the main image, namely, the bullring—a theme Picasso had often drawn and painted in the preceding twenty years. The only addition to the bullfight scene as we know it from his past work is the extended arm of the woman, unlike an earlier picture of the woman with a lamp (which I shall discuss presently).

Fig. 3 Another sketch—really, more than a sketch, a considered drawing on wood—elaborates the scene more clearly. Here are two new features: a soldier instead of a bullfighter, but a soldier in Greek costume, an archaic type that transports the tragic theme of struggle and death to a literary, half-mythical world. We notice, too, that from a wound in the flank of the dying horse springs a little horse with wings. It is Pegasus.

Why Pegasus in *Guernica*? Pegasus is the mythical figure in Greek myth who has come to signify art; it has many beautiful meanings (to whoever reflects on its sense), allusive for Greek and later thought about the arts.[2] Pegasus is the winged horse that springs from the Gorgon Medusa's body when she is slain by Perseus. According to one legend, this flying creature is the offspring of Medusa and Zeus, or of the Gorgon's blood and the earth. Perseus is able to slay the Gorgon without being turned to stone by her fearful glance: He does not look at her directly but instead views her in a mirror given to him by Athena, the goddess of wisdom; or he looks at her image on his shining bronze shield. By looking at the image of reality, by not confronting reality directly, one is able to master it. Pegasus ascends, and with his hoof he stamps on Mount Helicon, the sacred site of the Muses; from the spot that he strikes issues a refreshing spring, the living water of the Muses. Pegasus is mounted then by Bellerophon, who is able to slay a monster, the Chimera, with the help of Pegasus. Pegasus is the creature who signifies art and is also the victor over monsters; he is himself the offspring of a monster's blood and the earth's soil. By placing this figure of Pegasus into a scene that symbolized the destruction of a sacred Spanish

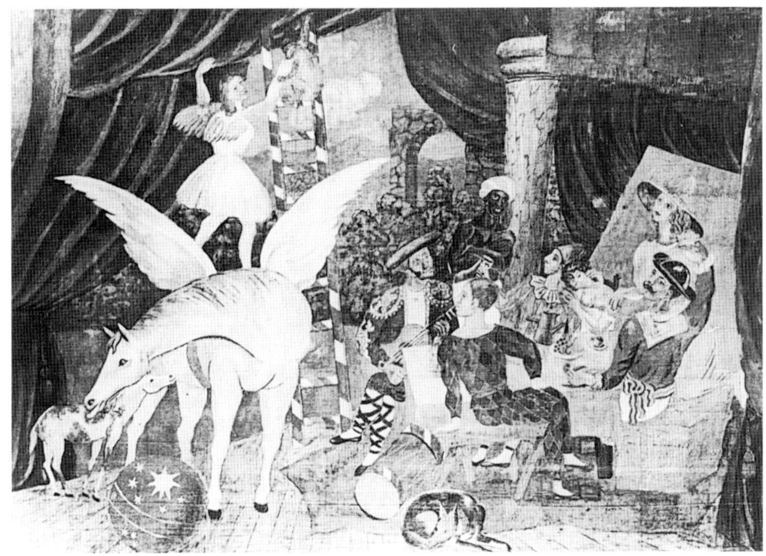

Figure 4. *Curtain for ballet "La Parade,"* 1917, tempera on canvas, 34'9$\frac{5}{16}$" x 56'7$\frac{1}{8}$" (10.60 x 17.25 m), Musée National d'Art Moderne, Centre Georges Pompidou, Paris.

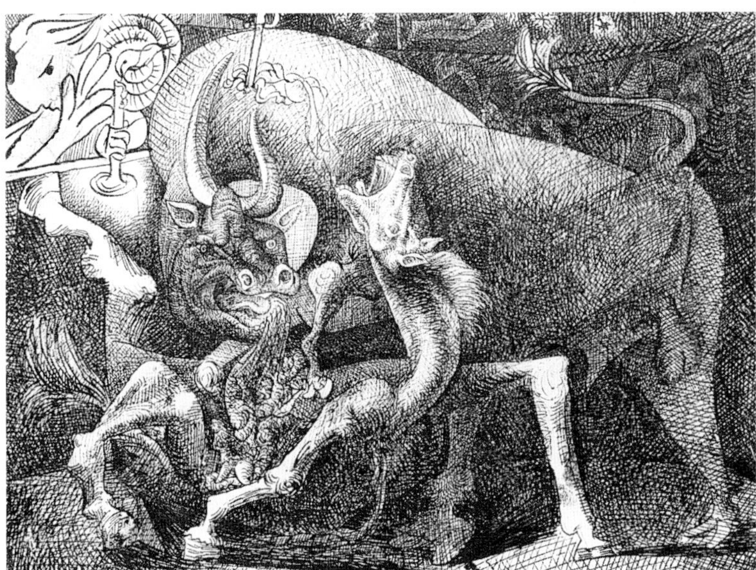

Figure 5. *Woman with a Candle, Fight between Bull and Horse,* July 24, 1934, pen and India ink, brown crayon on cloth pasted on plywood, 12$\frac{3}{8}$ x 16" (31.5 x 40.5 cm), Musée Picasso, Paris.

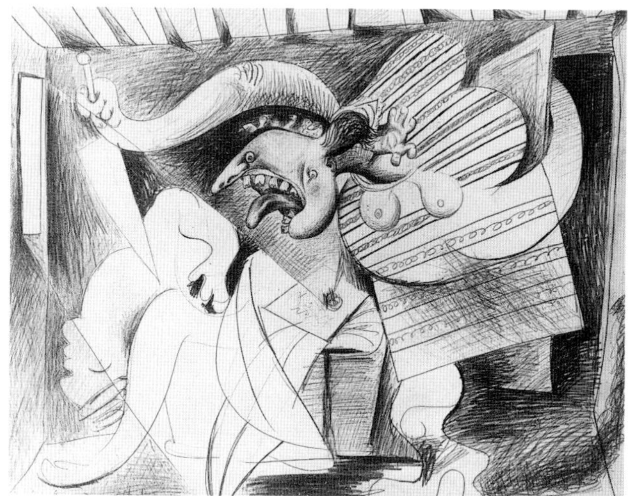

Figure 6. *The Murder (Death of Marat)*, July 7, 1934, pencil on paper, 15¾ x 19⅞" (39.8 x 50.4 cm), Musée Picasso, Paris.

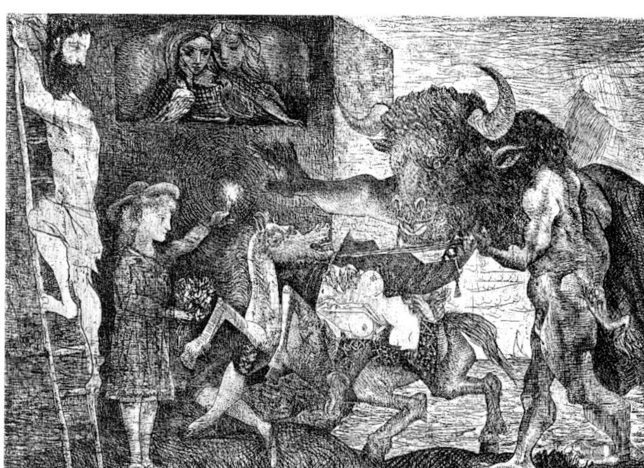

Figure 7. *Minotauromachy*, April 1935, etching and scraper, 19½ x 27⅜" (49.6 x 69.6 cm), The Museum of Modern Art, New York, Abby Aldrich Rockefeller Fund.

Figure 8. *Crucifixion*, February 7, 1930, oil on plywood, 19¾ x 25⅞" (51.5 x 65.5 cm), Musée Picasso, Paris.

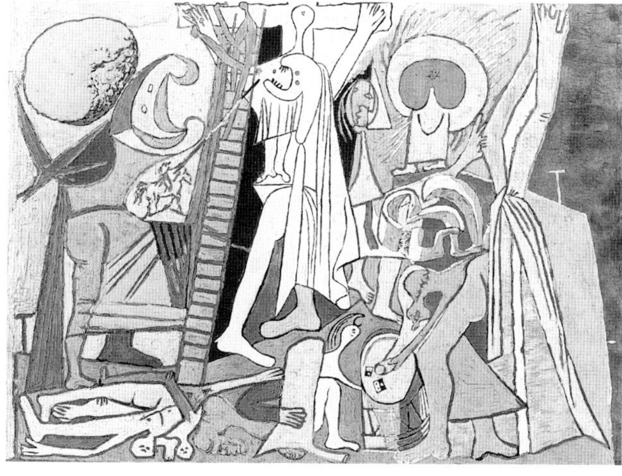

town, Picasso wishes to say, I suppose, that art will remain, even ascend, after that disaster, after the death of the horse.

Perhaps he was influenced, too, by a personal association: In Spanish, Pegasus is *Pégaso*, and the stab of a pike on the horse is called a *picazo* (the pike's stab). Since you may think this is just a piquant guess, I shall recall to you that when Picasso was asked why he changed his name from his father's Ruiz to Picasso (his mother's), he answered that not only was it less common—an unusual and foreign name—but it had two *s*'s in it, like Matisse and Poussin; he also said to his interviewer, Brassaï, "You, too, have adopted a name with two *s*'s in it." To him, names are clearly significant and important. The similarity of *Pégaso* and *picazo* to Picasso permits us to suppose that he in particular is able to invent an image that calls up an association relating to art and to the conquest of evil; Pegasus owes his origin to both evil blood and the earth (and was released from the dreaded mother by Perseus).

Picasso painted Pegasus once before, when he made the backdrop for the ballet *Parade* in 1917. On the left side is a winged horse, a mare, Fig. 4 however, with a young foal, and standing on Pegasus was the winged ballet dancer who was to become his wife. She points to a monkey that had climbed to the top of the ladder as part of the circus performance, perhaps a playful reference to himself as the "*simia naturae*." The ladder, Pegasus, and the woman are bound together in a personal fantasy that I do not venture to fathom; I only indicate its existence and note that these elements reappear together at a later time in other works.

I have said that in undertaking this commission to create a mural symbolizing a sensational, horrifying recent event and not just a personal experience—it concerns a nation and is a shock to the whole civilized world—he returns to the bullfight, which had been for him an absorbing, even an obsessive theme for twenty years in his preceding art. A drawing he had done of a bullfight in 1934 is so astonishingly like Fig. 5 his first thought for this new picture that we must pay more attention to it. Not only is the horse overwhelmed by the bull, but the bull is stabbed by a sword, and in the corner at the left is the girl with a lamp. If we pursue this subject in other works of the same period, we discover

that he has used the theme of the bull mangling the horse with a most intense rage, as if he wished to discharge an uncontainable anger against some creature—see the bull's immense horns and its tongue hanging down into the entrails of the disemboweled horse. The image springs from a will to destroy, an absolute personal hatred. It is not the Spanish bullring that has inspired this fantasy, but his own personal life; the evidence will appear in another drawing made in the same year. The crea-
Fig. 6 ture corresponding to the bull is an ugly, repulsive woman with an immense tongue; it spells imprecation and slander, the destructiveness of speech. She stabs a beautiful woman with a frightful instrument. Her unwholesome, demonic nature is marked by a heavy foot on a high heel; we shall see her costume again in *Guernica*.

How to explain this passionate imagery? I venture a guess suggested by the artist's biography in the catalogue of the current exhibition; next to the year 1934, in which this drawing was done, is the one event, "Difficultés conjugales." In the following year, when his wife refused to divorce him and he found a new mate, he represented in a magnificent etching—and outstanding one in the immense body of Picasso's prints—
Fig. 7 the scene that he called *Minotauromachy*, or the Battle of the Minotaur. I need not go into the sense of the Minotaur as a monstrous creature—it is evident to everyone—only I must add that Picasso had already identified the Minotaur as himself, and he had spoken of the bearded man as his father. In this work the Minotaur stands over a horse and a dying woman, a toreador who lies on the horse's back; beside this group stands a child holding a lamp and flowers; above, at the left, two girls with a dove look down from a window; and at the left a figure climbs a ladder (set against a wall of their house), a type one sees often in Spanish seventeenth-century popular art; it is Christ about to mount the cross. What does all this mean? It suggests a family history, a scene from private life enacted by figures of myth, religion, and the bullring, a tragic moment in which the horror of sudden death evokes also memories of childhood and love. The artist is satisfied to be able to express through fantasy intense anger and strain in a great image where every detail is an object of thought and emotion and from which an arresting, beautiful whole emerges.

One cannot ignore this work as a factor in the series of stages of *Guernica*. We understand better from it that the core of the large picture of *Guernica* was a direct transposition of an imagined scene symbolizing the most intimate and personal aspects in the artist's private world in a shocking, terrifying public event. He did not reconstruct that event in its material details; nor did he try to relive or reenact precisely how those other Spaniards had died; nor did he show the German bombers in action. He transported to the space of the canvas the objects of his immediately preceding fantasy of himself and his family, and the animal analogs of his own rage, anxiety, and feelings about death; and he tried to build with them an image that would have a meaning to others beyond his own personal situation.

Another painting, dated 1930, is the *Crucifixion*. It was inspired by an earlier work of art but was radically changed from the old version, a work in which that ladder appears prominently. In the *Crucifixion*, too, we observe elements of the ferocious, the sadistic, in the deformed human body; the great weight of the limbs, enlarged beyond any perspective requirement; we sense it as contributing to the strained effect of the body in a spasm of pain. Here, too, are fallen figures, broken and extended limbs, enormously prolonged gestures, excited and passionate, in the corners of the space. It is a tiny picture in strong colors, very different in range of shapes and relationships from the final *Guernica*. Fig. 8

So far, I have spoken about the subjects of the first studies for *Guernica* as themes from life rather than from forms, though one cannot ignore the shapes altogether in discerning the sense of a theme. The motifs of action present great forceful thrusts of line, a restless complexity of shapes, contrasts of the left and right, the top and lower part of the work, which are effective for expression and provide the energy of increment. Picasso returns here to a particular sense of form. In one stage, at the lower left are two extended severed arms that do not look quite human—they are cut too cleanly—and between them is a head that also seems to be cut mechanically. These are dissections or dismemberments of the body, in which no blood flows; the parts exist fully detached as separable inorganic entities. He had already conceived these

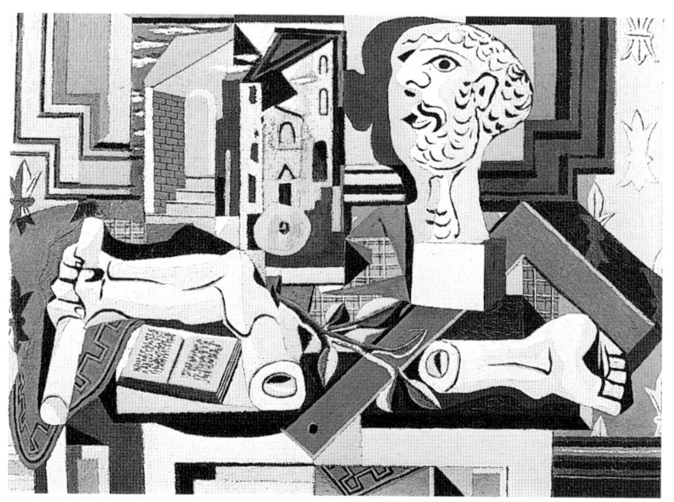

Figure 9. *Studio with Plaster Head*, summer 1925, oil on canvas, 38⅝ x 51⅝" (98.1 x 131.2 cm), The Museum of Modern Art, New York. Purchase.

Fig. 9 forms in 1925 in large still lifes, such as the *Studio with Plaster Head*, where we recognize the same limbs spread out, one of them clutching a staff or rod; above is an isolated head. These are plaster casts, studio props, not the organic living body. They belong, we may say, to the realities of art. He places them in correspondence and in a dense, divided field with so many contrasts of shapes and rivalry of abrupt tones that we sense the whole as a continuous clatter. He inserts in this stratified horizontal-vertical field a T square, a triangle. Forms like these appear in several places in *Guernica*, also associated with dismemberment—in one case a dismemberment arising from the earlier Cubist play with single stokes or lines. It is as if, having detached from a drawing the single straight lines, curves, and other marks that are no longer seen as parts of the body, and therefore not properly called dismembered, these become elements of the medium—the paint, the brush, and the surface—rather than of represented objects. They are marks rather than mimetic signs. Having given them value as signs, they retain as signs some of the qualities of the isolated units that had appeared in his Cubist phase. Besides that figure from earlier art, he applies in *Guernica* another, or a rather different artistic and expressive sense, and particularly in the drawings and paintings made on the way. (In painting *Guernica*, he has reserved certain discoveries for separate pictures, just as a scientist in the course of investigation may observe a relationship or phenomenon that he proposes to study separately.) Among these postscripts to *Guernica* are several paintings no less impressive and powerful than *Guernica*. I have already cited the one with the isolated horse's head.

I digress now to speak of this head. A central feature of Picasso's representation of feeling emerges here more clearly than in any other work. Fig. 10 It is this: In depicting pain, he shows the insides of the body. The pain is perceived not only in the posture, it is expressed through the agonized response of the body's interior. We see the mucous parts, the palate, the tongue fully exposed; even the undersurfaces of the teeth are visible. On the face, the texture of the skin, its hairiness, all that belongs to the close-lying surface becomes tangible. To realize that effect, Picasso resorts to a new proportioning of the inwardly sensed body. Just as in a toothache one side of the mouth feels much bigger than the other, so in these pains one part of the face feels larger, more strained, in sharper spasm. Other features become recessive and tiny: The passive eyes, which bring us the surrounding world, are secondary and cease to function as visual organs. What we feel most as our own bodies, the inner somatic sensations, the physiological, is made more visible. To render

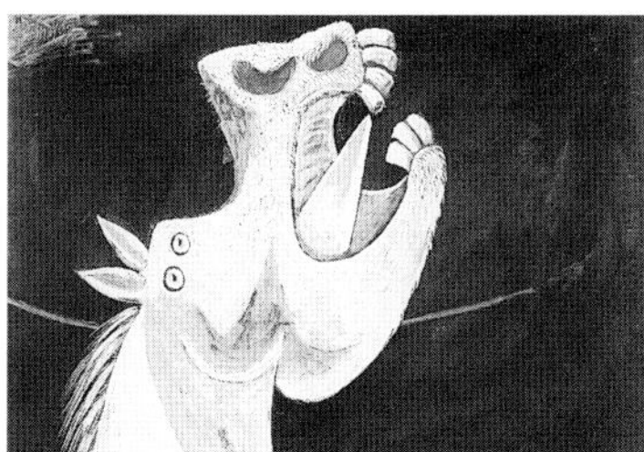

Figure 10. *Horse in Agaony*, May 2, 1937, oil on canvas, 25½ x 36¼" (65 x 92.1 cm), Museo del Prado, Madrid.

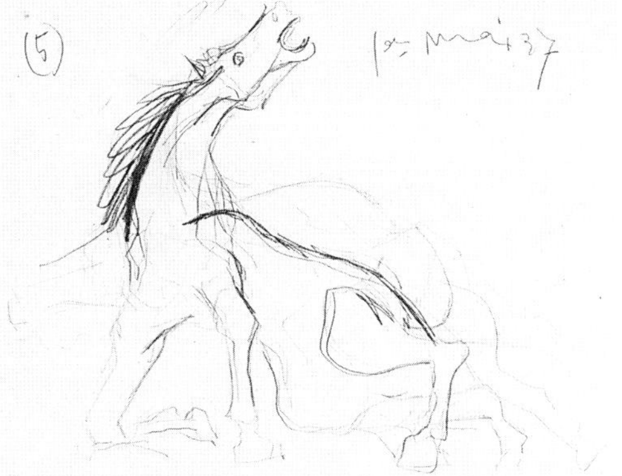

Figure 11. Sketch 5. *Study for Horse*, May 1, 1937, pencil on blue paper, 8¼ x 10½" (21 x 26.8 cm), Museo del Prado, Madrid.

this experience more intense, he contrives, within that pronounced contrast of white against black (a chalky white and an absolute black), the shadows on the inner jaw and on the neck and divides the neck into big contrasting areas, one white and sharply triangular and the other roughly triangular, complementary to it, and blunted. On the jaw and cheek, a black triangle with two wings, forms that echo the rigidity and sharp point of the tongue, the shadow on the nose beside the nostril, which inverts the triangle of the tongue, and the subdivision of the open mouth into related symmetric areas—all of these form a scale of poignant elements that we see as a powerful coherent whole. They are not derived directly from observation but come from an imagination that dwells on the rigid and spasmodic in the human organism as felt from within. This form, already half anticipated in a different guise in a
Fig. 11 picture of 1907, is found also in a study for *Guernica* that does not exhibit these features; it has its own convincing pathos and naturalism of movement, but it does not force upon us the agony as a sensation endured by the horse internally. It is an evisceration, an extrusion of the inner-bodily sensations of the suffering creature.

In the painting of the nude of 1907, a subject altogether remote from
Fig. 12 the horse, it might occur to one that behind this strange figure lies also a latent feeling like the stricken animal's pain. Picasso had discovered here, perhaps through the example of African tribal art, a new force of expression in treating part of the face as a triangular shadow that resonates in the void between the arm and the face. We see these two shapes together; in their likeness they are coupled harmonically and expressively, each referring to the other. The reserved hollow reappears again between the legs and in patterned areas below; that sharp, angular form fills the body in several other parts and also determines the zigzag cascading of the curtain. Here the conception of a distinct large unit, which is repeated in rotation throughout the whole, is not conceived to make a pleasing ornament but rather becomes the argument of an intensified feeling or mood that is connected with a derangement of the body. There is a strong note of trouble in it: The eyes are not a level pair, with a common axis; they cannot focus; they will not produce

corresponding images. The nose is cut, the mouth is twisted off axis, and the lower body strangely deformed, though it is of a dancer, a figure normally graceful with supple command of its limbs. In Picasso's art, the association of these two themes is maintained already in a remarkably consistent way.

Another example is the *Weeping Woman* of June 26, 1937, which came out of *Guernica*—a far more moving version of the two; it is poignant and superior to the heads at the sides of the large canvas. Her mouth is exposed as a deep cavity, disclosing the ungainliness of the large teeth in this intense pain with even more power. Most remarkable of all is the distorted drawing of the organs of sense. The ear is turned backward, it cannot hear; the eyes are twisted, deranged, and pricked by the hairs of the eyelids, drawn as little darts or arrows directed inward. The painful sensation of the eye is referred not to a blow from outside but to a shock from within, to internal stresses and tensions. The added diagonal and descending lines, altogether arbitrary, look like the path of tears falling grotesquely; but we may also suppose a suggestion from a source in a diagram the artist might have seen of the crossing of the optic nerves; they seem to bring the hidden nerve structure to view on the surface of the head and make it visible, not as an apparatus of vision in relation to the external world but as the unstable cross pattern of suffering and destruction. So, too, the nostrils are shifted from the smooth, elegantly rounded forms of the other pictures to angular, sharply pointed openings—signs of disturbing sensations, a dislocation in the normal, ordered, symmetric structure of the sense passage. Picasso has achieved here what Arthur Rimbaud, in another writer, called "derangement of the sense"—not, however, as the condition of inspired visionary experience of a transcendent or occult sphere but rather as the result of an overwhelming shock, a real torture of the human being who cannot for the moment see or hear, knowing only its inner state of blinding pain. It is, as I have said, a largely physical state detached from perception of its objective outer cause and circumstance. Picasso was prepared by his Cubist work for that freedom in rearranging and deranging the senses; he had, with that extraordinary daring

Fig. 13

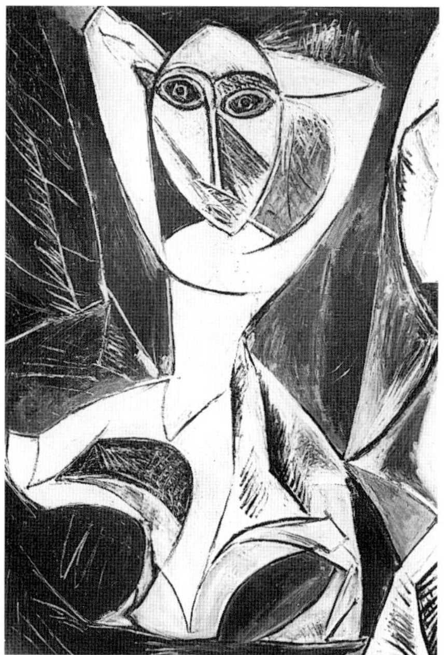

Figure 12. *Nude with Raised Arms*, spring–summer 1907, oil on canvas, 59⅛ x 39½" (150 x 100 cm), Private collection.

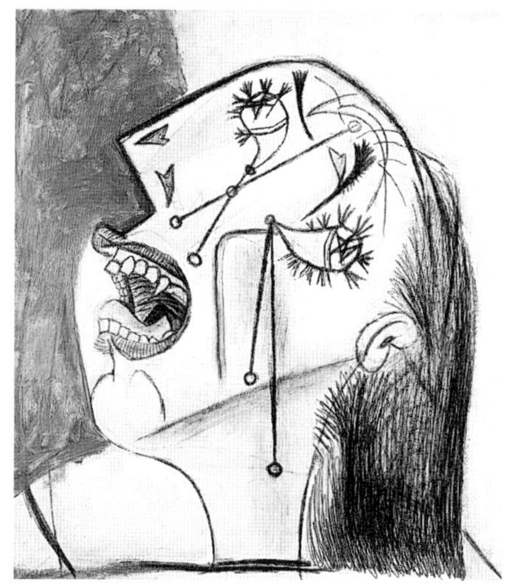

Figure 13. *Weeping Woman*, June 26, 1937, gouache and color crayon on canvas, 21⅝ x 18⅛" (55 x 46 cm), The Museum of Modern Art, New York.

that initiated a new kind of painting in our century, already drawn a head by isolating its contours as discontinuous lines or strokes, and adding (and crossing them with) others, without a necessary sign-reference or meaning, while retaining a vague allusion to a submerged starting point in an original head through vestigial circles and angles, and the suggestion of a neck. He could not have moved from that art to the poignant somatic (physiological) reality of *Guernica* without a subject matter that called for the disturbing representation of intense pain. Here we see how absurd it is to generalize, as some have done, that one picture produces the next, that a new art comes about from the painter's meditation on a preceding work or style of art rather than from a new situation or experience. If that were the case, it would be altogether mysterious how Picasso could have moved on, through the aesthetic basis or from the play with the artistic matter itself, from that Cubist conception of the head to the later work, though the second presupposes the first.

Fig. 14

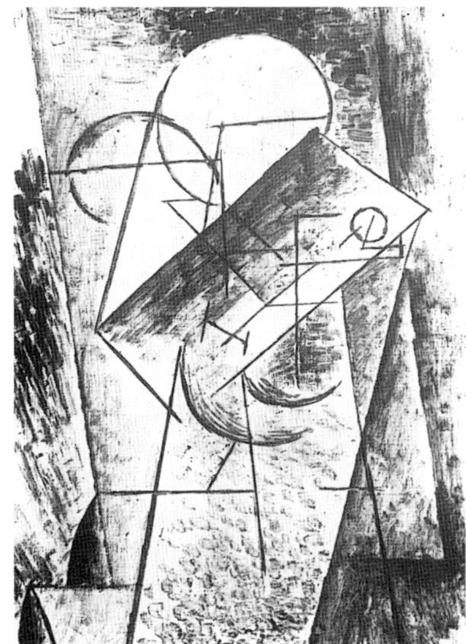

Figure 14. *Head*, late 1912 or early 1913, oil on canvas, 21⅝ x 15" (55 x 38 cm), Private collection, Westport, Eire.

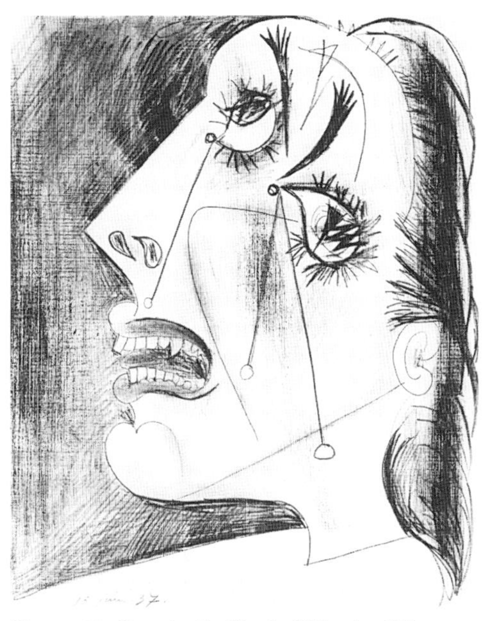

Figure 15. Sketch 48. *Head of Weeping Woman*, June 13, 1937, pencil, colored crayons, and gouache, 11½ x 9¼" (29.2 x 23.5 cm), Museo del Prado, Madrid.

I have said that this postscript is one of the most gripping results of the work on *Guernica*. I should like, as far as it is possible, to confirm such a judgment of pictures, by comparing it with another version of the same idea by Picasso. In this drawing the mouth retains its natural symmetry—a dull form, lacking in pathos. The conception of these lines has far less interest and strength; you have only to compare the nostrils as drawn elements with the others to make the difference clear. The silhouetting against the background in this drawing will appear obvious, even banal, when set beside the other work. We see Picasso's self-criticism at work; he has been impelled not only by a requirement of coherent form but also by a mimetic goal, the goal of an emotion to be depicted, for which an effective expression or correspondence had to be realized in the tension and rhythm of accented shapes and contrasts of light and shade. Fig. 15

Let us return to Picasso's work on the large canvas. One of the remarkable facts about the execution of the final picture is that, after so

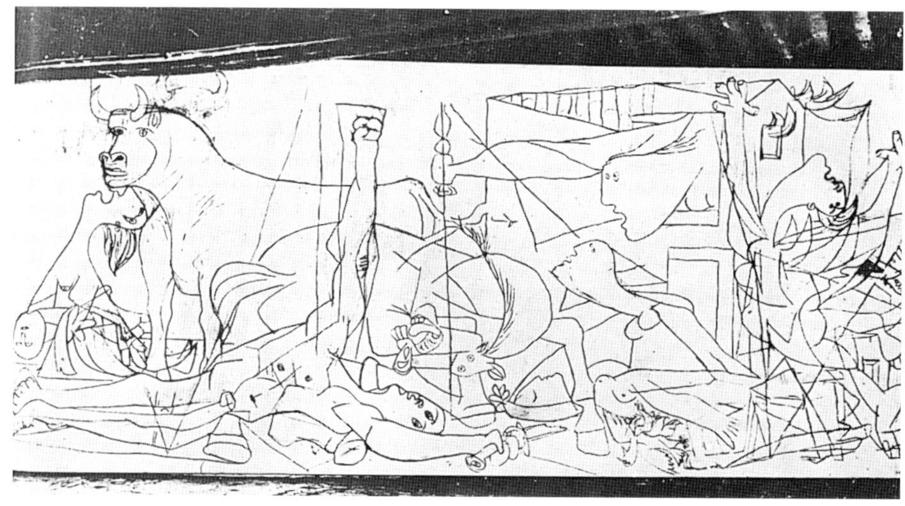

Figure 16. *Guernica* (1st state), May 11, 1937. Photograph by Dora Maar.

Fig. 16 many sketches and detailed drawings on paper and board, the first drawing on the canvas underwent so many changes in the course of the painting. In the past the work on a wall or mural-sized canvas was not usually begun until the artist felt sure he had reached his final composition; he did not alter the composition so drastically with brush in hand as did Picasso in *Guernica*. One could imagine this happening on a small canvas executed *alla prima*, but on a work of the scale of *Guernica* that would be exceptional. When the artists of the Renaissance were certain of the Fig. 17 final form of so large a painting, they traced a grid of lines over a drawing on paper and directed assistants to enlarge and transfer grid and drawing to the wall or canvas, outlining the whole composition, which could then be completed by the artist himself. When we compare the photograph of the first state on Picasso's canvas with the fifth and nearly final state, we are struck above all by his continuing self-criticism and corrections. He is like a general who, having planned a strategy, is able to plan freshly in the midst of battle, to maneuver his troops in new ways, to call them back, bring more to one wing, withdraw some from another, and continue to command fresh moves up to the last stage of the battle. Eugène Delacroix, in a comment on the problem of retouching, compared the artist to the general. "One can't know in advance what the finished picture will be, even though one has an approximate idea of

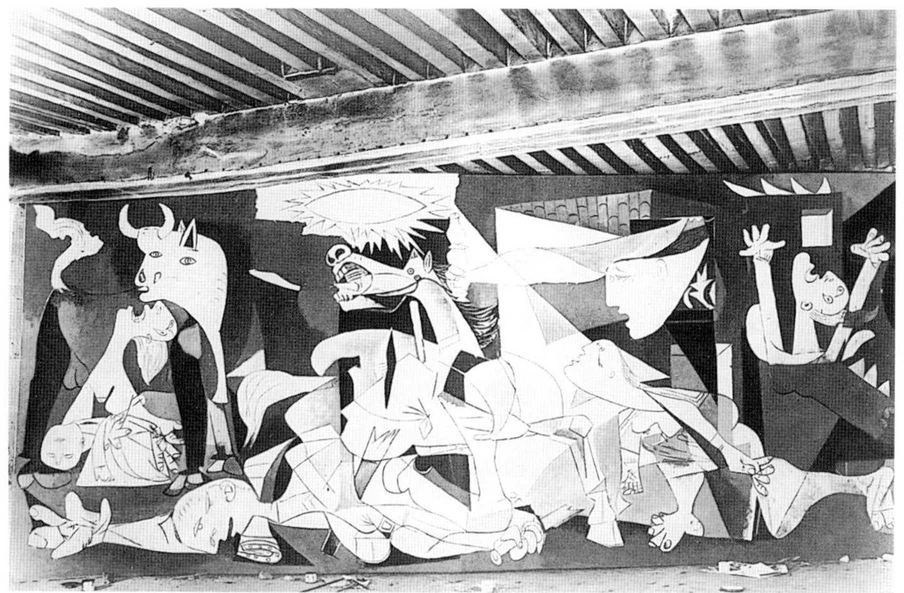

Figure 17. *Guernica* (5th state), May 27–June 4, 1937. Photograph by Dora Maar.

it at the start. . . . There are so many things one has to take into account." And then, citing the example of Napoleon: "He conceives the best possible plan of a battle, but with every incident that arises in the course of the action, he sprouts a new idea. 'It's beyond understanding,' cries the enemy, 'Napoleon offers you battle in one way and wins it in another.' But," added Delacroix, "he wins it! he wins it! that's the essential."[3]

Let us consider the lower part of the first stage. On the left side, the legs of the fallen soldier are extended to the left and the right arm is stretched upward. The head is turned upward. This stage, reached after a dozen trial drawings of different positions, was changed in the course of painting, in a surprising way. The head was shifted from the middle to the far left; the legs were eliminated entirely; a second arm, which had been raised to the top of the picture, is finally brought down, its hand, at first a clenched fist, is opened and extended. It is as if the artist were directing a plan and continually changing his instructions to the actors up to the last rehearsals, even after the first performance. Picasso rejudges his scene with sovereign assurance and replaces or reorders parts in a most drastic way, not simply through small retouches that refine a detail, but with great bold shifts that other painters would not dream of risking in the final stages of so large a work. He not only brings the high fist down, but raises the horse's head to the top from below. And the body of the bull, while maintaining the same position of the head, is turned around 180 degrees; his hind parts are now near the edge of the canvas. Equally radical changes are made in the figures of the women and especially the one who seems to dance like a maenad under the burning roof—she recalls one of his earlier figures of dancers. That liberty in treating figures as if they were freely disposable unity—like the lines in Picasso's earlier Cubist paintings—is unthinkable without his long experience of Cubist painting. They are not abstract forms, however, but the forms of bodily parts, detachable members that can be separated from the rest of the body and placed above, below, left, right, middle, or anywhere.

On the advanced version of the canvas, he resorts to another device, the persistent variation of small paired elements. It is clearest in the bull's head, with its two horns, two ears, two eyes, two nostrils, two lips—in each coupling the symmetry is a different pattern. In no pair do we see quite the same relation of size, interval, and axis. The eyes are tilted downward, the nostrils have another turn. The nostrils of the horse are different from those of the bull, the teeth in two sets (three against four), the little eyes, different again from the eyes of the bull, two ears of another shape, rounded and pointed rather than triangular. The eyes of the woman below the bull are paired horizontally. The bull's testicles are, like the breasts of the woman, another coupling. The tail and mane of the horse are like the woman's falling hair, the same substance but distinct in both, yet reminding us vaguely of each other. The man's hand is outstretched, the horseshoe is contracted, but both are marked by lines that invite interpretation as vaguely significant—contrasted symbols of destiny. Such devices of variation appear throughout the work, and always with an obvious coupling and equally obvious distinction—so frequent as to appear almost mechanical, a habit of work. I do not regard that as more than a device; it does not in itself contribute greatly to the expressive character of the whole or to its fullest meaning. It belongs to a mode of composition that in France was called, since the eighteenth century, a machine; large compositions are complex machines that are set up and tightened; the screws and bolts and nuts are inserted in the right places, and everything holds together; all builds up to the stable triangle or a slightly labile one. You can read the whole; there is no mystery in such conceptions; they belong to the mechanics of composition.

Another example of such correspondence: the woman in the burning house, whose hands form little projecting tongues; above are the analogous zigzags of the flame. While her arms are raised toward these flames, the woman beside her lets her arms fall and her two hands are opposed. The effect here is somewhat harsh, brusque, and cold. That is partly a calculation, I think; the painter, having to fill the large field and sensing the voids as a challenge to his desire to create a pervasive emotional stress, a sustained vehemence of expression throughout, continues to fill all points. It is not the primitives' habit of ornamental design but serves a conception of overwhelming violence, of outcry; in all these heads, the mouth is open, even of the dead and the dying. It is this that leads him to stabilize the whole, by isolating at the extreme left and right larger groups in contrasted patterns. Between them, in the middle of the field, the horse is more broken and chaotic, less distinct but also more agonized. This, I believe, is the expressive sense of the composition.

The repetitious quality, the somewhat mechanical compulsion in the constant assertion of the same affect, will be more evident if we compare Picasso's use of gesticulation with a figure of equally poignant character, in Piero della Francesca's *Crucifixion* in Urbino. The Virgin Mary raises her hands in anguish to Christ. She cries out to him; her two arms become one and branch into what seems a single hand with ten fingers. A similar tremor of feeling appears also in the rhythmical folds of Christ's loincloth, a softened reflection of the stark gesture of the Virgin' s hands that breaks through the massive, stable form. On the other side, John's hand extends outward and produces again a break in his compact form—a hand in fullest tension repeated in the folds of his robe but also contrasted with a compact form on one side, a broken one

Fig. 18

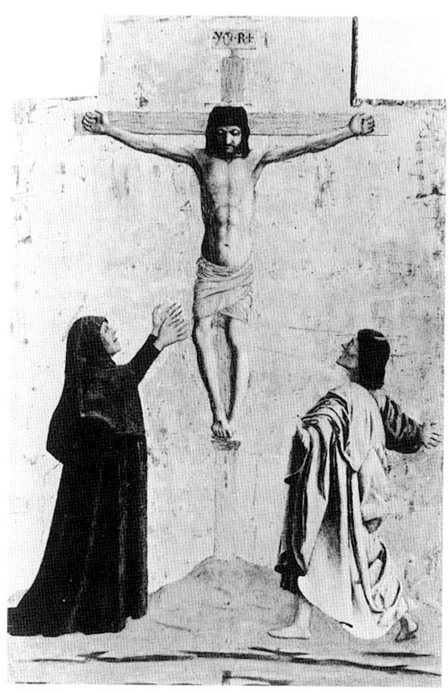

Figure 18. Piero della Francesca, *Crucifixion*, c. 1445–60, from *Madonna della Misericordia*, polyptych, oil and tempera on panel, 31⅞ x 22 7/16"(81 x 57 cm), Pinacoteca Comunale, Borgo Sansepolcro.

on the other, with much empty space. Though ordinarily so restrained and stable in his forms, Piero displays here a deeper sense of drama than Picasso, an artist of striking vehemence and force. Picasso's drama is clamorous, crying, howling throughout the canvas; he allows no rest for the spectator. He stuns you wherever you look; Piero, by contrast, not a dramatic or tragic artist, is able to conceive those two gestures within the boundaries of nature, which beget at a certain point the most extreme anguish, emerging from bodies that preserve their stability, their normal axis. It is of a nobler order of imagination and design than the segment of *Guernica* at the right.

I should like to consider the sense of the whole as a political image addressed to the world. There is, of course, much more to be said about the work. But I shall venture a description of the work in relation to the theme as proclaimed through the title *Guernica* and its destination as a mural for the Spanish Pavilion in 1937, during the Civil War. One could easily imagine a painting of the "event" Guernica, in which an enemy is identified and the issues of brutality and suffering are located in a time and place. Picasso chose rather to convey the shock of the event and his protest through an image of animal as well as human victims, a universal suffering. His attitude depended, I believe, on the political situation in France at that moment. We must turn back to the early spring of 1937, before the bombing of the town. In those months, the outcome of the Spanish Civil War had begun to appear increasingly hopeless; for many who had been drawn by a liberal outlook and humanitarian feeling to support the Loyalist government as the democratically elected regime, the accounts of events in Spain, of the role of Communists, the involvement of Russia, Italy, and Germany, had led to anxiety and disillusionment. The confession trials in Moscow also created doubts of the sincerity of the Russian government's commitment to truth and justice. The reports of massacres by both sides and of the destruction of churches had made French Catholics, who were at first friendly to the Republican government, less eager to speak in its defense or to express sympathy for it. There was also dissension among the Left because of repression by Communists at the front in Catalonia, which George Orwell described in his *Homage to Catalonia*. In France and elsewhere the original sympathy for the legitimate Spanish government was beginning to wane. When Guernica was bombed, there was an immediate resurgence of indignant feeling; Catholics, especially Georges Bernanos, spoke out strongly condemning the fascist leader, Francisco Franco, and his Moorish troops as enemies of mankind and not only of the Spanish Republic. The fact that the invited German planes had destroyed Guernica, an ancient religious capital of the Basque Province (the Basques themselves had won sympathy because of their separateness, their desire for autonomy, as well as for their opposition to Franco)—all this revived the sentiment for the Loyalist cause. At the same time the Communist Party proposed for the defense of Republican Spain antifascist rather than revolutionary slogans. Writers and painters were urged to support the Spanish Loyalist government in the name of humanity and justice without political scrutiny. There

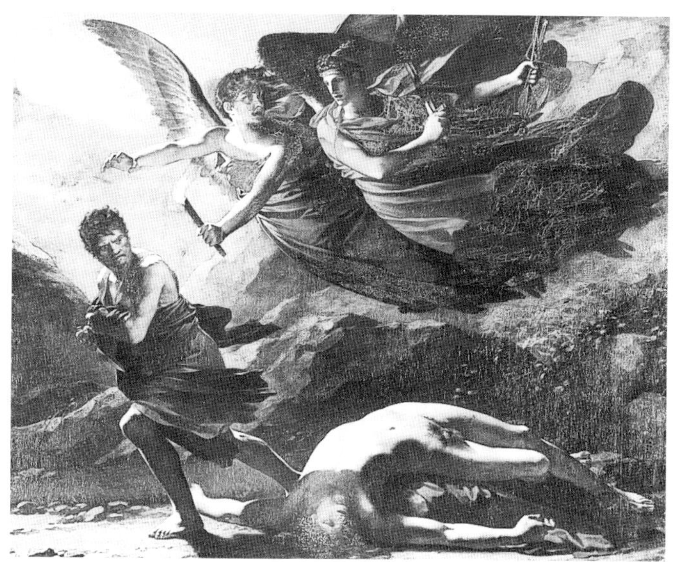

Figure 19. Pierre-Paul Prud'hon, *Justice and Divine Vengeance Pursuing Crime*, 1808, oil on canvas, 7'11⅝" x 9'7" (2.34 x 2.92 m), Musée du Louvre, Paris, Département des Peintures (INV 7340).

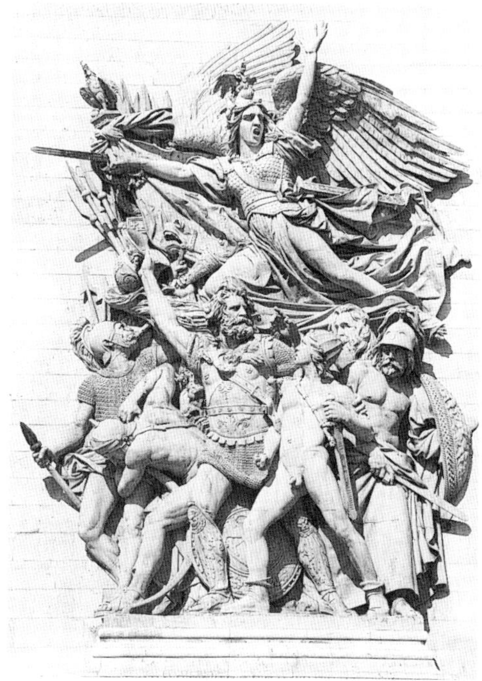

Figure 20. François Rude, *"La Marseillaise" (Departure of the Volunteers in 1792)*, 1833–36, stone relief, c. 42 x 26' (12.80 x 7.92 m), Arc de Triomphe, Paris.

arose then, typically, under the Popular Front in France a conception of the Civil War as a struggle between light and darkness, the lovers and the enemies of humanity. It was more and more depoliticized, at least in the appeals made to people of goodwill to back the victims of Nazi terror in Guernica. In that context, and with the state of mind in Paris in April and May 1937, we can grasp the aptness of a painting called *Guernica* in which the theme of suffering was made the chief vehicle of the message and of the Spanish Republicans' point of view. If such a work had been proposed earlier or in another period, it is less likely to have had the same impact. Another factor in the response was the readiness of those who wished to influence painters and sculptors toward a politically effective art to eliminate revolutionary political slogans from that art and to regard the commitment as one to general ideals of democracy, humanity, and goodwill, without reference to Communist or Socialist aims. In this atmosphere, much was written in that vein; André Malraux's *L'Espoir*, a novel about the war in Spain, is an example. Essentially apolitical, it was addressed especially to those who regarded politics and art as incompatible but approved a concern with suffering and justice as an admissible content of art.

In the situation I have outlined, certain works of French art of the nineteenth century, symbolizing justice, protest, victimization, heroic resistance, and revolt—works that stood in Paris prominently and were known to everyone—entered into the conception of *Guernica*. In the Louvre was Pierre-Paul Prud'hon's painting of *Justice and Divine Vengence Pursuing Crime* (1808), with a dead figure below and a Fig. 19
woman holding a torch in her extended arm. Another example is François Rude's great sculpture *The Marseillaise* on the Arc de Fig. 20
Triomphe, with the volunteers marching to the front in 1792: A woman with outstretched hand holds a sword, under her you see the horse's head with open mouth and exposed teeth, and above them the great zigzag of the wings and the weapons. How did these come into Picasso's picture? Is it by chance, or is it a coincidence? Do similar situations stimulate artists to invent corresponding symbolic figures of heroic will, of illumination and moral truth? In any case, it is to this

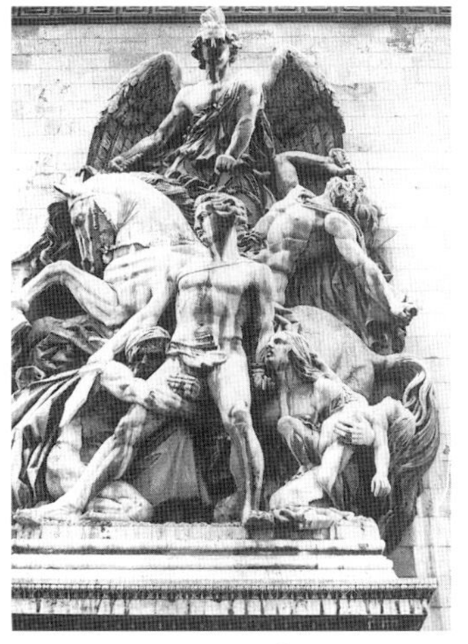

Figure 21. Antoine Étex, *La Resistance* (1814), stone relief, Arc de Triomphe, Paris.

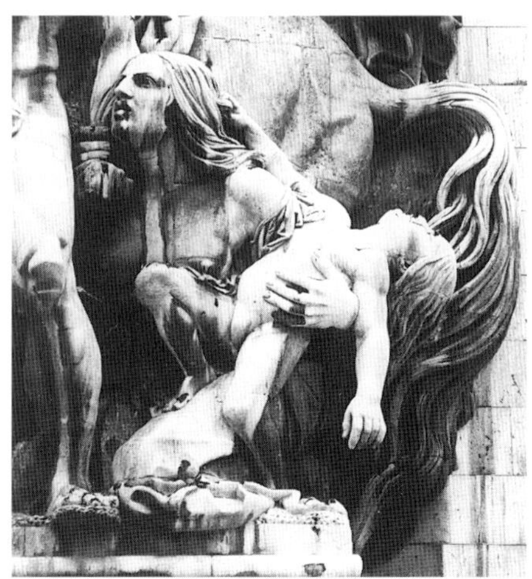

Figure 22. Detail of fig. 21.

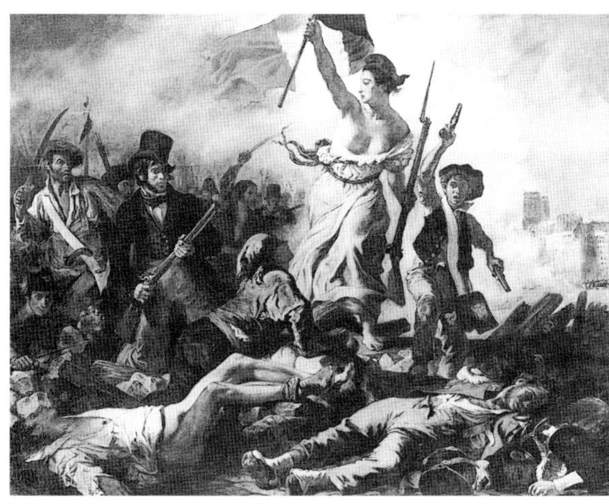

Figure 23. Eugène Delacroix, *Liberty Leading the People*, 1830, oil on canvas, 8' 5¾ x 10' 6" (2.60 x 3.25 m), Musée du Louvre, Paris.

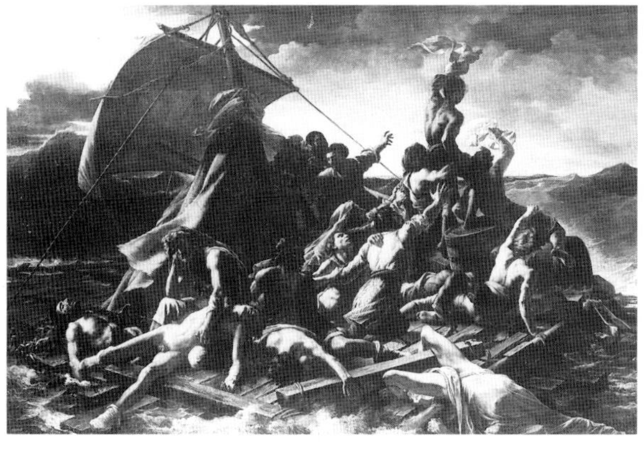

Figure 24. Théodore Gericault, *Raft of the "Medusa,"* 1818–19, oil on canvas, 16' 1¼ x 23' 4⅞" (4.91 x 7.16 m), Musée du Louvre, Paris.

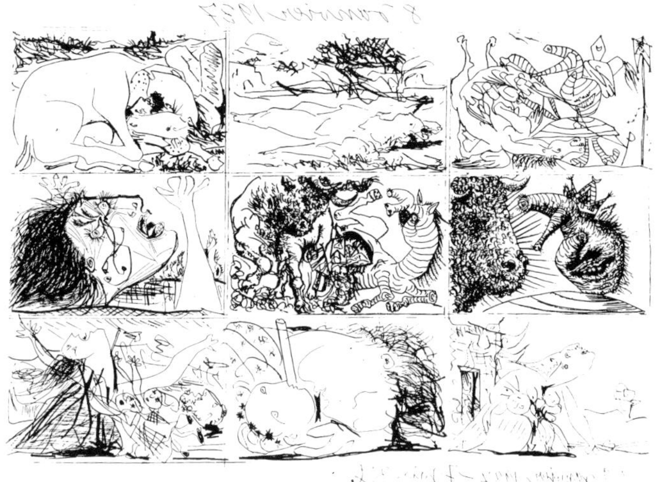

Figure 25. *Dream and Lie of Franco, II*, January 8–9, June 7, 1937, etching and lift-ground aquatint, 12⅜ x 16 $^{9}/_{16}$" (31.4 x 42.1 cm), The Museum of Modern Art, New York. The Louis E. Stern Collection.

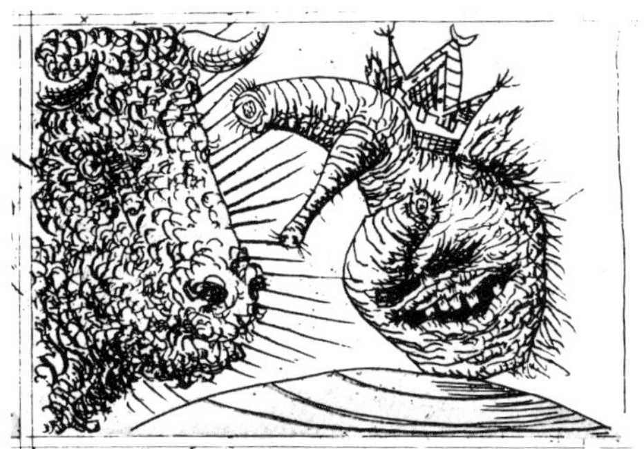

Figure 26. Detail of fig. 25.

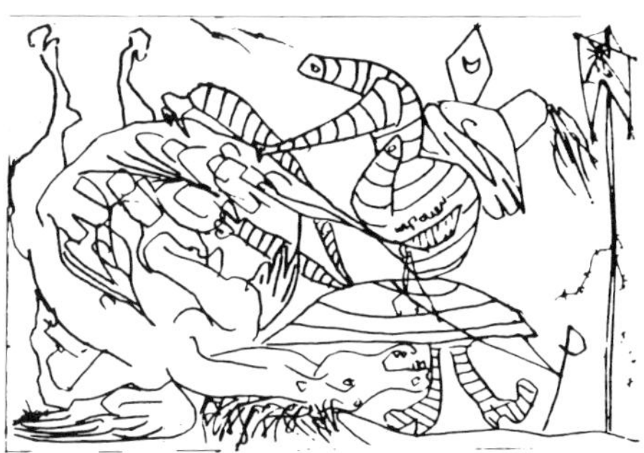

Figure 27. Detail of fig. 25.

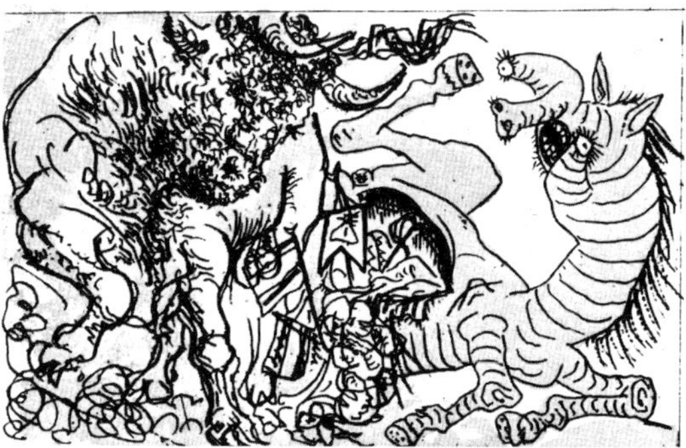

Figure 28. Detail of fig. 25.

kind of image that we turn for parallels to certain figures of *Guernica*.
A second, less-known example is on the other side of the Arc de
Figs. 21-22 Triomphe: a dull group by the sculptor Antoine Étex. At the base
beside the horse and tail, is a woman with her dead child. Another
Fig. 23 example in the Louvre is Delacroix's *Liberty Leading the People*, where
we see the woman with the arms outstretched holding the flag, the
dying fighters, and the kneeling figure who looks upward like the
woman raising her head to the light in *Guernica*. Still another great
Fig. 24 example in the Louvre is Théodore Géricault's *Raft of the "Medusa,"* a
painting of protest against the Restoration regime, accused of responsibility for the fate of the sailors abandoned at sea by officers of the royal navy. The dying and the dead are below; above them a surging movement from both sides forms a peak. The first to see on the horizon the boat that was to deliver them is a black man who holds a flag aloft to catch the attention of that distant boat. This kind of large-scale dramatic image with the contrast of the dying and the living, and with these balanced movements of powerful bodies, has been a tradition in French official painting.

Because of this allusive context of *Guernica*, the image is full of meaning. The content of suffering, diffused throughout the work, has evoked different interpretations; the bull especially has been described in contradictory ways. Placed at the extreme left, and seemingly no victim, the bull with mouth slightly open and tail raised was interpreted by Picasso's friend and editor, Zervos, in 1937 as a symbol of resurgent life in that devastation. He wrote the following:

> And above so much sadness, the bird which launches his song of life, and the bull, like those winged genii of ancient mythology, contemplate the destructive work of man. What a palpitating life full of promise beside this most desolate vision that has ever occurred! A feeling of permanence, of imperishable force, emerges from it. The serenity of his gaze convinces us that nothing essential has been lost, that one will always find them again among the ruins.

Others, among them Herbert Read, however, saw the bull as Franco; it represented the destructive force in Guernica.

The question was put to Picasso in 1944. An American soldier, in an interview with him published in a Communist magazine in New York, asked, "Doesn't the bull represent Franco?" Picasso replied, "Not at all. The bull doesn't represent Franco." "But Franco is evil, isn't he?" "Of course he is evil." "And you made the picture as propaganda?" "Well, generally I don't, but this is the only one I have done as propaganda." Under persistent questioning by the American soldier, Picasso finally conceded, "Well, of course the bull is Franco since Franco is darkness and the bull is darkness." Set down in print, it has been quoted as often as Picasso's explanation. Yet in an etching that he began in January and finished on the seventh of June, the bull appears, threatening a caricatural figure—a piece of Picasso's invective—which is Franco. The gruesome being wears a mock crown. He appears again with a North Figs. 25-26 African fez and carries a little standard with a crescent moon to indicate his Moorish cohort; he is disemboweling a fallen winged horse, Fig. 27 Pegasus. Franco is also the enemy of art. The bull who threatens him here disembowels a second horse, who is Franco, this time not a beautiful white horse, not a feminine horse, but a grisly, ugly creature. It is Fig. 28 Picasso's clear avowal of what he means by the bull in this cycle of pictures; and yet he could be led to make the statement that the bull is Franco and darkness and evil long after his spokesman, Zervos, who published the series of photographs of the stages of *Guernica* in the *Cahiers d'Art*, had declared the bull to be the ongoing life and invincible strength of the Spanish people. We see how the interpretations of *Guernica* had already become part of the history of the work.

The Spanish Civil War continued for eighteen months after June 1937; then the Second World War, foreshadowed in the events of the Spanish Civil War, broke out. In all that time, Picasso, I believe, was moved by those events; he felt himself deeply involved in them; yet he seems to have produced no works that pictured them or alluded to them as did *Guernica* or his etchings of Franco. But in 1951, as a loyal member of the French Communist Party, he painted another political

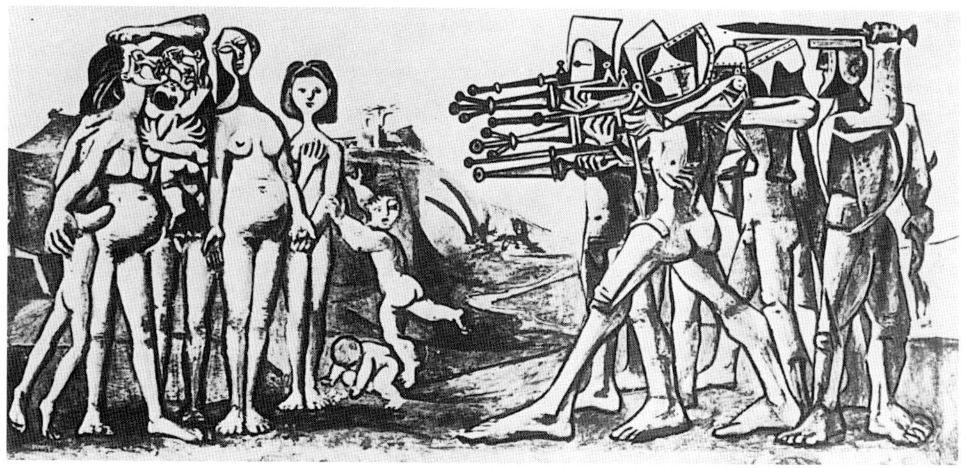

Figure 29. *Massacre in Korea,* January 18, 1951, oil on plywood, 43⅜ x 82⅝" (110 x 210 cm), Musée Picasso, Paris.

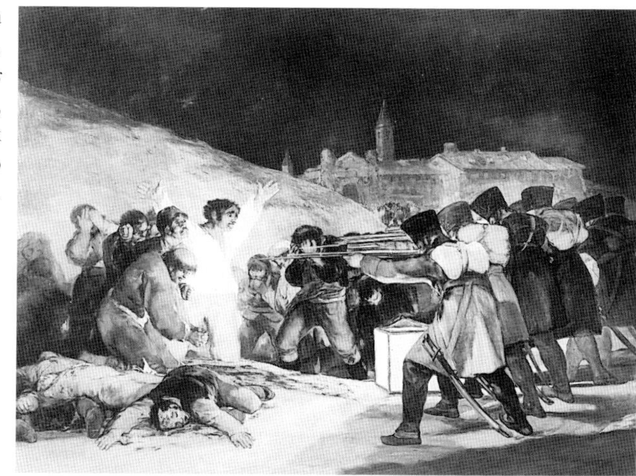

Figure 30. Francisco Goya y Lucientes, *The Third of May, 1808, at Madrid: The Shootings on Principe Pío Mountain,* 1814, oil on canvas, 8'8¾" x 11'3⅞"(266 x 345 cm), Museo del Prado, Madrid.

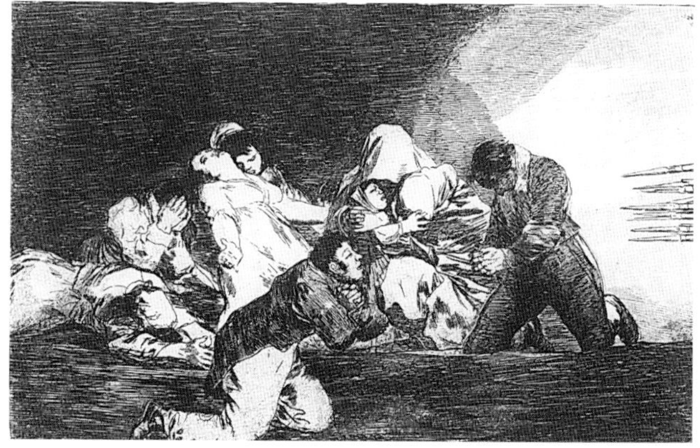

Figure 31. Francisco Goya y Lucientes, *"No se puede mirar"* [One cannot look at this], c. 1810–12, etching, 4¾ x 7¾" (15.2 x 19.7 cm), plate 26, *Disasters of War,* The New York Public Library, Prints Division, S. P. Avery Collection.

picture, which he called *Massacre in Korea*. He represents the war by a group of soldiers in strange antique costume, with swords and blunder- Fig. 29
busses, shooting in a bare landscape, with naked, defenseless women and children standing before them; some of the women are pregnant. It is a cold, dry, unemotional, though emphatically drawn work. It fails to move—at least I find little in it to move me either as a conception or as an artistic structure, although I am impressed as ever by Picasso's ability to make a line move, to render a body solid and rounded—forms contrasted with great force. This overtly political work, a propagandist's message, was evidently modeled on Francisco de Goya's painting of the massacre of Spaniards by French soldiers in 1808. Goya, too, represented the soldiers as faceless automata equipped with engines of Fig. 30
destruction; but the power and pathos of the work as an image lie in the picturing of the human response, the dramatic imagination and artistry in the varied postures and expressions as well as in the light and color of those victims; there is within that variation a stirring reenactment of a human process, from the initial fear through all the stages leading to death. Goya went further in an etching of the same scene; here he omits the soldiers and allows guns to exist by themselves as if those who aim Fig. 31
the guns are not there as human agents—one could say perhaps that they are present as human in the guns—but for him at least, the power of the image depends on that separation. He redraws the dying and threatened figures in the most moving representation of collective despair before a brutal anticipated death that I know. In doing that, his use of these startling flashes of light and dark in different degrees of density and different axes is an inspired invention, a living part of the conceived action and reality. To see Picasso's *Korea* beside Goya's two works is to see the difference between Goya, who, remembering the scene some years afterward, could write, "I saw all this," and the modern image made as an effort of propaganda about an event Picasso has not seen, or imagined, or felt deeply, but to which he applied his unrivaled powers of construction, drawing, and the realization of bodies.

From this account, I believe one can learn something about the issues that were discussed so often in the 1930s and then forgotten and that have arisen again in our own time. To what extent can an artist, and ought artists, express in their art their feelings about experiences common to all, artists and nonartists, about issues in which humanity is inescapably concerned, and that must affect the existence of their own art in the future? It was assumed at one time that artists who took these situations seriously, and were true to their own experiences, would be able to transform their art so that it could express the fullest content of their thought, including their sense of actuality and their partisanship. The model of old religious and state arts, the example of men like Goya and Honoré Daumier, were the acknowledged precedents for the modern artist who in loyalty to his social and political partisanship could draw inspiration from them and see his own role as a fellow human more clearly. But we have observed in Picasso's work that the greatest living artist, who has said so often that he has always painted from feeling and that the aim of art is to be true to the fullest perception, experience, and imagination of the individual, when confronted by a situation that impels him to express his awareness and perceptions, must struggle as Picasso did in this work with the incompatibility between the character of his art as practiced daily and the new problems arising from an exceptional, challenging situation. We see that the artist's response depends also upon the lifelong habit and experience of his art; for an artist in ancient times to express a religious attitude was no break with his ordinary practice, since his art was formed in the context of religious tasks that, in turn, shaped his way of imagining any theme. Insofar as the main content and functioning of art within our culture do not serve any institution, in fact have arisen and developed in the effort to create a freer way of life outside the frame of political ends, constraints, and institutional demands, work for party or a collective occasion can only be episodic, exceptional. It cannot easily be sustained as a life commitment. For that reason, the statements of Picasso and others that their art deals with the totality of their lives and their experiences also cannot be accepted. Only in admitting the constraints and limitations, arising from the marginal position of painting in our society, is he able to produce as he has done. It follows, then, that large sectors of his experience and awareness are not eligible for a painter's art. And if, under special circumstances, they suddenly become a theme or problem of art, they are subject to confusions, difficulties, and constraints that are built into the kind of practice normal at the time. Moreover, since such occasions are episodic, they cannot be the ground for a development of that type of art, and they cannot easily change the art that is to follow. Where there is a sustained situation of that kind, which sets a permanent direction for the art, it must enter into a conflict with a fundamental value of painting and of lyrical art in general within our own society, namely that it exists as a field of individual choices, perception, and discovery.

(1966)

[1] Rudolf Arnheim had recently lectured at Harvard University on *Guernica*.

[2] Pegasus was a symbol of immortality in Roman and Early Christian tomb decor.

[3] The conversation was preserved by Delacroix's friend Theophile Silvestre, in *La Galerie Bruyas, par Alfred Bruyas* (Paris, 1876), 290–91.

Illustrations

All works are by Pablo Picasso, unless otherwise noted.

THE UNITY OF PICASSO'S ART

Figure 1. *The Blind Man's Meal*, autumn 1903, oil on canvas, 37½ x 37¼" (95.3 x 94.6 cm), The Metropolitan Museum of Art, New York, Gift of Mr. and Mrs. Ira Haupt, 1950 (50.188). Photo: © The Metropolitan Museum of Art.

Figure 2. *The Aficionado*, summer–autumn 1912, oil on canvas, 53⅛ x 32¼" (135 x 82 cm), Kunstmuseum, Basel. Gift of Raoul La Roche, 1952. Photo: Giraudon/Art Resource, New York.

Figure 3. *The Crucifixion*, February 7, 1930, oil on plywood, 19¾ x 25⅞" (51.5 x 65.5 cm), Musée Picasso, Paris. Photo: Giraudon/Art Resource, New York.

Figure 4. Jean-Baptiste Siméon Chardin, *The Monkey as Painter*, c. 1740, oil on canvas, 28¾ x 23⅞" (73 x 59.5 cm), Musée du Louvre, Paris. Photo: Erich Lessing, Art Resource, New York.

Figure 5. *Three Musicians*, summer 1921, oil on canvas, 79 x 87¾" (200.7 x 222.9 cm), The Museum of Modern Art, New York. Mrs. Simon Guggenheim Fund.

Figure 6. *Mother and Child*, summer 1921, oil on canvas, 38 x 28" (97 x 71 cm), Private collection. Photo: Sarah Wells.

Figure 7. *Evocation* (*The Burial of Casagemas*), summer 1901, oil on canvas, 59⅛ x 35½" (150 x 90 cm), Musée d'Art Moderne de la Ville de Paris.

Figure 8. *Harlequin*, autumn 1901, oil on canvas, 32⅝ x 24⅛" (80 x 60.3), The Metropolitan Museum of Art, New York, Gift of Mr. and Mrs. John L. Loeb, 1960 (60.87).

Figure 9. Raphael, *The Betrothal of the Virgin ('Sposalizio')*, 1504, oil on panel, 66 15/16 x 46 7/16" (170 x 118 cm), Pinacoteca di Brera, Milan. Photo: Archivi Alinari/ Art Resource, New York.

Figure 10. Raphael, *Transfiguration*, 1517-20, oil on panel, 13'3 7/16" x 9'1 7/16" (4.05 x 2.78 m), Musei Vaticani, Pinacoteca, Rome. Photo: Scala/Art Resource, New York.

Figure 11. *Guitar*, spring 1913, pasted papers, charcoal, chalk, and India ink on blue paper mounted on ragboard, 26 1/8 x 19½" (66.4 x 49.6 cm), The Museum of Modern Art, New York. Nelson A. Rockefeller Bequest. Photo: © The Museum of Modern Art, New York.

Figure 12. Arthur G. Dove, *The Critic*, 1925, collage of paper, newspaper, fabric, cord, and broken glass, 19¾ x 13¼ x 4¾" (50.2 x 33.7 x 12.1 cm), Collection of Whitney Museum of American Art, New York. Purchase, with funds from the Historic Art Association of the Whitney Museum of American Art, Mr. and Mrs. Morton L. Janklow, the Howard and Jean Lipman Foundation, Inc., and Hannelore Schulhof, 76.9.

Figure 13. *Dancing Dwarf (La Nana)*, 1901, oil on cardboard, 41 1/8 x 24" (104.5 x 61 cm), Museu Picasso, Barcelona. Photo: Giraudon/Art Resource, New York.

Figure 14. *A Woman Ironing*, 1901, oil on canvas mounted on cardboard, 19½ x 10 1/8" (49.5 x 25.7 cm), The Metropolitan Museum of Art, New York, Alfred Stieglitz Collection, 1949 (49.70.2). Photo: © 1998 The Metropolitan Museum of Art.

Figure 15. *The Old Guitarist*, autumn 1903, oil on panel, 47¾ x 32½" (122.9 x 82.6 cm), The Art Institute of Chicago. Helen Birch Bartlett Memorial Collection, 1926.253. Photo: © 2000 The Art Institute of Chicago. All rights reserved.

Figure 16. *La Toilette*, early summer 1906, oil on canvas, 59½ x 39" (151 x 99 cm), Albright-Knox Art Gallery, Buffalo, New York. Fellows for Life Fund, 1926.

Figure 17. *The Old Jew ("The Old Man")*, 1903, oil on canvas, 49¼ x 36¼" (125 x 92 cm), Pushkin Museum, Moscow.

Figure 18. *Boy Leading a Horse*, early 1906, oil on canvas, 7'2 7/8" x 51 1/8" (220.6 x 131.2 cm), The Museum of Modern Art, New York. The William S. Paley Collection, 575.64. Photo: © The Museum of Modern Art, New York.

Figure 19. *Woman with a Fan*, early 1905, pen and black ink on paper, pasted on white cardboard, 12¾ x 8 7/8" (32.7 x 22.5 cm), Allen Memorial Art Museum, Oberlin College, Oberlin, Ohio, Charles F. Olney Fund, 1949.

Figure 20. *Woman with a Fan*, late 1905, oil on linen, 39½ x 32" (100.3 x 81.3 cm), National Gallery of Art, Washington, D.C. Gift of the W. Averell Harriman Foundation in memory of Marie N. Harriman.

Figure 21. Jean-Auguste-Dominique Ingres, *Tu Marcellus eris*, fragment cut from a version of *Virgil's Reading from the 'Aeneid' before Augustus and Livia*, 1813–14, oil on canvas, 54¼ x 55⅞" (138 x 142 cm), Musées Royaux d'Art et d'Histoire, Brussels. Photo: Giraudon/Art Resource, New York.

Figure 22. *Acrobat on a Ball*, 1905, oil on canvas, 577/8 x 373/8" (147 x 95 cm), Pushkin Museum, Moscow. Photo: Giraudon/Art Resource, New York.

Figure 23. Paul Cézanne, *Self-Portrait with Palette*, 1885-87, oil on canvas, 36¼ x 28¾" (92 x 73 cm), Foundation E. G. Bührle Collection, Zurich. Photo: © Erich Lessing, Giraudon/Art Resource, New York.

Figure 24. *Self-Portrait with Palette*, autumn 1906, oil on canvas, 36¼ x 28¾" (92 x 73 cm), Philadelphia Museum of Art. A. E. Gallatin Collection. Photo: Graydon Wood, 1990.

Figure 25. *Nude with Raised Arms*, spring–summer 1907, oil on canvas, 59⅛ x 39½" (150 x 100 cm), Private collection.

Figure 26. *Houses on the Hill, Horta de Ebro*, summer 1909, oil on canvas, 25⅝ x 31⅞" (65 x 81 cm), The Museum of Modern Art, New York. Nelson A. Rockefeller Bequest. Photo: © 2000 The Museum of Modern Art, New York.

Figure 27. *Head of a Woman (Fernande)*, summer 1909, oil on canvas, 25⅝ x 21¼" (65 x 54 cm), Museu de Arte Moderna, Rio de Janeiro.

Figure 28. *Girl from Arles*, summer 1912, oil on canvas, 28¾ x 21¼" (73 x 54 cm), Private collection.

Figure 29. *Girl with a Mandolin (Fanny Tellier)*, late spring 1910, oil on canvas, 39½ x 29" (100.3 x 73.6 cm), The Museum of Modern Art, New York. Nelson A. Rockefeller Bequest. Photo: © The Museum of Modern Art, New York.

Figure 30. *Standing Female Nude*, summer 1910, charcoal, 19 x 12⅜" (48.3 x 31.2 cm), The Metropolitan Museum of Art, New York, The Alfred Stieglitz Collection, 1949 (49.70.34).

Figure 31. *Portrait of Daniel-Henry Kahnweiler*, autumn 1910, oil on canvas, 39⅝ x 25⅝" (101.1 x 73.3 cm), The Art Institute of Chicago. Gift of Mrs. Gilbert W. Chapman in memory of Charles B. Goodspeed, 1948.561. Photo: © 2000 The Art Institute of Chicago. All rights reserved.

Figure 32. *Violin and Grapes*, spring–early autumn 1912, oil on canvas, 20 x 24" (50.6 x 61 cm), The Museum of Modern Art, New York. Mrs. David M. Levy Bequest. Photo: © The Museum of Modern Art, New York.

Figure 33. *Bottle on a Table*, winter 1912-13, pasted papers, charcoal, and pencil on newsprint, 24⅝ x 17⅜" (62.5 x 44 cm), Musée Picasso, Paris.

Figure 34. *Still Life with Chair Caning*, spring 1912, oil and oilcloth stuck on oval canvas framed with rope, 10⅝ x 13¾" (27 x 35 cm), Musée Picasso, Paris. Photo: Lauros-Giraudon/Art Resource, New York.

Figure 35. *Portrait of Ambrose Vollard*, 1915, pencil, 18⅜ x 12⅝" (46.7 x 32 cm),

The Metropolitan Museum of Art, New York, The Elisha Whittelsey Collection, The Elisha Whittelsey Fund, 1947.

Figure 36. *Sergei Diaghilev and Alfred Seligsberg* (after a photograph), summer 1919, charcoal and black pencil on paper, 25½ x 19⅝" (65 x 50 cm), Musée Picasso, Paris. Photo: Art Resource, New York.

Figure 37. *Three Women at the Spring*, summer 1921, oil on canvas, 80¼ x 68½" (203.8 x 174 cm), The Museum of Modern Art, New York, Gift of Mr. and Mrs. Allan D. Emil. Photo: © 2000 The Museum of Modern Art, New York.

Figure 38. *Mother and Child*, 1921, oil on canvas, 56½ x 64" (143.5 x 162.5 cm), The Art Institute of Chicago.

Figure 39. *The Red Tablecloth*, 1924, oil on canvas, 38¾ x 51¾" (98.4 x 131.4 cm), Private collection, New York.

Figure 40. *The Ram's Head*, summer 1925, oil on canvas, 30½ x 39⅛" (77.5 x 99.4 cm), Norton Simon Museum, Pasadena, California. Gift of Alexandre P. Rosenberg.

Figure 41. *Studio with Plaster Head*, summer 1925, oil on canvas, 38⅝ x 51⅝" (98 x 130 cm), The Museum of Modern Art, New York. Purchase, 1964, Inv. no. 116.64.

Figure 42. *The Dance*, June 1925, oil on canvas, 84⅝ x 55⅞" (215 x 142 cm), The Tate Gallery, London/Art Resource, New York.

Figure 43. *Girl before a Mirror*, March 14, 1932, oil on canvas, 64 x 51¼" (162.3 x 130.2 cm), The Museum of Modern Art, New York. Gift of Mrs. Simon Guggenheim. Photo: © The Museum of Modern Art, New York.

Figure 44. *Seated Bather*, early 1930, oil on canvas, 64¼ x 51" (163.2 x 129.5 cm), The Museum of Modern Art, New York. Mrs. Simon Guggenheim Fund. Photo: © The Museum of Modern Art, New York.

Figure 45. *Minotaurmachy*, spring 1935, etching and scraper, 19½ x 27 7/16" (49.5 x 69.7 cm), state V, The Museum of Modern Art, New York. Purchase Fund.

Figure 46. *Woman with a Candle, Fight between Bull and Horse*, July 24, 1934, pen and India ink, brown crayon on cloth pasted on plywood, 12⅜ x 16" (31.5 x 40.5 cm), Musée Picasso, Paris.

Figure 47. *Guernica*, May 1–June 4, 1937, oil on canvas, 11'5⅜" x 25'5½" (349 x 776 cm), Museo Nacional Centro de Arte Reina Sofía, Madrid.

Figure 48. François Rude, *"La Marseillaise" (Departure of the Volunteers in 1792)*, 1833–36, stone relief, c. 42 x 26' (12.80 x 7.92 m), Arc de Triomphe, Paris.

Figure 49. Pierre-Paul Prud'hon, *Justice and Divine Vengeance Pursuing Crime*, 1808, oil on canvas, 7'11⅝" x 9'7" (2.34 x 2.92 m), Musée du Louvre, Paris, Département des Peintures (INV 7340).

Figure 50. Eugène Delacroix, *Liberty Leading the People*, 1830, oil on canvas, 8'6⅜" x 10'7 15/16" (2.60 x 3.25 m), Musée du Louvre, Paris.

Figure 51. *Horse in Agony*, May 2, 1937, oil on canvas, 25½ x 36¼" (65 x 92.1 cm), Museo del Prado, Madrid.

Figure 52. *Weeping Woman*, June 26, 1937, gouache and colored crayon on canvas, 21⅝ x 18⅛" (55 x 46 cm), The Museum of Modern Art, New York.

Figure 53. *Head*, late 1912 or early 1913, oil on canvas, 21⅝" x 15" (55 x 38 cm), Private collection, Westport, Eire.

Figure 54. *Woman with a Cockerel*, 1938, oil on canvas, 57¼ x 47⅝" (145.5 x 121 cm), Baltimore Museum of Art.

Figure 55. *Painter with a Model Knitting*, 1927, Plate IV from *Le Chef d'oeuvre inconnu* by Honoré de Balzac (Paris: Ambrose Vollard, Editeur, 1931), etching, 7$^{9}/_{16}$ x 10⅞" (19.2 x 27.7 cm), The Museum of Modern Art, New York, The Louis E. Stern Collection. Photo: © The Museum of Modern Art, New York.

Figure 56. *Painter and Model*, 1928, oil on canvas, 51⅛ x 64¼" (129.8 x 163 cm), The Museum of Modern Art, New York. The Sidney and Harriet Janis Collection. Photo: © The Museum of Modern Art, New York.

Figure 57. Man Ray, *Pablo Picasso*, 1932, photograph, *Les cahiers d'art*, Nos. 7–10, 1935.

Figure 58. *Mother and Child*, 1905, gouache on canvas, 34⅝ x 27⅜" (88 x 69.5 cm), Staatsgalerie, Stuttgart.

Figure 59. *Seated Woman*, 1931, wood, 22 x ¾ x 2" (55.7 x 2 x 5 cm), Musée Picasso, Paris.

Figure 60. *Head of a Woman*, 1931–32, bronze, 33½ x 14½ x 17⅞" (85 x 37 x 45.5 cm), Galerie Louise Leiris, Paris.

Figure 61. *Le Belier* [The Ram], 1942, lift-ground acquatint, etching, and drypoint, 16$^{5}/_{16}$ x 12$^{7}/_{16}$" (41.5 x 31.5 cm), pl. 5 from *Histoire Naturelle (Textes de Buffon)*.

Figure 62. *Man with Sheep*, 1944, bronze, 86⅝ x 30¾ x 28⅜" (220 x 78 x 72 cm), Philadelphia Museum of Art, Gift of R. Sturgis and Marion B. F. Ingersoll.

Figure 63. *She-Goat*, 1950, bronze (after assemblage of palm leaf, ceramic flowerpots, wicker basket, metal elements, and plaster), 46⅜ x 56⅜ x 28½" (117.7 x 143.1 x 71.4 cm), The Museum of Modern Art, New York, Mrs. Simon Guggenheim Fund.

Figure 64. *Baboon and Young*, 1951, bronze (after original plaster with metal, ceramic elements, and two toy cars), 21 x 13¼ x 20¾" (53.3 x 33.3 x 52.7 cm), The Museum of Modern Art, New York, Mrs. Simon Guggenheim Fund.

Figure 65. *Pregnant Woman*, 1950, bronze, 41¼" (104.8 cm) high; at base 7⅝ x 6¼" (19.3 x 15.8 cm), The Museum of Modern Art, New York, Gift of Mrs. Bertram Smith.

EINSTEIN AND CUBISM: SCIENCE AND ART

Figure 1. Marcel Duchamp, *Nude Descending the Staircase, No. 2*, 1912, 58 x 35" (147.3 x 89 cm), The Philadelphia

Museum of Art (Louise and Walter Arensberg Collection). Photo: Graydon Wood, 1994.

Figure 2. Edward Burne-Jones, *The Golden Stairs*, 1876–80, oil on canvas, 9'1" x 3'10" (2.69 x 117 m), Tate Gallery, London/Art Resource, New York.

Figure 3. *Pitcher, Bowl, and Fruit Bowl*, spring–summer 1908, oil on canvas, 31⅞ x 25⅝" (81 x 65 cm), Philadelphia Museum of Art, A. E. Gallatin Collection.

Figure 4. *The Harbor at Cadaqués*, summer 1910, oil on canvas, 15 x 17⅞" (38 x 45.5 cm), National Gallery, Prague.

Figure 5. *Woman*, autumn 1910, oil on canvas, 39⅜ x 31⅞" (100 x 81 cm), Museum of Fine Arts, Boston. Charles H. Bayley Fund and partial gift of Mrs. Gilbert W. Chapman.

Figure 6. *Wooden Panel of Hesy-Ra*, from the northern edge of the Saqqara Cemetery, mid-Third Dynasty (c. 2686-2613 B.C.), wood, height: 45¼" (115 cm), The Cairo Museum. Photo: Bildarchiv Foto Marburg.

Figure 7. *Adoration of the Magi: Their Arrival and Departure*, The Pierpont Morgan Library, New York, PML 710, fol. 19V.

Figure 8. Gentile da Fabriano, *Adoration of the Magi*, 1423, commissioned by Palla Strozzi for the Strozzi Chapel, Santa Trinità, Florence, tempera on panel, 9'10" x 9'3" (3 x 2.82 m), Galleria degli Uffizi, Florence. Photo: Alinari/Art Resource.

Figure 9. Paul Cézanne, *La Route Tournante à Montgeroult*, 1898, oil on canvas, 32 x 26" (81.2 x 66 cm), The Museum of Modern Art, New York. Bequest of Mrs. John Hay Whitney. Photo: © 2000 The Museum of Modern Art, New York.

Figure 10. *Still-life with Guitar (Glass, Guitar, and Bottle)*, early 1913, oil, pasted papers, lead white, and pencil on canvas, 25¾ x 21⅛" (65.4 x 53.6 cm), The Museum of Modern Art, New York, Gift of the Sidney and Harriet Janis Collection, 1967. Photo: © 2000 The Museum of Modern Art, New York.

Figure 11. Georges Braque, *Clarinet*, 1913, pasted papers, charcoal, chalk, and oil on canvas, 37½ x 47⅜" (95.3 x 120.3 cm), The Museum of Modern Art, New York. The Nelson A. Rockefeller Bequest.

Figure 12. Edouard Manet, *The Races at Longchamp*, Paris, 1867, oil on canvas, 17¼ x 33¼" (43.8 x 84.5 cm), The Art Institute of Chicago, Potter Palmer Collection, 22.424.

Figure 13. Giacomo Balla, *Dynamism of a Dog on a Leash*, 1912, oil on canvas, 35⅜ x 43¼" (89.8 x 109.8 cm), Albright-Knox Art Gallery, Buffalo, New York. Bequest of A. Conger Goodyear to George F. Goodyear, life interest, and Albright-Knox Art Gallery, Buffalo, New York, 1964.

Figure 14. J. Kepler, *Rudolphine Tables*, frontispiece from *Tabulae Rudolphinae Ioannes Keplerus*, Ulm, 1627.3

**GUERNICA:
SOURCES, CHANGES**

Figure 1. *Guernica*, May 1–June 4, 1937, oil on canvas, 11'5$\frac{3}{8}$" x 25'5$\frac{1}{2}$" (349 x 776 cm), Museo del Prado, Madrid.

Figure 2. Sketch 1. *Composition Study for Guernica*, May 1, 1937, pencil on blue paper, 8$\frac{1}{4}$ x 10$\frac{5}{8}$" (21 x 27 cm), Museo del Prado, Madrid.

Figure 3. Sketch 6. *Composition Study for Guernica*, May 1, 1937, pencil on wood panel, 21$\frac{1}{8}$ x 25$\frac{1}{2}$" (53.7 x 64.8 cm), Museo del Prado, Madrid.

Figure 4. *Curtain for ballet "La Parade,"* 1917, tempera on canvas, 34'9$\frac{5}{16}$" x 56'7$\frac{1}{8}$" (10.60 x 17.25 m), Musée National d'Art Moderne, Centre Georges Pompidou, Paris

Figure 5. *Woman with a Candle, Fight between Bull and Horse*, July 24, 1934, pen and India ink, brown crayon on cloth pasted on plywood, 12$\frac{3}{8}$ x 16" (31.5 x 40.5 cm), Musée Picasso, Paris.

Figure 6. *The Murder (Death of Marat)*, July 7, 1934, pencil on paper, 15$\frac{3}{4}$ x 19$\frac{7}{8}$" (39.8 x 50.4 cm), Musée Picasso, Paris.

Figure 7. *Minotauromachy*, April 1935, etching and scraper, 19$\frac{1}{2}$ x 27$\frac{3}{8}$" (49.6 x 69.6 cm), The Museum of Modern Art, New York, Abby Aldrich Rockefeller Fund.

Figure 8. *Crucifixion*, February 7, 1930, oil on plywood, 19$\frac{3}{4}$ x 25$\frac{7}{8}$" (51.5 x 65.5 cm), Musée Picasso, Paris.

Figure 9. *Studio with Plaster Head*, summer 1925, oil on canvas, 38$\frac{5}{8}$ x 51$\frac{5}{8}$" (98.1 x 131.2 cm), The Museum of Modern Art, New York. Purchase.

Figure 10. *Horse in Agony*, May 2, 1937, oil on canvas, 25$\frac{1}{2}$ x 36$\frac{1}{4}$" (65 x 92.1 cm), Museo del Prado, Madrid.

Figure 11. Sketch 5. *Study for Horse*, May 1, 1937, pencil on blue paper, 8$\frac{1}{4}$ x 10$\frac{1}{2}$" (21 x 26.8 cm), Museo del Prado, Madrid.

Figure 12. *Nude with Raised Arms*, spring–summer 1907, oil on canvas, 59$\frac{1}{8}$ x 39$\frac{1}{2}$" (150 x 100 cm), Private collection.

Figure 13. *Weeping Woman*, June 26, 1937, gouache and color crayon on canvas, 21$\frac{5}{8}$ x 18$\frac{1}{8}$" (55 x 46 cm), The Museum of Modern Art, New York.

Figure 14. *Head*, late 1912 or early 1913, oil on canvas, 21$\frac{5}{8}$ x 15" (55 x 38 cm), Private collection, Westport, Eire.

Figure 15. Sketch 48. *Head of Weeping Woman*, June 13, 1937, pencil, colored crayons, and gouache, 11$\frac{1}{2}$ x 9$\frac{1}{4}$" (29.2 x 23.5 cm), Museo del Prado, Madrid.

Figure 16. *Guernica* (1st state), May 11, 1937. Photograph by Dora Maar.

Figure 17. *Guernica* (5th state), May 27–June 4, 1937. Photograph by Dora Maar.

Figure 18. Piero della Francesca, *Crucifixion*, c. 1445–60, from *Madonna della Misericordia*, polyptych, oil and tempera on panel, 31$\frac{7}{8}$ x 22$\frac{7}{16}$"(81 x 57 cm), Pinacoteca Comunale, Borgo Sansepolcro.

Figure 19. Pierre-Paul Prud'hon, *Justice and Divine Vengeance Pursuing Crime*,

1808, oil on canvas, 7'11⅝" x 9'7" (2.34 x 2.92 m), Musée du Louvre, Paris, Département des Peintures (INV 7340).

Figure 20. François Rude, *"La Marseillaise" (Departure of the Volunteers in 1792)*, 1833–36, stone relief, c. 42 x 26' (12.80 x 7.92 m), Arc de Triomphe, Paris.

Figure 21. Antoine Étex, *La Resistance* (1814), stone relief, Arc de Triomphe, Paris. Photo: Yve-Alain Bois.

Figure 22. Detail of fig. 21. Photo: Yve-Alain Bois.

Figure 23. Eugène Delacroix, *Liberty Leading the People*, 1830, oil on canvas, 8'5¾ x 10'6" (2.60 x 3.25 m), Musée du Louvre, Paris.

Figure 24. Théodore Gericault, *Raft of the "Medusa,"* 1818–19, oil on canvas, 16'1¼ x 23'4⅞" (4.91 x 7.16 m), Musée du Louvre, Paris.

Figure 25. *Dream and Lie of Franco, II*, January 8–9, June 7, 1937, etching and lift-ground aquatint, 12⅜ x 16 9/16" (31.4 x 42.1 cm), The Museum of Modern Art, New York. The Louis E. Stern Collection.

Figure 26. Detail of fig. 25.

Figure 27. Detail of fig. 25.

Figure 28. Detail of fig. 25.

Figure 29. *Massacre in Korea*, January 18, 1951, oil on plywood, 43⅜ x 82⅝" (110 x 210 cm), Musée Picasso, Paris.

Figure 30. Francisco Goya y Lucientes, *The Third of May, 1808, at Madrid: The Shootings on Principe Pío Mountain*, 1814, oil on canvas, 8'8¾" x 11'3⅞"(266 x 345 cm), Museo del Prado, Madrid.

Figure 31. Francisco Goya y Lucientes, *"No se puede mirar"* [One cannot look at this], c. 1810–12, etching, 4¾ x 7⅜" (15.2 x 19.7 cm), plate 26, *Disasters of War*, The New York Public Library, Prints Division, S. P. Avery Collection.

Index

R

S

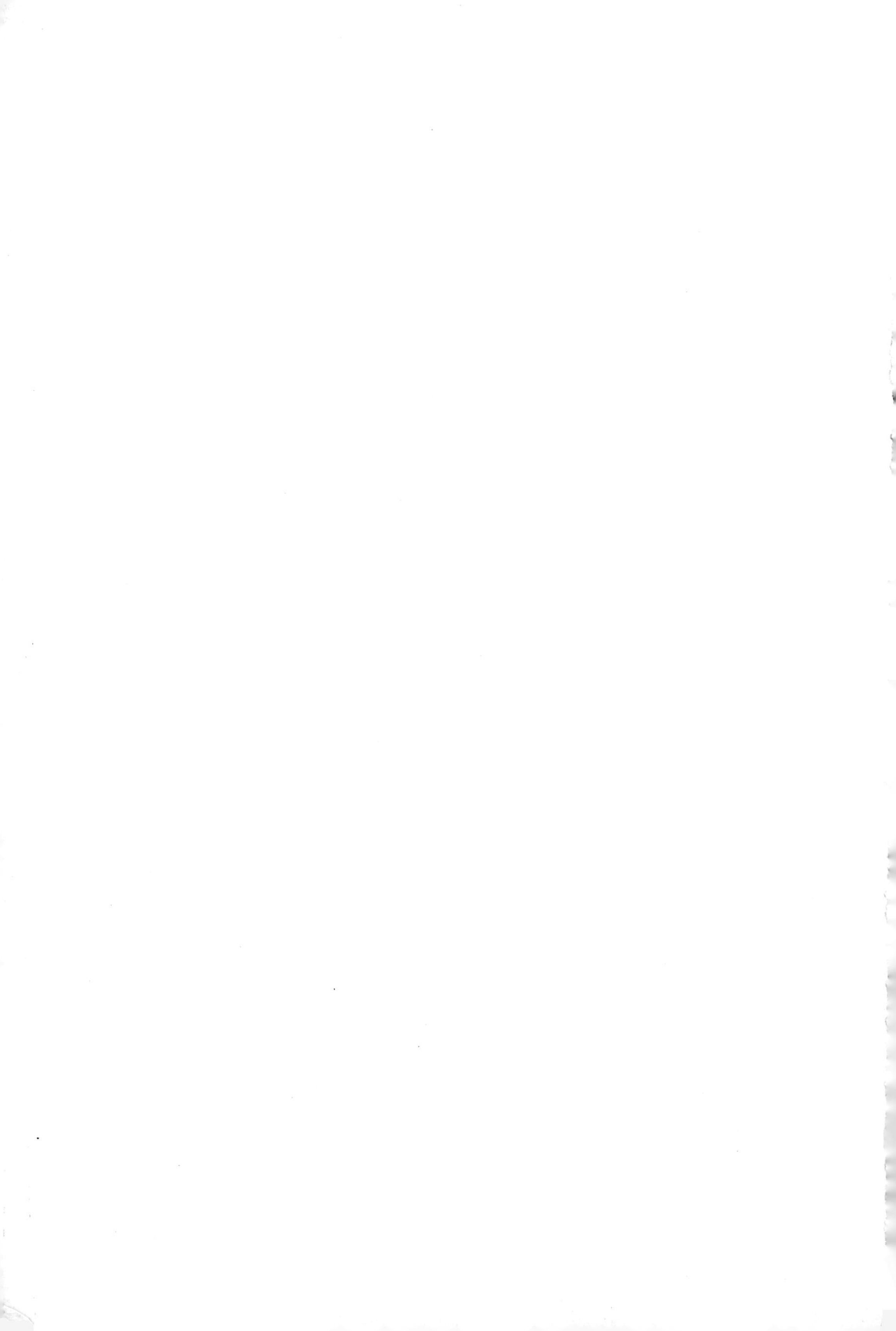